Seas the Day

Seas the Day

THE TRUE STORY OF FEAR,
FRIENDSHIP, AND FAITH WHILE
STRANDED AT SEA DURING COVID-19

JOHNNY VRBA

Foreword by
Archbishop Bernard A. Hebda

YES PRESS

Copyright © 2024 by Johnny Vrba

U.S. Copyright Case Number: 1-13486955651

All rights reserved. No part of this book may be reproduced or transmitted in any form or by any means, electronic or mechanical, including photocopy, recording, or any information storage or retrieval system, without permission in writing from the copyright owner except in the case of brief quotations embodied in critical articles or reviews.

Seas The Day is a work of non-fiction. The events and conversations from this book are a reflection of the author's experiences, recollections, and inferences. Some names have been altered to honor the privacy of those involved.

Edited by Susan Keillor and Cindy Doty
Cover and Interior Design by Jeremy Taylor

Publishing and Media Inquiries:

STRATEGIES PR
Contact: Jared Kuritz
jkuritz@strategiespr.com

ISBN: 979-8-9893137-3-0 (paperback)
ISBN: 979-8-9893137-4-7 (hardcover)
ISBN: 979-8-9893137-5-4 (eBook)

FIRST EDITION

First Printed in the United States.

First Published in the United States by Yes Press.

DEDICATION

For my family, who gave me the world.

Table of Contents

Foreword 1
Nautical Directional Terms 4
Introduction 5
Holy Ship! 18
Chapter Two 28
Making Friends 40
College at Sea 55
Sweet Life on Deck 66
Oops! 76
Flexibility—Level One 83
Twenty-Three Hours and Fifty-Three Minutes 100
Burberry & Birkenstocks 108
Hau Will We Get There? 114
Pu Mat 130
Ponderings, Poops, and a Spider 146

Pocket God 161
Flexibility—Level Two 167
The Twelfth Man 175
Wanderlist 182
Out to See 188
Still Out to See 199
Flexibility—Level Three 208
Johnny's Quiet 226
Moreitius 237
Confronting Lions 246
Flexibility—Final Boss 259
Dear Reader, ...269
Holy Spirit! 278
Afterword 290
Acknowledgments 303
About the Author 306

Foreword

IN 2019, POPE FRANCIS wrote to the young people of the world and offered the following advice: "Don't observe life from a balcony. Don't confuse happiness with an armchair, or live your life behind a screen .... Take risks, even if it means making mistakes. Don't go through life anaesthetized or approach the world like tourists. Make a ruckus! Cast out the fears that paralyze you, so that you don't become young mummies. Live! Give yourselves over to the best of life! Open the door of the cage, go out and fly!"

A few months later, as if on cue, Johnny Vrba, a sophomore from Arizona State University, embarked on what he believed would be the adventure of a lifetime: a semester at sea. Along with six hundred other college students, he boarded the *MV World Odyssey* in January of 2020 and set out across the Pacific to earn a semester's worth of college credits by exploring a significant slice of the world on three continents. The coursework promised to be stimulating and the settings unparalled.

Given that context, it is not surprising that Vrba's daily journal entries, documenting the entirety of his trip and now published as

Seas the Day, would be both informative and engaging. With an extraordinary gift for self-reflection and a knack for finding humor in even difficult situations, Vrba offers us a unique opportunity for sharing his experience of the semester at sea. I consider it a blessing that he would have allowed himself to be so vulnerable as to share with the readers of his journal not only his emotions but also what he learned about himself in the course of the journey.

And what a journey it proved to be. When the ship left the port of Ensenada, just south of San Diego, no one could have foreseen that the itinerary of the *MV World Odyssey* would be impacted by the outbreak of a previously unknown coronavirus, Covid 19. In *Seas the Day*, Vrba manages to chronicle the first days of the pandemic from the unique perspective of an American university student travelling in Asia by ship. More importantly, he shares how that situation unexpectedly opened him up to a transformational appreciation of the importance of relationships and community that continues to give meaning to his life today.

Nearly 35 years of priestly ministry have given me a privileged ring-side seat for witnessing the many ways that God manages to break into the lives of those he created. *Seas the Day* indirectly tells the story of a God who creates each of us with a plan, and who used the events of what might seem on the surface to have been an ill-fated semester at sea to open the eyes of a young man to an amazing purpose and potential.

I am very grateful that God's loving plan has brought Johnny Vrba to the University of St. Thomas, the largest Catholic institution of higher learning in the Archdiocese that I am privileged to

Foreword

serve. His work among university students as a missionary for Saint Paul's Outreach, a national apostolate on college campuses across the USA, seems to be bearing fruit in his life as well as in the lives of the young people he accompanies. He still has the quick wit, charm and sense of humor that helped him to navigate the fraternity scene at Arizona State and that would have made him memorable among the students on the *MV World Odyssey*. But now he uses those gifts to draw attention not to himself but rather to the Creator who is their true source.

In the tenth Chapter of Saint John's Gospel, Jesus explains to his disciples that he had come "that they may have life, and have it to the full." It never ceases to amaze me that God can use even the most difficult experiences in our lives to prepare us, sinful and wounded as we are, to live life to the full and to accomplish the marvelous work that he has intended for us from the beginning of time. I am grateful that Johnny continues to allow the Lord to use him.

As *Seas the Day* enables us to reflect on one young man's extraordinary experiences, it will be my prayer that his story might inspire us to take Pope Francis' words to heart and not approach our world simply as tourists. Let's not be afraid to make a few mistakes but rather give ourselves over to the best of life. It's worked for Johnny. Let's trust that it can work for us.

~ Most Reverend Bernard A. Hebda
Archbishop of Saint Paul and Minneapolis

Nautical Directional Terms

Port: left side of ship
Starboard: right side of ship
Forward/bow: front of ship
Aft: back of ship

Introduction

IN THE BEGINNING of my freshman year at Arizona State University, I was a dog with two tails, drooling over the brunette bombshells I'd walk past on Palm Walk, and marking my territory in the classroom. I was captivated when I stepped into my first class, Computer Information Systems (CIS 105), which had more seats than a movie theater. I plopped down in the front row and asked a lot of questions, most of which were not about the material, but rather its professor.

"Why are your toenails painted?"

"Why did you get that tattoo?"

"Why did you go to jail?"

The usual, get to know you, surface level kind. Sometimes I would ask relevant questions about trojan horses, random access memory, or floppy disks. Two weeks went by, and my hand shot up again. Professor McCarthy interjected, "Why don't you come up here and help us out?"

I knew he was serious because he had taken off his over the ear microphone and extended it to me. Dr. McCarthy sat down in my seat. "Go ahead, do that external processing thing."

I introduced myself and ran my mouth until the end of the period. The following week, the Brittney Spears microphone was sitting on my seat. "You cool to get up there and do that again?"

"Hell, yeah!"

While I helped move the lesson along, Dr. McCarthy was fielding questions. Nobody wants to raise their hand in a room that size and nobody wants to swim upstream after class, so bringing answers to the people was a genius solution for one of the nation's largest face-to-face classes. This continued for the remainder of the semester.

I never visited Professor during office hours, but I wanted to pick his brain outside of class. He loved his wife, wine, and mountain biking. I could only partake in one of those, so we hit the trails off Pima and Dynamite. Professor has a YouTube channel and posted a video of our ride. (Bonus points if you find it). Having such a unique relationship with one of my professors so early on solidified Arizona State as home. Or maybe the campus just reflected my perfectionism.

Nothing was ever out of place. It seemed as though everyone and everything around me was photoshopped. Often I would walk up to things and touch them to be sure they were real, but sometimes that wasn't possible. From the immaculately combed hair of my classmates, to the oasis of manicured grass outside the rec in the middle of the desert, this place was a full-time amusement park and part-time college—but not everyone was tall enough to ride.

Introduction

One of the largest attractions on campus was Greek life. I had no idea if I wanted to rush, so I went to a "walk around" event where all of the fraternities open their doors and showcase what they have to offer. I wasn't sold on Greek life, but I wanted to meet as many people as possible, so I rushed all sixteen fraternities. One by one, I shrunk my list until two remained, Sig Tau and Sigma Alpha Epsilon (SAE). SAE was a colony with less than twenty members and not recognized as a fraternity with ASU. They were on track to receive their charter back if they continued good behavior. I had written and rewritten a pros and cons list between the two houses and was about to flip a coin when I decided to reach out to both recruitment chairs one final time with a question. I asked, "Give me one reason why I should choose you over the other?" Sig Tau said, "We can give you what you want." SAE said, "You can make what you want." Forty-eight hours later I was an initiated brother of SAE.

It didn't take long to wonder if we were all barking up the wrong tree, but it didn't matter as long as a few coconuts fell from time to time, of which the overwhelming majority were young and green. They were dense as a rock, falling with such speed they'd knock somebody out, breaking open on impact, then others would swarm to enjoy the fruit. It was a flawless system. What's a few less brain cells and a few more bumps and bruises for a succulent nut? ASU has been ranked number one in innovation for the past seven years, so I was sure we'd eventually find a more sustainable process.

By the end of my first winter break, I couldn't wait to get back to campus. Within a few weeks, the fraternity I joined last semester,

Sigma Alpha Epsilon, earned our charter back simultaneously launching us into a record-breaking growth spurt. I felt a few inches taller wearing letters around campus and from time to time I'd bump into one of my former CIS 105 classmates who didn't drop out and they'd say, "You're the CIS guy! Thanks again bro... could you teach my ENG class?"

"HA! I can't write!" I'd shout back as I dapped up another fraternity brother.

As my network grew and I made friends from around the world, it was difficult to maintain a domestic mindset. I studied in Europe for two weeks with my high school and I caught the travel bug on the flight over, so I knew I wanted to study abroad again in college. I just needed to make sure that the study abroad option I chose would be more fun than ASU so I wouldn't get FOMO (fear of missing out).

I waltzed into the study abroad office and the smell of freshly printed paper ran under my nose. I waited for three minutes, fifty minutes in Johnny time, and a tall slender man named Andrew came out to greet me. The chair he sat me down in was unusually comfortable and his office was decorated better than most elementary school classrooms. His walls could have entertained me for days, but the vibrant colors of his scratch off world map took my full attention. I spent half our allotted time pointing to country after country, listening to Andrew retell extraordinary stories that deep inside I yearned to someday share myself. In transition to bring the conversation back towards me, Andrew affirmed my desire to see the world and my seemingly unquenchable curiosity.

Introduction

Consumed by wanderlust, I said, "I want to see as much of the world as possible, and there's just so many options I'm not sure I could ever pick one."

"Well, you don't necessarily have to pick just one," Andrew replied with a slight smirk.

Grinning from ear to ear, I asked, "How many can I see?"

Relaxing back into his chair, Andrew articulated, "Well, there is a program called Semester at Sea (SAS) where you could visit a dozen countries..."

I perked up in my seat like someone stuck a tack in my butt.

"However, living on a cruise ship for one hundred days makes it the most expensive program available, and it requires nearly an entire year of preparation and paperwork. Many students steer away in fear of seasickness—"

Before he could finish, I declared, "I'm in!"

I had a vision of the trip so grand that even the largest IMAX theater in my imagination could not bring it into full resolution. I needed to live it. Andrew quickly brought me back down to earth when he handed me a Bible-length to-do list. My chin raised as I pushed a huge gulp down my throat.

"Are you serious?"

Nodding his head, Andrew mumbled, "Yes, and unfortunately this is only ASU's side of things; you'll need to do even more on Semester at Sea's end."

My extensive task list was found on a private portal called MyVoyage, which would become my second home. Suddenly, this semester-long cruise didn't seem so glorious. The voyage I would embark on was just shy of twelve months away, but then again, nothing good ever comes quickly.

I would be sailing in the spring of 2020, on Semester at Sea's

128th voyage since the program's birth in 1963. Our itinerary was extremely impressive: Hawaii, Japan, China, Vietnam, Malaysia, India, Mauritius, South Africa, Ghana, Morocco, and the Netherlands, with Hawaii and Mauritius being single day provisioning stops required for refueling. Approximately six hundred college students and fifty-seven faculty members and staff would be living aboard the *MV World Odyssey*, a 22,496-ton ship. For reference, Royal Caribbean's largest ship, *The Wonder of the Seas*, is 236,857 tons. Having sailed on a few of Royal Caribbean's largest ships and still being able to feel the waves, I was nervous about what the ocean would feel like on a ship over ten times smaller, but I was excited I wouldn't have to run as far to find my friends. To help tame my nerves, I started to watch dozens of YouTube videos about SAS. I stumbled across a video of the ship off the coast of Alaska rolling around like a toy in a bathtub, which didn't help in the slightest. But no video could have prepared me for the workload I'd face before stepping foot on the ship.

While working simultaneously on both ASU's and SAS's checklists, I was feeling confident and actually beginning to make a dent in the process. The first obstacle came when I discovered I needed a bigger passport. SAS requires that voyagers have a minimum of seventeen blank pages, which was a completely blank US passport. I had sixteen. Hiring a visa concierge service was one of the best decisions my mom and I made. After giving countless documents to my agent, he sent them onward to India, Ghana, and China for approval. The slightest inaccuracy would restart the process, having to continually resend documents until they were satisfied. I learned about four months into the process that getting these visas was not even guaranteed; my Semester at

Introduction

Sea was entirely at their mercy.

    I was also less than excited about planning out my malaria pills and other medications. Thankfully, my mom really wanted me to come back from this trip, so she did a lot of the heavy lifting. Traveling in and out of malaria-risk countries, I had a full schedule of the days I needed to start and stop taking pills. In terms of shots, thankfully I needed just one poke for my yellow fever card. Seasickness patches were also purchased in abundance, even though I told my mom I wouldn't use them.

    Heading into my sophomore year, there was only one semester left before I would set sail in the spring. Planning for SAS was basically equivalent to adding a three-credit course to my schedule. There came a point when I entertained the thought: *Is this really worth it?* At this point in the process, I was throwing a mini celebration every time I checked an item off my list no matter how significant it was. Whether it was a dinner out or a dance party, just something to acknowledge I was taking a step in the right direction. I trusted that my SAS experience would be well worth the strenuous planning process, but I wondered how many days on the ship it would take to break even.

Almost halfway through my sophomore year, I knew I was still barking up the wrong tree, "chasing tail" as my friends referred to it and those little headaches developed into migraines. I either needed to stop barking or find a new tree, and Lord knows the former wasn't going to happen. If I'm being honest, the latter was equally arduous. All of the trees were so tantalizingly tall and skinny. I was lost, frustrated, and running out of steam while simultaneously beginning to make a name for myself. I was *well known,* but deep down I knew I was not *known well.*

I was raised Catholic and if you asked me if I was a believer I'd say "yes." If you asked me if I wanted to get back into my faith, I'd say "yes." If you asked me to come and see on a retreat, I'd say "yes." If you asked me to sleep with you, I'd phone a friend first and then say "yes." In high school, I used to feel guilty, but as the years went by, this feeling ran away. God was probably important, but I was already in so deep I figured that train had left the station. I thought: *If I just gave my buddy a second chance at being my designated driver after passing out in the bathroom with an IV in his arm, I can give God a shot.* I had permission from my friends to fornicate all week long. All I needed was permission to stop.

I started giving God a few yesses. I showed up to Mass every Sunday, but I was not interested in mingling afterwards. There were always missionaries posted up outside of church and they wouldn't let me get away without at least handing me info on the next event. It never felt quite right to walk away from all the commotion, considering I usually ran towards it. On November 5, 2019, I hopped off my longboard, took a shaky deep breath, and pushed open the door to my first "Jesus thing."

The following weeks before the semester ended, I met a caliber of men the Greek system didn't have the tools to manufacture. I was embarrassed at times to be seen in daylight with them because I had an image to maintain. I hated writing that sentence. I would sport my letters during the day, avoiding interactions with my new friends and then attend their events by night. Other times I would seek their counsel during the day and party by night. *The best of both worlds,* I thought. But my new friends were persistent, and for the first time in my life, *I* was the one being pursued. I only took one step into their home to understand these

Introduction

guys barked up the right tree... a tree that hung in every room of their house.

It was only two months before the voyage when I found out there were a few other Sun Devils sailing on my voyage, one of whom I was able to grab lunch with, Julia. We shared an awesome conversation—I was astounded as she retold the story of her parents meeting on SAS back in the day! She also invited me to a group chat of spring 2020 voyagers.

When I joined, there were just under two hundred people, but at its peak, the group chat was four hundred and fifty strong, roughly 80 percent of the students on board. From this gigantic group chat, we broke out into smaller chats on the hunt for a suitable roommate. The very first person I connected with was a Minnesotan named Jimmy. It didn't take long to run him through my roommate examination consisting of just one question.

"Do you snore?"

"No."

Jimmy and I signed on the dotted line and later found out we had similar organizational and cleanliness habits. We were also both gifted at spending other people's money. We deemed ourselves to be ultra-compatible, so on top of taking the exact same classes, we even booked the same SAS field programs. Voyagers have three options when it comes to traveling within each country. First are preplanned adventures packaged together by SAS using their decades of relationship with each country. Three to four months before the voyage, the field office finalizes a catalog of more than two hundred programs ranging from single day, multi-day, all the way to the entire length of the stay in port. Program costs vary from as low as $25, to upwards of $3,000. There is no stress involved because purchasing a field program simultaneously books any hotels, flights, bus, or train tickets involved in the trip. Other important logistics, like clean food and water, and safety, are taken care of. The largest downside was the cost, little flexibility within the itinerary, and that I might not get to travel with the friends I make on board.

Second, every voyager was required to take three courses with three corresponding field classes. It's a field trip but SAS likes to create their own words for everything. Global studies was an interdisciplinary course that was required for all voyagers regardless of their major and it did not have a required field class. In the routine of regular college campus life, twelve credits hardly registers as a full-time student, but on SAS there would be far more to balance, including balancing itself.

The third and most obvious way was to make plans independently. This was the most common form of travel because of the freedom to change the itinerary at any time and it's generally the cheapest option. The major downside to independent travel is the intense planning and logistics, which can end up being half of the fun anyway.

Having a pretty good understanding of the information above, Jimmy and I booked the same field program in every country as opposed to planning our travel independently. We valued the time and stress saved over the opportunity cost of being flexible with more spending money. We also knew that SAS had been to these countries hundreds of times, so we thought they would be able to show us around better than we could. I also figured having a normal guy around me in class, in country,

Introduction

and in our cabin would keep me in line. I was impressed by how much we accomplished over a few phone calls. We didn't really communicate much outside of what was absolutely necessary. If becoming close friends was in our future, that was for the future to figure out.

With my immunizations, patches, pills, insurances, extra-large passport loaded with visas, class schedule, field programs, seamail account, and John Hancock on over one hundred forms, I was ready to board my new campus. SAS CEO Scott Marshall says, "There is only one Semester at Sea in the world... because it's damn hard to do!" The time and effort spent preparing for my voyage as a student was not even a fraction of the hard work the employees put into the logistical miracle that is Semester at Sea.

I had an idea of the man I would see in the mirror after sailing around the world, and I am grateful that I don't ever have to meet him. Somebody had a much bigger plan for my life than I did. Even though our voyage didn't end up needing any of the extra passport pages, the three visas, or any of the malaria medication, planning for 365 days was worth one at sea.

Every single day on board the *MV World Odyssey* was like an award-winning film. Every single day presented an obstacle that culminated in a concrete life lesson. Therefore, every single chapter of this book will be independent of the next, as were our days on the 128th mission of Semester at Sea.

In four days, my friends and I completed the following:
- Visit the Cape of Good Hope
- Walk the beach with Cape penguins
- Shoot the big five (on a camera)
- Jump out of a perfectly good airplane
- Stretch out the world's longest bungee cord
- Swim with the world's largest colony of seals
- Hike Lion's Head Mountain
- Drink wine in the Stellenbosch vineyards
- Dive with great white sharks (in a cage)
- Hand feed pineapples to elephants

Some of these activities were completed within an hour of each other. None of which would have been possible without our tour guide Machiel and his glorious van the thirteen of us stuffed into. After crossing off our bucket lists in less than a week, we were finally able to entertain the idea of going home. By some miracle, the whole squad except for Jacob was able to get on the same flight to Newark, NJ, where we would say final goodbyes and take our respective connection flights.

The Cape Town Airport was bustling with people who all seemed to have just left the operating room of an open-heart surgery. Folks were wearing full masks, shields, gloves, and even shoe coverings. We were completely unprotected, which warranted glares as if we were walking around naked. At this time, there were no laws requiring us to put on a mask and staying updated on the current news proved difficult while constantly cheating

Introduction

death in South Africa.

Nineteen squirts of hand sanitizer later and we were finally boarding our plane. The feeling of plopping down at last into my seat after never-ending lines was euphoric. My body molded into the cushioning, I slowly closed my eyes, and the weight of my experience fell into my lap like a ton of bricks. My muscles froze and my mind went into overdrive, as the flight attendant reminded me for the fourth time that buckling my seatbelt was not simply a suggestion. Sinking deeper into my seat, my skin bubbled with goosebumps; it felt as though I was morphing into the next stage of my life. I learned more about myself and the world this semester than I had in my previous eighteen and a half years. I quickly reached for my journal and flipped to its first entry. As I slowly began turning the pages of my manuscript, an enormous herd of life lessons and memories stampeded through my mind.

Holy Ship!

*"The sea, once it casts its spell,
holds one in its net of wonder forever."*
—Jacques Cousteau

Day 1 | Jan 4, 2020: The sensation of waking up this morning was like the bliss of one hundred Christmas mornings wrapped into one!

I JUMPED OUT of bed in my hotel in downtown San Diego with more energy than a nuclear power plant. The feeling of Christmas morning was so intense I actually looked around the hotel room for presents. My gift, however, was much larger than anything I had ever received on all my birthdays, Christmases, and graduations combined. My gift was the world.

Unsurprisingly, being gifted the world takes an astronomical amount of time, effort, and money as we've already learned. The logistics of day one opened my eyes to the incredible feat Semester at Sea truly is.

Running around my hotel room, I just finished stuffing the seventy-third protein bar into my suitcase and I was still in my underwear. I threw on the plain white t-shirt and tan shorts that I had set out the night before. My logic was simple. I wanted everyone to meet me on a blank slate, no logos or fraternity letters, just Johnny.

I was finally ready to head to the staging area, but I needed to leave a few important things behind—my parents. My mom squeezed me as if it would be our last embrace while my dad stood beside us chuckling at her torrential downpour of tears. Letting go of what must have been a ten-minute hug, I pressed hard against my dad's chest, allowing me to feel his racing heart, giving him away. One hundred and five days was going to be the longest time I had ever spent away from my family.

Pulling away from the hotel in my Uber, I turned around in my seat for the classic goodbye wave through the back window. "Byeee!" I said aloud, as if they could hear me. Sitting straight again, I gripped the passenger side headrest for support as I twisted my back in both directions, popping so many vertebrae my driver said, "Ooo, good one." I took a deep breath and mentally checked that I had everything. When I came to the end of my list, I looked up and noticed a neon-green rosary hanging from the rearview mirror. *I forgot that.*

A few months before the voyage, I encountered a group on campus who lived very differently than me. They were part of an organization called Saint Paul's Outreach (SPO). I'd become close with a few of the guys before setting sail: JP, Jeff, and Mike.

Legend has it when Jeff came out of the womb, the doctors shouted, "It's a man!" They had heard the *Urban Dictionary* definition of Semester at Sea "offshore drilling" and were worried for my soul and that they might never see me again. But as badly as I wanted to sail around the globe, I desired what they had more than anything I've ever wanted in my life. An authentic community, a real brotherhood, freedom that couldn't have been curated in-house. These were gifts.

I was just beginning to start a prayer life, and the guys encouraged me to bring along my rosary, which I hadn't touched in years, tucked away in the depths of my boxes in storage. Praying the rosary takes about fifteen to twenty minutes and consists of reciting prayers in sections called decades while meditating on the mysteries of Christ's life. Somehow all the beads were intact, but for whatever reason, it never made the trek to San Diego.

Since there's not much discretion between my thoughts and words, my Uber driver knew the dilemma. Without hesitation, he removed the rosary from its place and handed it back to me. I immediately asked for his name. "Maslah," he responded. Before I could even form words to thank him, he said the following recounted from my journal: "There is nothing you will experience on this adventure that will fully satisfy the desires of your heart."

Gosh, Maslah, just what I wanted to hear! I thought to myself. His words pierced my heart like a two-edged sword. This adventure was all I had been thinking about for over a year now and if it wasn't going to satisfy, I'm not sure what would. I gave Maslah a firm handshake, and he bid me farewell.

The staging area which weaved through the ballrooms of a large hotel was infected with enthusiasm! This was confirmation everyone was receiving the same gift I was. Folks from all

Holy Ship!

over the world stood beside me, their entire lives packed into a few containers on wheels. After waiting through a number of Disney-length queues, I boarded a bus destined for Ensenada, Mexico, where we would finally board our glorious new campus. Since our ship sails under the flag of the Bahamas, we were not allowed to sail between two US ports, so sailing from San Diego to Honolulu was not possible, hence our departure from Mexico.

I sat in the front row of the bus next to a girl named Emily, who waved a bittersweet goodbye to her boyfriend outside as our wheels lurched forward. The slight nudge that pushed my back into my seat triggered a smile on my face that I could not suppress. The bus was almost uncomfortably quiet. I sat silently holding a wide grin until we came to a halt at the border.

An agent hopped on and explained in very broken English that she would need to take a roll call of every passenger on board. As she began, we realized that the language barrier rendered our names incomprehensible. A few names into her list, a student named Kat stood up and offered to help, which inspired me to do the same. We took her packet of names, split it in half, and started to rattle them off.

Funny enough, we couldn't read the names either! I had forgotten that our voyage would have students from all over the world. Our smorgasbus represented four continents! I felt pretty stupid continuing to butcher one name after another, but at least the pressure was off somebody else.

Back on the road again, we passed over the Tijuana canal and I began to comprehend the fact that this was actually happening. After planning for a trip long enough, you start to forget there is a light at the end of the tunnel. We were an hour into the drive, and I was still having trouble shaking the smile off my face. It seemed as if everyone was holding their breath. We were literally on a constant cliffhanger, cruising along the never-ending coastline, cornering one humongous bluff after another. Each hairpin turn we hugged brought us closer to embracing our new home.

I had so much adrenaline pent up inside I wanted to scream at the top of my lungs but that could very well send us plummeting to our death. I felt like I was at the starting line of a drag race with the gas and brake pushed down to the floor and it took four hours for the light to turn green. I probably set the record for most calories burned on a coach bus.

Then, out of nowhere, we screeched around an enormous rock face and our floating campus, the *MV World Odyssey*, was revealed in our direct line of sight, glistening in the sun with an almost supernatural hue. My mouth shot open, and I let out everything I had inside of me—the rest of the bus followed suit—erupting so loud I thought the windows would surely shatter! I hadn't even boarded the ship and the stress of over a year of preparation instantly melted away.

After a few security lines, everything around me seemed to be moving in slow motion, except for me. I approached the gangway, and the aroma of the ship drew me in. You would have thought I snorted crack by the massive inhales I was taking in, but I'm just a big smells guy. High on life, I glided across the ship to my cabin, 5016, where I found my cabinmate, Jimmy. We literally high-fived until our hands went numb! I met Jimmy for the first time just two days prior to our embarkation, and we were getting along better than MJ and the rock.

Jimmy and I didn't realize we had been spoiled with electronic key cards our entire life, so once we learned how to use a traditional key, we dropped off our things and levitated to the top deck where there were hundreds of people to meet. Embarkation day on Semester at Sea is comparable to the first day of grade school. Everybody is brand new and eager to make as many friends as possible. I found myself hanging out on the aft of the ship, sitting on a barstool, sparking conversations as people strolled by.

I yelled "Jake!" when I read one guy's name tag; I could tell he was confused about how I knew his name.

"Whadup! Forgot I was wearing a name tag!" Jake replied excitedly.

Jake introduced me to his roommate, Chris, and we made conversation about video editing, one of my favorite hobbies. We all had dreams of creating an edit in all the countries we would visit. Rather than getting their phone numbers, I asked for their cabin number, which turned out to be right down the hall from mine on the fifth deck.

Many months later, Jake shared a memory with me from his point of view that happened just a few hours earlier that day. He was in the staging area of the hotel in San Diego when his dad (ASU alumni) caught a glimpse of the pitchfork on my luggage tag.

"Jake! That guy over there must go to ASU! You've gotta go talk to him!"

Jake refused to walk over. "I've got all semester to meet this kid. When it happens, it happens."

I must have met over a hundred new faces within the first hour on board. Jimmy and I were on a mission to meet as many people as possible, and eventually we sort of came up with a slogan. "Johnny and Jimmy fifty sixteen" we would yell, parading through the ship, as if our Portillos order just got called.

The sun began falling out of the sky as evening rolled around, abruptly transforming the ship from an international networking spectacle to an organizational nightmare as the staculty (SAS's combination of staff + faculty) attempted to categorize the mammoth onslaught of wide-eyed college students. All voyagers had to pass through a multitude of tables to officially check into the ship before we were allowed to leave port.

After checking in with the passport station, I moved along to the medical table where one of the shipboard nurses, Kim, asked me if I had placed my seasickness patch because we would be setting sail in the next few hours. I responded as I did to my mother, insisting that I would not get seasick the entire voyage. She rolled her eyes back and replied, "Ahhh, you're one of thooose."

The time spent on the ship had felt like a week, and we had not even untied from the dock. As night fell, I ventured over to the bow and leaned over the side railing to see Captain Kostas with his right hand on a joystick. I instantly threw up my arms and waved everyone around me over to watch our campus take her first steps of the journey. The dock crew on land untied our ropes while the ship's crew slowly cranked them inside. One of the ropes slid over a sea lion lying on the shore and it let out a hilarious yelp of disapproval!

The scene was picture-perfect; I was in a state of pure bliss. More and more people began to flock to the top deck of the ship to take in this incredible moment. No more than a hundred yards offshore, our ship let out a gigantic horn blast that shook me into another dimension, and the crowd viscerally roared back in response.

Holy Ship!

Day 1 | Jan 4, 2020: Screaming into the sky with a few hundred of my new friends secreted more adrenaline than any other time in my life. This is why I chose SAS!

Beep-boop! The overhead speaker sounded and brought everyone's conversations to a halt. "Welcome aboard the beautiful *MV World Odyssey!*" the voice overhead began. One of the most important jobs on board was held by Daniel, aka the Voice of the ship. Every day the Voice would come on the overhead speakers located throughout the ship to provide important news and updates. Day one on board was not even finished before I started to lose my own voice. One of the many reasons I would never be fit for Daniel's job.

I figured this was a perfect opportunity to explore the nooks and crannies of the ship by myself. I always enjoy having a solid awareness of my surroundings whenever I'm in a new city, regardless of if it floats or not. Prancing to the aft, I ran down several decks before I noticed a seating area guarded by a string of red felted ropes. Not being allowed entry in places only makes me want to enter more, so I hopped the rope and opened a heavy wooden door to reveal a bar. Jackpot! I couldn't wait to tell everyone about my discovery, but my fantasies were cut short when an older woman stepped into the room.

"Oh my! You scared me. You're not allowed to be here!" She extended both her hands to push me out.

"I'm sorry, I was just exploring," I replied.

The door she pushed me out of was different from the one I had come in, so when she closed the door behind me, she pointed to a sign that read: NO STUDENTS BEYOND THIS POINT.

"I can read, but I never saw this sign because I hopped over the ropes guarding the back entrance," I said smartly.

The woman finally introduced herself as Kathy, the Karen of the Seas, one of the lifelong learners on board.

Students, staculty, crew, family, and lifelong learners (LLL) all make up the shipboard community. The crew ran the ship that students took classes on, which staculty taught, who were supported by their families, and the LLLs were the oil that kept the engine running smoothly. LLLs are the ones behind the scenes helping the staculty organize clubs, proctor exams, and run ship-wide events like Sea Olympics and Neptune Day. They can sit in on any class they wish but don't take any exams—pretty sweet, right? They do all the same things the students do besides returning home with a transcript. LLLs even get a few special areas of the ship all to themselves, one of which happens to be the Fritz Bar.

I retold this story to Jimmy as we started unpacking all of our bags. Thankfully, both of us were neat freaks, so we agreed that everything must have its own space. Snacks in this drawer, pens in that drawer, undies over here, camera equipment over there. There were two closets in our cabin, one of them just slightly larger than the other. Jimmy made it into the cabin before me, so he claimed the larger side, which was no problem at all because he let me use a portion for my camera gear. Once everything was out of our bags, I noticed all of Jimmy's shirts were still in their original Gap packaging. He explained that he had bought them just for the voyage and that they were something he would wear the majority of the time. However, they weren't worth bringing back home so at the end of the voyage he would simply throw them away, lightening his load on the way home. I thought, *I sure hope he meant donate.*

Fully satisfied that every little item had a home, I organized the medicine cabinet in our bathroom and hopped into my first shower. Swaying side to side ever so slightly was a funny feeling. I wondered if there may come a time when I'd lose my balance altogether.

I was exhausted crawling into bed, but the second my head hit the pillow I realized I forgot to journal. A month and a half before the voyage, on November 14, 2020, I purchased my first journal, and I was determined to write in it every single night of the trip before going to sleep, so I got out of bed, grabbed a pen, and wrote the wonderful happenings of the day.

> Day 1 | Jan 4, 2020: WHAT A DAY! Semester at Sea eats expectations for breakfast!

In bed for the second time, I turned over on my side to face Jimmy and confirmed that he did not snore.

He exhaled. "Negative, Cap."

Jimmy said that I started asking another question, but I was out cold before I could finish. All he heard was: "But... if you do..."

That night, I set the world record for fastest entry into REM, making it my second world record of the semester, and I didn't even have to move for either one.

Chapter Two

*"You don't know what tomorrow will bring,
so bring it to tomorrow."*
—*Zohnay*

Day 2 | Jan 5, 2020: Today started with a bang when I drilled my left shin into my nightstand drawer that I definitely closed before jumping into bed.

THE TINY SWELLS that jumped up and kissed the hull of the ship effortlessly rocking me to sleep apparently culminated into a greater love affair, fully opening my nightstand drawer. Jimmy confirmed that he did not simply forget to close the drawer. Leaving my cabin, the ship life was beginning to show its true colors, making me use the handrail while walking up to breakfast at Lido.

There are two dining rooms on board the *MV World Odys-*

Chapter Two

sey. Lido, which is located on the top deck, features unbelievable views and outdoor seating. And Berlin, the main dining room centrally located in the belly of the ship, which offered only indoor seating with large porthole windows. Very similar foods could be found at either location.

I was sitting with new people at every meal, but regardless of my company, I would always make the sign of the cross and say grace. On occasion, people would ask me if I was a practicing Catholic, to which I'd sometimes joke, "I'm no longer practicing, I've perfected it." January 5 was our first Sunday at sea, and I remembered JP, Jeff, and Mike's encouragements to pray the rosary, so I listened.

After a long day of meeting new faces, our entire evening was dedicated to joining and creating student organizations. One of the fascinating aspects of SAS clubs was that they came and went with the students. Every voyage required clubs to be created from scratch because its members would eventually return to their home institutions. Joining some sort of Bible study was at the top of my list, so I scoured around looking for a sign-up sheet. I faintly heard someone say "Jesus" while handing off a piece of paper to a friend. By the time I had gotten hold of the sheet, every single line was full, so I happily wrote my information on the other side.

We were a very creative voyage coming up with everything from rave club to pancake club. I was excited to check out all the different organizations, but I had yet to explore the entire ship! Flying down a few decks into the belly of the beast, I stumbled upon what's known as the "pamper room," equipped with an indoor heated pool, sauna, private bathtub, and an army of heated stone massage beds. Robert California would certainly approve!

The spa made me realize our campus was a cruise ship, not that our cruise ship was a campus. When SAS was not leasing the ship during the school year, our vessel doubled as a German cruise liner during the summer months. Built originally in Germany in 1998 as the MS *Deutschland*, our ship was renamed the *MV World Odyssey* in 2015, from September to April each year. The ship is decorated in 1920s style and certainly uses no shortage of high-caliber materials. Maintaining the *MV World Odyssey* costs Semester at Sea $25,000 per day and from the conception of SAS in 1963, the program has been hosted on six different vessels.

The largest space on board the ship was known as the Lastinger Union, a mammoth multifunctional room used for classes, logistical pre-ports, lectures, talent shows, etc. When global studies was not being taught, the room was curtained off into four smaller classrooms. Every class period in this room was a true production, with chairs so plush they swallowed you whole.

> Day 3 | Jan 6, 2020: Our first global studies class consisted of two middle-aged men making impossibly accurate animal noises, a woman singing a lullaby to 250 college students, and a chart detailing how much time we have left before our carbon emissions kill us all. Oh, and they said that the closest human being to our ship was above us, floating on the international space station.

That synopsis of global studies (GS) pretty much sums up the entire semester. Global studies was an interdisciplinary course that was required for all voyagers regardless of their ma-

Chapter Two

jor. The class was taught by Professors Manietes, Denning, and Wildermuth, who took turns lecturing each week. The feeling of looking outside and watching the waves pass by washed away any stresses the class was creating. The same space that birthed many of our stressors also doubled as our means of therapy—now that's renewable energy!

Sitting beside Jake, there was never a dull moment. We were both going back and forth, lamenting about the lack of testosterone on board. We were trying to determine if the scarcity of men was a pro or a con. Jake and I turned our heads in a circle, casually making eye contact with about forty girls in a matter of seconds. "It's a pro." We nodded to each other. One girl in particular, Ashley, forced me to hold my gaze until Jake nudged me forward.

Giving our attention back to the professors on stage, Wildermuth stepped forward. "So tell us, why did you sail on Semester at Sea?" You would have thought a bottle rocket shot up my ass by how fast I leaped out of my chair to scream, "THE RATIO!"

Even the professors had a hard time containing themselves, as if the elephant in the room had just farted. I could individually hear all twenty men in the room laughing. A punch from Mohammad Ali wouldn't have knocked the smile off my face. I had earned respect from Jake and the attention of half the ship. To my astonishment, Wildermuth backed up my interjection with facts, transitioning to the next slide that revealed a whopping eighty-one percent of our voyage was female. There were quite a few fish in the sea.

Jake and I left class eager to get to know each other better, so we headed up to the top deck for a conversation.

"Bro, Arizona State! What's that like? Must be sick!" Jake

asked eagerly.

"You wanna do video work? Like, full time? No, that's sick!" I said, answering Jake's question with another question. Both of us were so anxious to learn about each other we didn't want to talk about ourselves. We hadn't sat down for more than a few minutes before an elderly man, one of the lifelong learners, interrupted us saying, "Boys, get up, we're gettin' ice cream."

He asked me not to disclose his name, so for the sake of this book, we'll call him John Shaw. Following John's orders over to the poolside bar, I had no idea I was entering one of the craziest conversations of my life. The second our butts hit the stool, he began firing off dozens of questions as if we didn't have over one hundred days at sea together. Jake's face was cringed slightly the whole time, skeptical about this old man's intentions. On the other hand, I was an open book and as long as John was pumping ice cream into me, I was going to keep talking.

Fifteen minutes into the conversation, John directed his attention toward me and asked candidly, "Have you ever worked a day in your life?"

I replied, "Yeah, I was a lifeguard for three years."

John grabbed both of my palms and lifted them up in front of me. Inspecting the creases in my hands, he exclaimed, "Nahhh, I think you're just really good at chokin' the chicken!"

I had never met a more presumptuous person than myself until I met John. I'm not sure what would have happened if he made that remark to the wrong person, but that didn't matter because he said it to me. And with the confidence that we had known each other since birth. Our incredibly unique first encounter was the foundation we would build upon for the remainder of the semester. But, by the end of our conversation, we

Chapter Two

hadn't just laid the foundation, we were already ten stories high.

John was a free spirit—at seventy-nine years young, he was the oldest kid I'd ever met. He didn't have a filter much like myself, a take it or leave it type of guy, so I decided to take as much as I possibly could. John had been a human sixty years longer than me, so I figured I might learn a thing or two. Aside from being at complete opposite stages of life, we were wildly similar, and we recognized that from the get-go. Besides sharing the same name, John believed that I was his teenage reincarnation. At the age of seventy-two, John jumped out of a perfectly good airplane. But I reminded him it wasn't the same as my jump because his wrinkly skin would have slowed him down substantially. John did not want to be treated like an old man. He wanted to be one of the boys.

On the fourth morning of our voyage, I was rudely awakened by what was known as "the cough." (This was not COVID.) This cough was part of a respiratory infection that normally happens at the beginning of every voyage. Living so close to one another, the entire ship gets sick at the same time. But this cough couldn't hold me back today because Jimmy and I had signed up to receive a tour of the captain's bridge. Walking through the CREW ONLY doors was even more satisfying than sneaking into the bar. The computer systems on the bridge were far more expansive and complex than I had imagined. I thought it was fascinating that the captain slept right in the back of the control room, which allowed for quick access in the event of an emergency.

Since there were no icebergs in any of the oceans we were to sail through, I tried to imagine what an emergency situation would look like when the sirens began to wail overhead! Our tour guide immediately stopped talking and Captain Kostas burst through his cabin door and grabbed a clipboard off a shelf. After scribbling down a few things, the sirens seized and in a thick Greek accent Kostas announced, "Do not fear, this was just a dummy... a test." Now that our hearts had resumed beating, we finished the tour by taking a few pictures behind the main steering wheel.

> Day 5 | Jan 8, 2020: The coolest part about my new campus is that I can make it to the pool, class, gym, and ping-pong table in less than ninety seconds.

Five days into the voyage, I was already taking for granted how close my cabin was to everything. Jake and Chris lived right down the hallway and most of the girls we were befriending lived directly below us on the fourth deck. By now, I had seen enough faces to know that Ashley was the most beautiful girl on board, and it just so happened that she was Julia's roommate. I thought my cabin would need a revolving door, but I was happy that the hangout spot was elsewhere because our room remained spotless. That place was Maddi's cabin.

It was this special place, the size of a walk-in closet, that I learned many things about myself and my friends. But for right then, I learned that my cough wasn't really something to complain about. Everyone expressed their dissatisfaction with the sea sickness patches. The mantra was: "I could not see this morning!" On top of drowsiness and constipation, losing vision was a pretty gnarly side effect. My friends envied me for not having opened the box.

Contrary to blindness, I was wide-eyed when Jake told me he

Chapter Two

had used "Corners of the Earth" by Odesza for one of his video edits. While explaining that I had just used this song in a documentary on summiting Kilimanjaro the previous summer he rolled up his pant leg revealing the icosahedron, Odesza's logo, tattooed on his thigh. A diehard fan indeed!

Jake and I resurfaced our conversation about the ratio on board. Just under a week into the voyage, we noticed that a healthy percentage of the girls were in a long-distance relationship, many of them for the very first time. We were shocked when we learned about some of the couples' dating rules. For most, their healthy and communicative relationship continued even as the two physically became farther and farther apart. For others, a "hall pass" was applied, meaning cheating was fair game. For those who were not so open about the terms of their relationship, they disguised their pass with a "break." Even though they had the full intention of getting back together after the voyage.

If there's one thing that my generation sucks at more than anything else, it would be commitment. And certainly not just in a dating relationship; this could mean showing up to club meetings each week, pulling through on vacation plans, or following up after saying, "Let's hang soon!" On Semester at Sea, however, it was harder to ghost someone knowing you might bump into them at any second. Anyone who missed a meeting vocalized beforehand, travel plans were far more inclusive, and dating relationships on board were some of the most committed I'd ever seen. Could this be solely due to our proximity? And how was all of this possible when one of our main modes of communication on board were Post-it Notes?

Some people got creative with their Post-its and wrote where they could be found on the front of their cabin door. Gone to:

"Library" or "Berlin." I thought it might be a cool idea, but I was never in one place for very long and Jimmy didn't want the public knowing his whereabouts, so our cabin door was clean. Naturally, sticky notes opened wide the opportunity for pranks, particularly fake love notes. It was middle school all over again. Our cabins were just a walk-in locker. We were taking Post-it notes to new heights even Mr. Post-it himself would have never dreamed, so I decided to ask Ashley out with one. In retrospect, she definitely should have said no.

As big of a role that sticky notes played in our lives, they couldn't help me keep track of the days of the week. Monday? Or should I say A7? SAS does not use the traditional calendar week, meaning classes held on Saturday and Sunday were fair game. Every day would switch off between A classes and B classes, the number behind the letter indicating the day into the semester.

> Day 6 | Jan 9, 2020: Military time has become the new norm. I cannot believe we don't use it back home.

Dinnertime was quickly becoming my favorite part of the day. Enough things had occurred by 15:30 to have several hours of conversation and luckily, we could! Breakfast and lunch were normally much quicker due to classes but dinners lasted several hours most nights. The length of the meals also could've been attributed to the sheer number of women involved in conversation. The ratio was always hilarious at each table, typically one guy for every four girls. It was the girls that started most conversations, and it was the girls that kept the guys at the table.

Constantly meeting new people in class, on the pool deck, and in the gym, I don't believe I sat with the same exact table of people

Chapter Two

twice. I was used to meeting new people every day back at Arizona State, but I wasn't used to *intentionally* pursuing relationships with guys; that was something reserved for girls. With so many females on board if I wasn't careful, I would end up with a friend group of girls, and I'd be stuck for the rest of the semester helping my girlfriends decide if a guy was "ship cute" or "cute cute." *But as long as I had Jake, I'd be okay*, I thought.

Just under a week into our voyage I had arrived to dinner at Berlin about fifteen minutes before the buffet opened to scout the place for some PNFs (potential new friends). This time I decided to do the reverse approach and sit at an empty table and see who came by. I had laid my phone face down on the table revealing the photo of Saint John Paul II I had behind my case on the back. One person after another strolled by and suddenly someone began speaking to me over the back of my head. "Why do you have his photo on the back of your phone?"

I swiveled in my chair and gave her my standard elevator pitch and arriving at the part where he plays a major role in the downfall of communism in Poland, she interjected, "And that's supposed to make me like the guy?"

I didn't know that was even an option for a response, so I sort of sat there blankly. We didn't end up sharing dinner together, but others filled the seats, and we stuffed our faces with the finest pasta the open ocean had to offer. After dinner I met Jimmy and Mackenzie in the Union for our first (and last) dance club meeting. The three of us had remarkably different dance experience. Mackenzie was professionally trained, Jimmy didn't have a rhythmic bone in his body, and people sometimes mistook my dancing for a medical emergency.

Mackenzie and Jimmy somehow found out that I would do

anything for attention, so they dared me to run up on stage, interrupt Madz, one of the club leaders, and do the worm. I stood up out of my chair and confirmed there was enough of an audience for a respectable ROI. Plopping back down, I handed Jimmy my glasses, dumped out my pockets, jumped onto the stage, kicked off my Birkenstocks hitting the chandelier two decks above, and performed a proper worm, ripping my loose-fitting elephant pants in the process. This stunt sent the club into a spontaneous dance party, but Jimmy and Mackenzie couldn't partake as they were paralyzed in laughter.

The seventh evening of our voyage I was on the top deck admiring the sound of the ocean when I heard a commotion coming from the pool bar. Walking up on the scene, I learned it was a guy's birthday who I had not had the chance to meet. So naturally, I began belting out the happy birthday song. The only issue came when it was time to sing his name, so when it did, I abruptly filled in this space with some random gibberish. Once the gobbledygook had left my mouth, the dude looked over to me and said, "It's Ben... but it's the thought that counts."

We were approaching our first port of call: Honolulu, Hawaii. Traveling across the globe at twenty knots, or roughly twenty-three mph, was almost comical. Jimmy and I enjoyed watching our cabin's miniature TV screen as the tiny arrow signifying our ship inched across a fully blue screen. I had no idea how disconnected I would feel after not seeing land for just a few days.

Chapter Two

Day 8 | Jan 11, 2020: I keep hearing rumors of people spotting whales and dolphins and I haven't seen shit!

This was the longest period of my life without seeing a single animal. I took for granted walking outside of my dorm and locking eyes with a pigeon. A pigeon! I was starting to believe I would only see the people on our ship for the rest of my life. I had not spotted another vessel or even a plane. I felt so out of control. I'm all for taking the path less traveled only when I'm the one steering the ship!

I was so desperate I leaned over the railing in search for garbage, really any sign of human life. But the crisp blue water was not interrupted by any foreign colors as far as the eye could see. I thought this thing was supposed to be filled with plastic! Frantically scanning the water like an anxious lifeguard, I figured there had to be a straw somewhere, or one of those plastic can holders that turtles seem to wear like it's the top trend.

Suddenly an awful sensation came over me unlike anything I had ever felt in my life. Picture that horrid feeling when you've got to sneeze but it won't come out, so you're stuck holding up your arm in front of your face, eyes squinted like you just ripped a bong. Now imagine instead of having to sneeze you felt like fainting. I have never fainted in my life, but I've watched four people collapse in front of me, and every time it disturbs me to my core. The lightheadedness came over me but rather than falling over I stayed in that state for a few seconds. Once I recalibrated and caught my breath, I assured myself I drank enough water; the problem was I'd seen too much.

Making Friends

"I don't like that person. I must get to know them better."
—*Abraham Lincoln*

STEPPING BACK ONTO solid ground for the first time in over a week was euphoric, but unfortunately, we wouldn't be there long enough for a stable shower. Since we were only staying for less than twelve hours, our options were limited to SAS sponsored adventures. We had a plethora of options: shopping, hiking, snorkeling, cleaning up trash on a beach with Jack Johnson, etc. Jimmy and I signed up to tour the Pearl Harbor Memorial.

At 8:00 a.m., we entered a 360-degree theater room and watched footage of the 1,800 pound Japanese bomb violently explode the USS Arizona on December 7, 1941 at 8:00 a.m. The hair on my arms stood up so high I feared it would touch the person beside me. Then I had a thought: *How many people have mournfully watched that video which invoked deep feelings*

Making Friends

of resentment towards Japan, and then set sail for Japan the same night? I simply couldn't wrap my head around what we were doing. This would be the first of many extreme shifts in perspective that only a program like SAS was able to pull off. A privilege I never fully understood until many months after the voyage.

When the video was finished, we promptly loaded onto a boat to visit the rectangularly shaped memorial built directly over the sunken ship. Walking through the pearly white memorial the contrast of the charred remains of the ship below drew me out of myself. Through one of the square openings in the floor a massive oil puddle was slowly making its way beneath our feet. Experts say that some 500,000 gallons are still left inside the belly of the ship, and about one gallon leaks out in the harbor every day. Making our way to the far end of the memorial we saw 1,177 names etched into a towering stone wall. We were informed that roughly 1,000 were entombed in the hull below.

> Day 9 | Jan 12, 2020: I learned more during my tour at the Memorial than any history book could have ever taught me.

After our somber experience we made a beeline downtown hoping to brighten our spirits. A few of us stumbled into a small burger joint and realized this would be our final American meal of the semester. What better way to honor the US than gnawing through the layers of a cheeseburger, treating our tongues to a grease bath? We knew there would be hamburgers available along our journey, but we wanted to do our best to eat the local cuisine to fully submerse ourselves in the culture.

Leaving lunch, my eyelashes caught the light drizzle as we

walked through the town. Eventually, our route led us onto a beach packed to the brim—I was shocked at the crowd for such an ugly day. Walking along the sand in the warm rain a fellow student, Mackenzie, and I started brewing a peculiar idea. You guessed it—a fake proposal! After a brief huddle, Mackenzie handed me a ring off her finger, and I dropped down on a knee to put it back on her. She played it perfectly: both hands over her mouth, an enthusiastic yes, and then we jumped for joy. We had sold sand to a beach.

We posed together for photos and shook a few hands before it was time to hop on the bus and head back to campus. Everyone was worn down by the end of the day, so our ride was mostly silent, except for the relentless vibrations in my pocket. I whipped out my phone to see all my new friends from the ship following me on social media, the vast majority on Instagram. What confused me the most was when I clicked on a profile and scrolled through their photos, it felt like I was meeting an entirely different person. I could not wrap my head around this phenomenon before it was time to unload our bags and make our way through security. I performed the hula for the Hawaiian agents—kudos to my dance class—which relaxed everyone in line, especially those who were attempting to sneak on alcohol. With everyone on board we set sail for the second time.

My day in Hawaii would be the last time I would go an entire day on land without seeing a mask for the next two and a half years. Little did we know that COVID was surging out of Wuhan, and with our bow still pointing westward, we were headed straight for it.

Making Friends

The day after leaving a port, everyone on board participated in a post-port reflection session. Groups of roughly twenty students led by either a dean or staculty member scattered to various spots around the ship for privacy. My group was led by the head academic dean, Gene, and Angela, a resident director. They started our first meeting by sharing some extremely personal details about themselves, teeing us up for the very vulnerable conversation to follow.

Since we were so early into the semester, Dean Gene asked how everyone was doing making friends and finding "their people." A few expressed the difficulty and stress while trying to balance coursework and travel plans but one student confessed they had not made any friends at all. Feeling an intense urge to yell out, "I'll be your friend!" I contained myself and tried to offer practical advice.

"You know, making friends is a lot like spreading jam on toast."

My group snapped their heads at me with a scowl thinking I was on my way to making fun of her.

"And your energy is the jam. If you put all your jam in one spot on the toast, sure that bite is going to be delicious, but you might not enjoy the rest of the toast as much as if you spread it evenly around. Spreading your jam doesn't mean you won't have those few who you truly connect with, it means you'll have a better chance of finding them."

I continued on, telling the student to sit with new people in the dining rooms, but this was much easier said than done. What was so difficult about this situation was that the socially affluent had already connected with "their people," meaning their table was already full. And even if there was an open seat it was not *really* open. The further we sailed it became exponentially harder to find new friends as if there was some sort of unspoken window where friendships were expected to be made. At the end of this window, everyone could take a deep breath, look around them, and prioritize those relationships. Ten days into the semester we were quickly approaching the end of said window if it hadn't passed already. The song had stopped in our imaginary game of musical chairs and some students had nowhere to sit. I just couldn't understand why the music wouldn't play all semester long.

When I entered one of the dining rooms, I would scan the place for a few seconds to locate my friends. Most of the time they were already sitting at the same table. Besides "my table" I also took notice of those who were eating alone. On occasion, I would ask that person if they wished for company and then sit with them. When "my table" noticed me eating without them I hoped they understood my intentions. I didn't try to explain to my friends what I was doing before I sat down with someone else. What would that even look like?

"I know you guys are my friends, I just want to sit with someone else that's not my friend that could potentially become my friend, but not to replace our friendship. Okay, bye!"

My friends weren't going anywhere, and if they were truly my friends, sitting at a different table here and there would not change a thing. While I was lucky enough for this to be my case, I know it was not this way for everyone. Sitting at a different table meant something must be wrong; it was making a statement.

Somewhere during this season of the voyage I wish the Voice had come over the loudspeaker and said something along the lines of, "Good evening! I see that everyone has found their

Making Friends

people, but how can you be so sure? Spend the next hour in the company of someone you'd like to know but haven't had the opportunity."

This "click shift" would be dreadful to some but for others it might have provided their only opportunity to seek out new relationships without the fear of breaking their own.

I pondered our reflection session for the remainder of the afternoon before it was time for my first fancy dinner orchestrated by Jimmy. For $29.99, this extravagant meal is held in the Four Seasons dining room and offers its meals from a special menu that changes throughout the voyage, along with two glasses of champagne. The most common reason to have a fancy dinner was to celebrate a birthday, but we were simply there to celebrate each other.

Thirty minutes before our fancy dinner some of the girls came knocking on our cabin to take pictures. This would be the only time the girls were ready before the guys the entire voyage. I scrunched up my tie and followed Maddi up to the bow sporting my American flag suit and immediately spotted Kathy waving me down.

"Where's my invite!" she snarled.

"Students only," I replied.

Everyone looked stunning. We felt like celebrities as people outside of our group stared and took pictures. As if the ocean view from the bow wasn't enough, we headed back to the aft to cap off the photoshoot. In need of someone to take a proper group photo, our good friend John turned the corner and offered to help. He was becoming known for impulsively buying dozens of people ice cream, so a small crowd was sure to follow close behind. Strangely enough, he was also dressed up, wearing all black with a cherry red tie.

> Day 10 | Jan 13, 2020: When John stood next to Kathy, I realized she must be his wife!

John was dumbfounded at the number of girls in our photo; surely, they were not all going to the same dinner. A few million pictures later we headed down a couple decks to the fancy dining room where our group of fourteen was split between two tables. A dozen women—six dates for me, six dates for Jimmy. I sat across from Kate, which was a terrible decision because I could hardly swallow my food as she joked that the Japanese flag reminded her of her first period. Kate's mannerisms were shockingly similar to mine, so we were on the same wavelength all night.

Just after we had dug into the bread our old friend John burst through the dining room doors hoping he could join us while Kathy scrambled up behind trying to pull him back. We welcomed him over, but the waiting staff vetoed and immediately threw him out, so we shouted that he and his wife could dine with us soon. John, now engaged in a door-pushing match with the servers, shoved one final time to stick his head through and shout, "My wife's dead, top that one!" All of us looked around at each other with blank faces—what the hell just happened?

Upon further review of the play and follow-up with John we learned that cancer had taken his wife years prior, yet he was incredibly open and willing to talk about his loss. He wore his heart on his sleeve and loved entertaining all types of questions—taboo was not a part of his vocabulary. We'd discuss everything from personal finance to underwear tags, but the most surprising part about John was the potential for our conversations to turn on a dime. John and I would be making small talk about no wipers, then he would say, "You know, life is just like a toilet paper roll, the further along you are the faster it goes." He was a master tattoo artist who loved spelling out his wisdom with my brain as his canvas.

After indulging in the finest food our ship had to offer, Maddi was inspired to burn it right off with a full-body workout in the morning. I rose at my usual time, 8:00 a.m., ate breakfast upstairs in Lido, and made my way to the gym. Now, I am very much an afternoon workout person, so getting into the zone this early was going to be interesting. I had heard once that if you're not motivated to work out, just try for the first two minutes and if you're still not feeling it, you can quit. Implementing this strategy I closely monitored myself for the first two minutes but as my body warmed up and I broke a sweat, stopping now was way harder than continuing. I guess the only thing harder than quitting cold turkey is quitting warm turkey.

We were dialed in, and our water breaks were few and far between. The humidity painted a thick glaze over our skin like a Krispy Kreme doughnut. Feeling the burn and smiling ear to ear I couldn't tell how long we had been working out. Both of us knew we eventually had to shower and get ready for our 10:30 global studies class so Maddi checked her phone for the time: 10:31. We raced to reset the gym, grabbed our water bottles, and flew over to the union. We jogged in dripping sweat, so rather than sinking into one of the plush red chairs we unfolded a few plastic ones and placed them as far away from other people as possible. My cotton shirt trapped all my body heat due to the lack of air flow in the union, so I took it off and folded it over my chair.

A few moments after class ended, I was in my cabin about to hop in the shower when the infamous *"Beep-boop!"* sounded overhead. The Voice said sternly, "Shirts must be worn at all times in class. We thought this was a given."

Guilty as charged.

The Voice continued on to remind us that our first drink night was later that evening. Since our ship was sailing through international waters, the legal drinking age was eighteen, and our captain reserved the right to determine how the drinking was to be carried out. To participate, we pre-purchased a drink card for forty dollars from the front desk on the fifth deck loaded with eight drinks. Our cards were punched in after each drink to monitor our progress. Each drink night anyone eighteen and up was allowed two beverages, either two glasses of wine or beer.

Some were content with two drinks, others were not. When someone was seen getting a new drink people would approach them to ask their price. I witnessed someone sell a glass of wine for thirty dollars—for a beverage valued at less than one dollar. There are roughly five glasses of wine in a bottle, and we were being served five-dollar cabs.

With at least one drink in everyone's system deck nine turned into a dance party. In a shouting match over the noise of the crowd between a few students I hadn't gotten to know yet, I learned of a rumor that the ship wouldn't port in Morocco due to "heightened middle-eastern tensions." But truly this was the least of our worries. In the heat of the evening, I stepped away from the action to have a word with a few of the deans and the Voice. I apologized about my wardrobe malfunction and assured it would only happen a few more times. All of the commotion

Making Friends

made it difficult to hear each other, so we all leaned in closer. Fully aware that the scent of alcohol was on my breath I tried to put my hand up in front of my mouth, which completely defeated the purpose of leaning in close. Even though I was legally able to drink on board I still felt like I needed to hide something. Drinking in front of the deans was quite the flip from those in high school who called me AND MY MOM into their office and warned me not to throw a party. The party was thrown, and I took pride knowing I gave the police a reason to visit a neighborhood they had never been to. Recognizing a few wounds, I eventually eased up, and we began our conversation.

We chatted about the drinking age in the US. The leadership team agreed that it's silly we are able to fight and die for our country yet cannot enjoy a beer. Maybe if alcohol was less taboo and more commonplace students would not get their first glimpse of freedom in college and dive right off the deep end. A glass of wine or beer with family might teach teens to respect alcohol and understand their limits before they disrespect themselves by desiring to blow past them. But who knows, at the end of the day there are so many variables that affect the consumption of alcohol. And I'm sure standing on the top deck of a German love boat in the middle of the ocean with some of the most beautiful and adventurous people in the world standing beneath a beautiful string of lights had little to no effect on our consumption.

Joining the crowd once again I was approached by a girl who confessed, "In all honesty, I'd date you in real life."

What the hell were we living in now? It's difficult to articulate what would lead to someone to describe the present as "not real life" but in short—it's too good to be true. While our voyage was soon going to give us a most impressive awareness of our global community, it simultaneously didn't feel real. Quite the paradox, huh? It all boils down to the simple fact that what we are doing was *insane*.

Some people's wildest dreams would still fall short of the adventure we were embarking on. And to think that SAS was not even a dream of mine until about a year before setting sail is mind-boggling. It would take a lifetime of planning and saving to sail around the world independently, while all we had to do was apply. Granted, our study abroad was the most expensive in the world. I'm dying to know what percentage of people would choose to sail on SAS if they would match the price of their single-country program.

During Semester at Sea, it is so easy to forget about life before the ship when every meal is cooked for you, your laundry is taken care of, your bed is neatly made, your professors are the best in their field, and all your best friends live in the same compound. So rather than pinching myself throughout the voyage to convince myself this was real life, I pinched myself as a reminder that this utopia would not last forever. It was going to be an awfully hard transition going from a fifty-second walk to a three-hour flight to knock on Maddi's door.

Two weeks into the semester I waltzed into Berlin with Jake for lunch. The topic was alone time. Jake enjoyed being alone; he viewed it as a time to recharge. On the other hand, when it was just me, myself, and I, even the three of us couldn't get along. When I am alone, I constantly think I must be somewhere else, where there's people, doing things. When I am alone, I am not building any relationships, therefore I am stagnant. All of the reasons I felt

Making Friends

like a kid in a candy store on embarkation day.

Jake said, "Where in the world does your energy come from?"

"I dunno, I guess I just feed off of people so being surrounded by them is when I'm most alive," I replied

"Do you feed off me?"

"Of course, I do!"

I feed off of everyone, but it is far easier to hand off the baton when two people are running at the same speed. In the race of life I picked up my head and found myself sprinting alongside Jake, so it was easy, even natural to hitch my wagon onto his, so to speak. Jake and I operated on the same frequency, like two Energizer Bunnies beating our drums in unison, but our energy came from wildly different places. Oddly enough, the Energizer Bunny's choice of footwear is the sandal, so maybe I was onto something with my Birkenstock obsession.

Basking in the sunshine that was our friendship, we reflected back to the first time we met and our impressions of each other were strikingly similar. This same question was brought up again at dinner sitting around one of the giant round tables in Berlin.

> Day 12 | Jan 15, 2020: The group of friends I surrounded myself with were beginning to call themselves "the squad." Maddi, Jake, Kate, Chris, Julia, Jacob, Ashley, Nic, Jenna, Riley, Lauren, and myself.

The squad humored each other by going around the table and sharing our first impressions of one another. I was up first.

Riley: "I loved how kind you were to everyone around you,

and I enjoyed your free-spirited energy; I didn't understand how you were so happy twenty-four/seven."

Jacob: "Well, honestly Johnny, I thought you were just a frat boy who loved to booze and didn't really care about school."

I couldn't even register Riley's wonderful comment because my brain zeroed in on Jacob's. I was pretty distraught that he had come to such a sadly unimpressive and specific conclusion. Desperate to understand what was going on, I tried to remember where I met Riley and Jacob. Both of them claimed it was at some point on the first day of the voyage. Then, a few moments later, Jacob added that technically he had followed me on Instagram prior to our first day. Bingo.

Now, stay with me for the next few minutes while I come to a conclusion in a roundabout fashion.

Like I was creating a constellation, I began connecting the dots in my head. In today's culture, we meet each other on social media before we meet in person. The recruiter stalks prospects via LinkedIn, messages for a potential opportunity, then meets for the interview. A guy stalks a girl's profile on Instagram then direct messages her to set up a date—if he's a man they're out on the town, if he's a boy they meet on the couch. Our interactions are becoming follow first, friend second.

Shortly after Julia had added me to the spring 2020 voyage group chat a few months before embarkation someone sent a message reading, "Send your Instagram @." Without delay, I—and hundreds of others—responded to the message with our Instagram account handles.

This was the point in time that made all the difference. I remember sitting at my desk in the fraternity house at Arizona State University irrationally overwhelmed with the amount of

Making Friends

people I could find and follow on social media. I was extremely tempted to try and follow as many people as possible, thinking I would start the voyage with at least a few friends. So, I joined the masses and sent my account handle. An hour later I had muted the chat and deleted my message because the bombardment of notifications tied me down to my chair preventing me from getting anything done. But there were a few, like Jacob, who managed to follow me before it was deleted.

Refusing to continue stalking my future voyagers' lives, I inadvertently assured that my first impression of my future friends was not skewed by the facade of Instagram. When I met a fellow voyager for the first time, I had no context about their life other than the fact that they were brave enough to sail on a ship for an entire semester. This was the only thing that every single voyager held in common.

Just as we find it difficult to quit working on a project that we have spent considerable time on, even if it is a failure, we do not want to cut off the fantasy friendships we fondle in our heads. I'd have had a list of those who I believed could be my friends based on the pictures I saw, and more importantly the amount of clout the person had. But just because someone has a large following on social media does not mean they are genuinely followed, well-liked individuals. This is the danger of subscribing to someone before you ever meet them.

I did not post a single photo including alcohol or related paraphernalia on my Instagram. The majority of my posts were something along the lines of skydiving, snow/watersports, and speaking engagements. So how did Jacob come to such a conclusion? Does my Instagram page accurately represent who I am? The answer is simple: no, and it never will.

This is because people do not see me the way I am, they see me the way *they* are. Jacob may not have even scrolled past my bio "ASU | ΣAE | '22," and determined that I was, in fact, a "frat boy." Ergo drinking habits and poor grades were assumed, so this was the bucket I was tossed into. Escaping my bucket would only be possible if we physically met in person. Jacob might've never voluntarily sat at the same table as me if the rest of the squad didn't exist. But Jacob, being the winsome man he is, probably would have intentionally sat across from somebody he was inclined to dislike in an effort to get to know them better.

Now, you may be thinking, "Goodness, Johnny, what did social media do to you?" and I will unpack and answer this question in spurts as our voyage unfolds. You might also be thinking, "Johnny, this is all far too extreme." So, in the least extreme case, I will offer one final example. Wouldn't you want to save yourself those awkward steps down that annoyingly long and narrow hallway with nowhere else to avert your eyes as you're quickly approaching someone who you've gotten to know so well online but who happened to act quite differently in person?

By doing my best to meet voyagers on a blank slate, I gave both parties the greatest chance to create a lifelong friendship based on authentic connection rather than Internet connection.

College at Sea

> *"How inappropriate it is to call this planet Earth, when clearly it is Sea."*
> —Arthur C. Clarke

ALMOST TWO WEEKS into my Semester at Sea I was becoming accustomed to my simple mornings. No longer was I able to grab my phone, roll back over, and refresh a social media feed. Getting out of bed was as easy as getting in it. I was overjoyed with my lack of options the same way I am more satisfied with my decision choosing between chocolate and vanilla ice cream than walking into a Baskin-Robbins and their thirty-one flavors. Once I made my bed, I opened my seamail to a Bible quote and a few words of wisdom from my grandparents. This was a surefire way to be grateful for the day ahead, especially when tomorrow does not exist!

That's right—I never lived on January 16, 2020. Our ship

crossed over the international date line in the middle of the Pacific Ocean, which meant the morning of January 17 we crossed off two days on our calendar.

> Day 13 | Jan ~~16~~, 17, 2020: I've had this lost day phenomenon explained to me roughly 622 times, and I am still beyond confused.

Nothing has changed so I won't even try to explain it here. Even more mind-boggling was that a fortnight into the semester our floating campus had traveled close to a quarter of the Earth's surface at a leisurely neighborhood speed. The only thing that seemed to move slower than our ship was seamail, our robust email system and main source of communication. Whether it was with friends on board or my grandparents back in Geneva, IL, seamail was the go-to. All announcements from the helm came through this platform because it worked 99 percent of the time.

The only thing that worked 100 percent of the time was an invigorating workout in our miniature gym! One of my biggest concerns before setting sail was how crowded the gym would be, seeing that it was about half the size of a boxing ring. Fortunately, I rarely found more than one other person using the weights at a time. I could comfortably work out alongside another person but three was company.

The coolest part about lifting on the ship was that some reps were much harder than others depending on the swells. On the bench press, pushing the bar up when the aft came down increased the weight substantially, so to show off you would push when the aft was on its way up using the waves as a spotter.

Rather than holding a medicine ball between my legs during pull ups, I could simply wait for the aft to come down and I would struggle to get my chin above the bar.

My most reliable workout partner was Dylan. We had similar builds and strength, and each of us were trying hard to put on muscle. On the seventeenth afternoon of the semester the two of us turned the corner of the seventh deck to find another guy bench-pressing. Letting out an audible sigh we figured we should just come back later. However, we were in a particularly amazing mood because the sun was shining brightly on our skin, and I remembered I was getting ice cream with Ashley after dinner.

Dylan said, "What if she gets cold eatin' that ice cream on the top deck and puts her hand around your arm...they need to be a comforting size."

"If my arms are comforting her more than my words—"

Dylan cut me off, "If your arms won't comfort her then mine will!"

"OK, LET'S GET SHREDDED!" I screamed.

After a few warm-up exercises we were already dripping in sweat. With our shirts off we began our chest and triceps workout. Neither of us were listening to music, just screaming like banshees as we pushed through our sets.

Feeling a good pump and respecting the other student's space the three of us carefully placed our steps. About halfway through our workout we needed to use the dumbbells that were lying beside our fellow shipmate. We watched him for a few moments and determined he was not using the weights anymore. I walked over and lifted both dumbbells then our friend cocked his head at me and muttered, "What the fuck do you think you're doing, bitch boy?"

I had never been in a fight, so I figured this was my chance. Staring him in the eyes I asked, "What'd you just say?"

"You heard me, buddy,"

I despise being called buddy, and I'm sure he did too, which is why he said it.

Dylan, now walking over with a stern voice commanded, "Johnny, walk away!"

Not moving an inch I watched him put his earbuds back in having a very difficult time following Dylan's orders. Against every cell in my body no further dialogue was shared then Dylan yanked me away from the gym to conduct a postmortem.

I was irate, yell-whispering to Dylan, "If he doesn't apologize, there's going to be some awkward moments ahead considering we see each other every day."

Dylan and I finished the second half of our workout just a few feet away from our new friend. Passing by him time and time again throughout the semester I held my breath, but the apology never came.

Later in the evening the first Bible study meeting was beginning in the Lido lounge. Floor seats were all that were available when I arrived as students poured through the port and starboard side doors. When the room finally quieted down to a whisper, we were informed that this meeting was heavily logistical and geared toward dividing out the various Bible study groups. Those who were interested in leading a group were asked to come up to the front of the room. I stayed put, knowing that there were plenty of far more qualified students up to the task. Next everyone was split up into groups of five to six with whom we would study the Bible for the remainder of the voyage. My group consisted of Sasha, Maggie, Kyra, and Zack, who was our leader. Our first small group meeting was the following day, and I was over the moon to get started.

I dipped out of the Lido Lounge and checked my teeth for crud in a hallway mirror before meeting Ashley at the pool deck bar. This was the first time we had conversation outside of a group setting. The bar stools were drilled to the deck, so we didn't waste any time adjusting how closely we sat. Locking eyes with Ashley I could see the rest of the squad sitting at a table in my fuzzy peripheral. A shot of nervousness went down my spine and for some reason my reaction was to call over Dr. Gentry, my marketing professor, who just walked out onto the top deck. From there I think I blacked out. I believe several minutes passed when I was completely turned away from Ashley and engaged in a conversation with Dr. Gentry about our upcoming exam. *Girls like a studious guy, right?*

"I didn't agree with the whole 'C's get degrees' mantra until I found Semester at Sea," I joked with my professor.

Girls like a funny guy too, right?

At some point my professor, who I sensed might've been slightly illiterate in the field of social cues, realized that I invited him into our date and vanished before I could offer him another bite off of Ashley's spoon. I felt all of the eyes on the pool deck watching. I feared somebody was recording this and would use it for quality and training purposes. It wasn't long before we sort of slid off our barstools and joined the noise and laughter emanating from the squad.

In bed, on my side, facing Jimmy about to fall asleep, he asked, "So, did Professor Gentry know you were bringin' Ashley on your guys' date?"

"You were there?"

"I'm everywhere." Jimmy yawned. "But don't sweat it, maybe Ash will invite me on your next date."

"Shut up, Jimmy," I said on the verge of snapping.

It was my first date on a ship, there are lot more variables to factor in, I reassured myself. I just hoped it wasn't bad enough to get booted from the friend group.

Two weeks into the voyage I realized that the larger the waves the lesser my appetite. While big swells meant walking funny and a wave pool neither of those mattered if I wasn't hungry. The sunny side up eggs I would scoop onto my plate from the buffet line in Berlin were always just less than room temperature if not outright cold. In line I saw people dousing their eggs in Tabasco sauce which made me want to hurl.

"You really like that stuff, huh?" I asked.

"Nah, not really, I just like hot food, and this tricks my brain," the guy responded.

I gave it a shot myself, and it was a game-changer.

At this point in the voyage my daily routine at sea was well established, and it was glorious. Breakfast, pool, class, pool, lunch, pool, class, pool, workout, pool, dinner. Because the pool was saltwater, I rinsed off at least five times a day in one of the two freshwater showers in the top deck in my swimsuit. When a line for the shower formed sometimes a few friends would go in together. About to hop in the shower solo I spotted Ashley jogging up to the front of the line. I thought: *There's no way she's getting in this shower with me.* I thought wrong as she latched the door closed and pumped some soap into her hands. I stood on my tippy toes, peaked over the top of the door, and locked eyes with the entire pool deck. I didn't think we'd be showering together before I asked her to be my girlfriend so what was the rush now?

The conversations I had later that day were firing me up for the content that was to be created in a dozen countries on the horizon. I had recently purchased my first DSLR and still being a rookie I hung it around my neck and walked around the ship asking for tips and tricks from anyone with experience. Jake and Jacob had a wealth of knowledge about cameras, so they were my number-one resource. They both agreed that just like anything practice makes perfect, so I set out to take some photos.

My first picture was of Jimmy lounging out on the pool deck with a book. Then I turned around to shoot Dylan as he walked by. I quickly realized I was only interested in shooting people's faces, so I set out to capture every single one. Running around the ship like a chicken with its head cut off, I asked for permission before snapping a photo then moved right along to the next person. Eventually, people were volunteering to have their photo taken. By the time Bible study began I had photographed half the faces on board and was excited to hear that all my friends still wanted to be friends with me after last night.

I was the last to arrive, finding my group sitting in a circle in the back of the union. Zack started us off with a prayer like any great adventure should. Immediately after, he shared that this was the first time he had ever led something like this before and my eyes lit up. I had thoroughly convinced myself that I shouldn't lead because there would be somebody out there who could do it better. Meanwhile, Zack was in my exact same shoes but decided to stand up and give it a shot. He knew he may not have the most experience but stepped into the role regardless and let God do the rest.

The vulnerability I experienced was unlike anything I had witnessed before; thoughts seemed to articulate themselves as we ventured deeper into conversation. By the end of our meeting, everyone had shared part or all of their testimony and it was clear how incredibly diverse our group was.

Brushing my teeth before bed I could barely feel the waves moving beneath me, but by the time my head hit the pillow the TV remote was moving ever so slightly across our glossy countertop. We were in for it tomorrow.

> Day 14 | Jan 18, 2020: In global studies I was made aware by a fellow classmate that it was, in fact, a Saturday. Halfway through the lecture and still wrestling with this fact, I had concluded that this was against the law. I uprooted from my seat and swiftly made way for a bathroom break on the pool deck. It appeared that nature called the rest of the class as well.

Contrary to my journal entry, school was the number-one priority on SAS, but a solid pool outing always left me refreshed and energized. With my first marketing exam later that day, I checked the syllabus for the location of Professor Lance Gentry's office hours. "Deck #7, Aft," which was not a very specific location considering most of that deck is littered with pool chairs. To my wonderment, I approached Dr. Gentry laid out with a drink in hand. These were the most productive office hours of my academic career. It's shocking how well class concepts travel through a salty breeze rather than a stuffy box with no windows.

Our exam was nearly upon us, but King Neptune had different plans. Inside the ship staculty and LLLs passed out puke bags which were apparently in high demand. I headed over to Berlin for a quick lunch but the entrance was stained with vomit, sending my appetite into hibernation.

Marketing was just an hour away, so I found some quiet space in the library to chill out before staring down one of those hideous Scantron sheets. I hadn't been sitting for more than ten seconds when the sheer size of a world atlas sitting tall on a shelf stole my attention. Flipping to a random page I opened to a map of South Africa. Drooling on the page, a bolt of excitement shot through me when I realized this would be one of our ports of call.

Guuush! The belly of our campus slammed into a humongous swell forcing me to grab hold of the shelving to maintain balance. The deep noise of the impact sounded like the ocean had blown right through our hull. Looking around at everyone's reactions in the library I spotted a small commotion brewing on the opposite side of the room.

A congregation was forming around Ashley; I wouldn't have been surprised if they were just there to stare at her, but it looked like she was holding something. Getting a closer look people were staring at the desktop keyboard and laptop in her hands as if these objects weren't the two most common things found in a library. Ashley's laptop keyboard had broken, so she was given a separate one which sat on top of the dead keys.

Leaving the library, the handrail assisted me to the top deck for my exam which happened to be where waves were felt the most. Sitting in my chair as exams were being distributed, three-story waves were smashing into our ship like a toy in a bathtub. Attempting to fill in my first bubble, the aft jolted down, raising the bow of the ship high into the sky. Filling in these tiny circles was harder than opening snacks in *A Quiet Place*. We must have hovered at the top of this wave for fifteen seconds until the bow slammed back down, which caused a thunderous vibration so vigorous that it sent my water bottle off my desk! Trying to hold a laugh, my chipmunk cheeks suddenly burst, breaking the silence in the room, and giving the rest of the class permission to follow suit.

> Day 15 | Jan 19, 2020: Marketing was something out of a movie! I asked Lance if the ginormous waves would curve our exam! LMFAO

Dr. Gentry honored our request and added a curve due to inclement weather!

School rocked, and I knew that the second I turned in my exam I would be rewarded with the thrill of our very own wave pool, courtesy of King Neptune. Dylan and Lucca bought floaties in Hawaii for this very purpose, but we needed to act fast before the crew closed the pool for our "safety." The swells of the ocean tossed our campus so much that the saltwater pool spit water twenty feet into the air. If so much as a drop hit my contacts I looked like I just stepped out of a recording session with Snoop Dog. On random days of the voyage, Captain Kostas and some of his bridge crew—dressed in white head to toe—could be found relaxing by the pool with a cup of coffee. Today was one of those days. The captain and his crew walked by and complimented our flotation devices. I shouted out to the captain, "Who's steering the ship?!" Kostas yelped back, "It is the chef... pray for us!"

Everything about our campus was top tier, especially our captain. If you open your dictionary to "stud" you will find a piece of wood with a picture of the captain nailed to it. Kostas was a large bronze Greek man whose accent and athletic short shorts gave the girls chills and whose poise couldn't be disturbed if his house fell on his head. When the captain walked by, I felt like I needed to stop and salute, and most times I did. He had the power to join two together in matrimony and blow a serve past anyone brave enough to stand on the opposite side of the ping-pong table. Frankly, if you found yourself across any table from the captain, you were either going to lose or be booted off the ship. This is why I preferred to hold my meetings with the captain in passing. Beyond our gorgeous captain, our staculty and crew were fantastic. SAS only brought on the cream of the crop.

The past week was as close to the *Suite Life of Zack and Cody* as our voyage came. These were the types of days I had envisioned living from my study abroad advisor's office. The lack of technology, abundance of sunshine, the coolest friends, the prettiest girls, the exams curved with the waves, the strangely attractive captain, it was really happening! We were liiiiiiivin' the suite life!

Sweet Life on Deck

"The heart of man is very much like the sea, it has its storms, it has its tides and in its depths it has its pearls too."
—*Vincent van Gogh*

ON THE SEVENTEENTH afternoon of our voyage I found myself engaged in a very competitive ping-pong match. Besides the table being positioned in a wind tunnel its location was terrific socially speaking because the designated smoking area was just a few feet away. Those with a nicotine addiction could not bring their vapes on board so some took up cigarettes. Go figure! A few backhands away from glory I spotted the Voice on his way for a smoke so I held off my serve and asked if I could join him after my game. My opponent insisted that we could finish another time, so I set the paddle on top of my ball and grabbed the cigarette he had sticking out of the top of his pack.

Lighting up both of our smokey treats the Voice asked, "So,

how long have 'ya been smoking?"

"This is my first time," I replied coughing my lungs out.

Daniel screeched and moved quicker than the Matrix yanking the cig from my mouth exclaiming, "HOLY SHIT! Then I must be the devil!"

I snatched it back from him and insisted it was okay, as long as my mom never found out. The gusts of sea air only allowed me to take three drags before my cigarette disintegrated before my eyes. Rookie move. Experienced smokers sacrifice the euphoria of leaning over the railing due to the wasteful wind gusts that burn the cigarette exponentially faster than standing back a few feet.

Deteriorating my body physically, I figured I could use some restoration spiritually by praying another rosary. I forgot last week because I was too busy eloping in Hawaii. Running into our cabin to grab my prayer materials Jimmy's nose perked up. "Why the hell do you smell like my mom?"

I left the cabin before answering Jimmy's question with haste as if I knew where I was heading, but I didn't. Like a vagabond I wondered about the ship looking for a place to call home for the next half an hour while I prayed. I wandered past the union and ran into a fellow student named Mitch. I had not spent much time with Mitch, so I was completely blindsided by the honoring he was about to deliver.

"You have a way of making everyone feel important. Your energy is contagious. I simply don't know how you manage to do it. You have time to make friends with everyone, while making them feel appreciated at the same time. You have a real gift."

"Thank you, Mitch," I said sincerely.

I invited him to pray the rosary with me and he accepted. On our search for a spot we bumped into Lizzie who was peacefully doodling on her iPad.

"I love to draw too!" I exclaimed.

"Oh, yeah? Let's see whatcha got!" Lizzie replied.

Lizzie handed over her device and I turned the screen away to conceal my drawing.

"I gotta say I can't believe this."

"Huh?" I mumbled not lifting my head from the screen.

"Johnny Vrba, sitting still in front of me, drawing, not shouting, not surrounded, not rushed," Lizzie said in a flirty tone.

"I'd tell you to take a picture, but I'm almost done with this beauty."

Counting down from ten I put the finishing touches on my incredibly realistic and life-sized you-know-what and then flipped the iPad for the big reveal.

"So, y'all comin' to pray or what?" I asked, starting to walk away.

The three of us found a lonely spot starboard side on the seventh deck and I pulled out the rosary Maslah gave me. Lizzie was raised Catholic, so she had prayed the rosary before, but this was Mitch's first time. Words could not describe how beautiful the waves looked that night. The breeze seemed to blow right through my chest, blowing out any debris that had collected in my soul scattering it across the sea. When we finished our fiftieth Hail Mary, a short prayer asking for the intercession of Jesus's mom, Mary, I found myself pondering the sheer power of the ocean.

Sweet Life on Deck

Day 17 | Jan 21, 2020: After a rosary with Mitch and Lizzie, I listened to Kanye West's "Water" gazing off the back of the ship as our wake rippled into pitch-black darkness. *Somebody authored this.*

It was about this point in the voyage that the smallest things became a much bigger deal. The first drops of sweat during a workout that disappeared into the sea as I leaned over the guardrail to taste the salty air. The way the ship moaned like an old man after plowing through waves by day, and then gently hummed me to sleep by night. The tone in which I'm greeted by Perry, the friendliest server in the dining room. I had spent enough time at sea to realize that they would need to drag me off this thing when the time came. I was already having trouble leaving the dining rooms during lunchtime.

Somehow my lunch schedule had begun to align with the staculty's children otherwise known as the ship kids. This lucky bunch were invited on board with their parents, while one parent taught, the other technically homeschooled them on the ship. I played with the youngsters while I ate; a passerby would consider it fighting. Nonetheless, their parents were overjoyed at the idea of me working some steam out of their kids. Since running was prohibited nearly everywhere besides the treadmill, and kids were not allowed on the treadmill, there was really no energy release for them at sea. The ship was large enough for the big kids, but it was too small for the little ones.

When I was finished eating, I would have to sneak out of the dining room. Most of the time someone would give up my position and I would brace as the swarm of overgrown fingernails pulled me back into their lair. Finn and his friends were the most aggressive on the ship and I liked to play that way too. One would rip off my backpack, another would snag my water bottle, and the remaining troops would hurl themselves onto me. My fight-or-flight response would immediately activate, always choosing the former: I began ejecting my professors' kids off my back (which is way more fun than any other type of kid). Two of my favorite things in life are deep conversations with the elderly and rough housing with kids, the last two things I expected to enjoy on Semester at Sea.

Beep-boop! The Voice came on overhead: "Don't forget to submit a tagline idea for our voyage, number 128! Two tickets to a fancy dinner will be awarded to the winner who will be announced during our Japan pre-port meeting! Can't wait to see you all at the talent show!"

Every voyage was given a tagline, which was submitted and voted on by the shipboard community. I had several ideas: 128, The World's at Stake!; 128, You're Great!; and 128, The World Awaits! Each tagline was awesome, but I saw a clear winner in my mind, so I submitted: 128, The World Awaits!

My thoughts now instantly drifted to the talent show. Do I have a talent? The show was just two days away! I knew I wanted to be a part of the show in some capacity. I almost felt some sort of obligation to participate, as if sitting in the audience wouldn't be fulfilling enough. I reached out via seamail to see if the show needed an MC, and it turns out they already had one. Crap! Who could be better than me on the mic? *They need me,* I told myself.

I contacted the student who had already secured the MC role. My email read:

Hey, Dalton!
I heard you were going to be the MC of the talent show. Congratulations! I'm not sure if I missed the sign-up/tryout but as a fellow microphone enthusiast I would love to get involved. I bring a ton of energy and I am curious if you would be open to having a co-MC?

Less than a few hours later Dalton agreed. I know if I were in his shoes, I wouldn't want someone storming into my limelight, so I was thankful for his yes.

Later in the evening the videography club invited the entire ship to the union to watch their first projects of the semester. Groups were split up and tasked with creating a music video to "Fergalicious." It came as no surprise that I made a cameo in the videos.

Filled with exuberance after watching a couple hysterical videos I made my way up to the top deck to smell the ocean. Strange, right? Turns out that during the day all of my other senses are so overstimulated that my nostrils seem to put up an OUT OF ORDER sign. Salt water alone does not smell—the sulphury scent is produced by bacteria as they digest dead phytoplankton.

Making my way down to my cabin to start counting sheep, I happened to bump into another student named Jordi. Jordi was quite the character; he sort of nonchalantly meandered about the ship, mostly minding his own business, until this conversation. He mentioned that tomorrow was his thirty-sixth birthday and all he wanted was a chocolate and strawberry ice-cream cake. I immediately chuckled to myself and asked how old he was really turning until he pulled out his driver's license. I told him that his friends would do their best to get him one. We agreed to meet in Berlin to enjoy dinner and eat the cake at 17:30 sharp the following day because afterward I would be co-hosting SAS's 128th talent show.

The sound of the waves thundering against the side of our ship made me think we might have caught air in the middle of the night. Like most mornings, Jimmy reached for the TV remote and pressed the power button. Those next five seconds were the longest of the day as we waited to see how far across the screen we had traveled. It was always anticlimactic, as if the captain slowed down to a stop while we slept. The only thing special about our travels last night was sailing across the Mariana Trench.

Leaving the cabin I set out to acquire a chocolate and strawberry ice-cream cake. I knew that birthday cakes needed to be ordered weeks in advance, so an eight-hour notice was not ideal. I approached one of the servers named Alphonzo. He and I had gotten in the habit of exchanging proverbial phrases every morning while I poured my orange juice and today was no exception.

"Speak of the devil and of course he's flying by the seat of his pants," Alphonzo exclaimed with a thick Jamaican accent.

"Another day, another dolla'," I replied.

"Money doesn't grow on trees."

Using my best Don Corleone impersonation I said, "Alphonzo, I have an offer you can't refuse."

"Spill the beans."

"Listen, I made a promise to a friend that I would get him a chocolate and strawberry ice-cream cake by dinner tonight. You help me get the cake and you can have some!"

"The road to hell is paved with good intentions."

"JEEZ, Alphonzo, I'm serious!"

"It's gonna cost ya an arm and a leg, but I might have an ace up my sleeve."

With that, Alphonzo darted into the kitchen, and I stood still, patiently sipping my orange juice with a grimace because I had just brushed my teeth.

"Stick a fork in it," Alphonzo said.

"Shoot! That's ok, thanks anyway for checkin'."

"No, you can actually stick a fork in it. LET DEM EAT CAKE!"

I let out a Shamu sized spit-take and rejoiced with Alphonzo. An invitation to Jordi's party was included in every conversation I had all morning and afternoon. Everyone seemed to be down to go but I wondered who would show. The rest of the day seemed to slip through my fingers as the sun slid into the ocean, effortlessly scattering billions of sparkles across the water. It was 17:15. We pushed multiple tables together, signed a birthday card, and positioned the cake at the center of it all.

Jordi's friends showed out in numbers, about twenty-five strong! In the blink of an eye, 17:30 rolled around as we stood ready for Jordi to walk through the Berlin doors. At 17:35, Jordi was nowhere in sight. At 17:40, the crowd started mumbling to each other. By 17:45 we questioned if Jordi had gotten cold feet? The scrumptious cake, still sitting on the table, stared back at us blankly. I quickly gathered the crowd into a large huddle and devised a plan.

Standing on a chair so that everyone could hear, I announced our reconnaissance mission. We would sweep the ship from bow to stern. Each search party consisted of two people. Three parties would tackle each deck, and we would report back to this rendezvous point in exactly ten minutes. I reminded everyone to clear bathrooms, the doctor's office, and knock on his cabin door. The party who came back with Jordi would be rewarded with extra cake.

Ready... I held my hands apart and clapped them together... BREAK!

Immediately a sea of people rushed out of the dining hall sprinting around the ship shouting, "Jordi!" It wasn't until writing this sentence now that I realized people may have thought he had fallen overboard. Regardless, our search party expanded well beyond Jordi's party—it was all hands on deck. I stayed put in Berlin to make sure Jordi didn't find his way into the dining hall with no one there.

Eleven minutes passed, and everyone had returned empty-handed. At 18:03 I decided to call it quits. In the realm of colossal surprise birthday party failures this one certainly takes the cake. I picked up the knife and as I made my way through the chocolate and into the strawberry, Jordi glided into the dining hall with the grace of a gazelle.

> Day 18 | Jan 22, 2020: I screamed, "JOOORDI" so loud my parents might have heard it from Illinois.

On the border of conniption and pure bliss I chose the latter and decided not to ask any questions. With the attention of all 250 people in the room I squeezed the life out of Jordi and brought him to his cake to the tune of the happy birthday song. As we were singing, it was clear that Jordi's guests were more surprised than Jordi. If you've ever been to a surprise birthday party, you know that this is usually not the case.

Jordi's face lit up when we handed him the card and we congratulated him on thirty-six glorious trips around the sun.

He dug into his cake, but he was better at wearing it, or maybe it was eating him. When everyone had their share, the cake was wounded but not dead so Jordi asked me if he could hand deliver the remaining cake to other people outside our party. With an enormous grin on my face, I explained, "It's your cake, you can do whatever you want!"

I helped Jordi plate the rest of the slices and followed him around the room as his assistant. He would walk up to a random table and say, "Happy Birthday!" then set a plate of cake down to which the most common response was, "Thank you so much, but it's actually not my birthday." Jordi, already moving on to the next table, shouted back, "It's mine, enjoy!" I guess you can have your cake and eat it too.

Oops!

"But the human tongue is a beast that few can master. It strains constantly to break out of its cage, and if it is not tamed, it will run wild and cause you grief."
—Robert Greene

AFTER DELIVERING THE last piece of Jordi's cake I ran back to my cabin and threw on my American Flag suit and a long winter coat so I wouldn't ruin the surprise. (Only a few saw the suit during my fancy dinner week one)

Volunteering to be an MC two days before the show turned out to be much less work than I had imagined. Watching the acts practice on stage I kept wondering why we weren't up there ourselves? With such a diverse range of performances requiring all sorts of different equipment, and a very small crew to help, transitions between acts were sometimes a few minutes long. We wouldn't be congratulating then cracking a quick joke; we needed to have a full-blown conversation.

As people flooded into the union, my blood pressure rose to that of a hiker summiting Mount Kilimanjaro. I darted backstage to find an equally amped Dalton. Normally when I am holding a microphone, I at least have the faintest idea of what I am going to say; tonight this was not the case. However, we did plan the first two minutes of the evening, hoping it would be enough to spike the energy in the room for the remaining two hours of the show. The MC's job is to bring a sense of humor to what is otherwise a bunch of people showing off their talents for a sheet of paper that says they have talent. I just needed to relax. The lights slowly began to dim... showtime!

The iconic guitar riff of "Thunderstruck" by AC/DC shattered the silence of the room. The lighting guy was sweating in the back using all his might to send strobe lights into every corner of the room. In the chaos of the flashing lights Dalton came running through the crowd and jumped onto the stage. I was still in position backstage right behind the crack in the curtains. Dalton hyped up the crowd then introduced me like a starter of the 1996 Chicago Bulls: "Jooohnnnnnnnyyy Vrrrbbbaaa!"

Throwing both curtains to the side I leaped out into the center of the stage, taking inspiration from Iron Man (my favorite superhero)—I wanted to mimic his famous entrance when he premiers a new suit.

> Day 18 | Jan 22, 2020: I quickly understood I wasn't Iron Man the second I drilled my knee into the stage and punched the hardwood with all my strength.

Slowly lifting my head for dramatic affect I smiled through the pain then pranced around the stage like a young gazelle screaming into the microphone. I probably blew the sound guy's eardrums. Our entrance was executed to perfection, now all we had to do was maintain the hype.

The first few acts flew by. I was still buzzing off my adrenaline rush, and anything that came out of my mouth felt like pure gold. But as the show progressed, I started to feel human again. Dalton and I tried hard to coordinate our next bit while an act was performing. Whispering as softly as possible, others backstage let us know we needed to be quieter. We tried everything to keep the crowd entertained, from singing "Ave Maria" to impersonating Kermit the Frog.

About halfway through the show, the six hundred and some bodies packed in the room combined with the lighting on stage turned my suit into a straightjacket. I was drenched, constantly running my fingers along my collar for air. Downing several water bottles still left me parched, but I knew if I kept drinking, I would have bigger issues. Two acts later the bigger issue presented itself.

There was no bathroom backstage; I would either need to hold it for the next hour or somehow get through the sea of people in front of me to the restrooms on the other side. I didn't want to just leave Dalton up there alone while I walked over everyone without telling them where I was going. Still processing our dilemma, the act on stage finished her dance.

Dalton began, "Wow! What a terrific performance Mackenzie, especially—"

"I have to go pee; I'll be right back!" I interjected.

Hopping off stage left, I parted the Red Sea and miraculously arrived just in time. The crowd was dead silent as I passed through. *Maybe I didn't need to tell them where I was going,* I thought. Walking up to the urinal I stood beside another student, AJ. He did a double take and with wide eyes exclaimed, "Wait, aren't you supposed to be on stage?"

With a smile I nodded. "Yeah, don't worry, I let 'em know."

Back under the lights I was as light as a feather. The extreme relief helped me get through the next couple acts with a renewed sense of confidence. Dalton and I were still trying our best to come out after each act with somewhat of a plan, so we stood side by side whispering into each other's ear. All of a sudden Abby, a fellow student and one of the directors of the evening, reminded us that the last act was on stage. All we had to do was close the show.

Trying to scheme up something good for our final remarks, we couldn't stay focused because of the powerful voice on stage delivering her poem. She kept saying, "My skin shines when... my skin shines when..." repeating this phrase enough times that I figured it had to be significant. As she finished her final line, Dalton and I took the floor.

Assuring I stayed relevant to the act I said, "Now that was awesome! Thank you so much for your words, Jennifer! I don't know about y'all, but my skin shines when I'm on the *MV World Odyssey!*"

Half the crowd erupted; the other half was quiet as a mouse. I could hear one guy, Van, distinctively cracking up toward the back of the room who was then abruptly hushed by his friends. After a thorough round of applause for all the acts the union slowly began to empty. I hung out on stage with Dalton and congratulated him on an awesome night, then we made our way over to the front of the stage for a few photos. I pulled off my jacket to let out the heat that had been trapped the entire show. My BO hit notes I never thought possible as my nostrils tinged. Cooling down and catching my breath I felt a tap on my shoulder.

One of Jennifer's friends, Aliaya, congratulated me and then asked, "Do you know what her poem was about?"

"Um, no, actually I don't," I replied with a confused face.

"That's what I hoped, because her poem was about racial injustice."

Oops!

> Day 18 | Jan 22, 2020: I felt like Juni Cortez from *Spy Kids* and the perfect ten on my chest just dropped to zero.

Here is Jennifer's poem.

The Sun Says Hello

The sun says hello
My skin shines when the sun says hello
My eyes sparkle in the darkness
My mouth speaks the untold truth
My ears listen to the pain of the voiceless
My skin shines when the sun says hello
My body curves like the ocean big beautiful and endless
My hands grab onto the shackles of oppression
My legs run the race of endless obstacles
My skin shines when the sun says hello
My feet touch the earth that my ancestors cultivated

Oops!

My soul feeds the mouth of the hungry
My heart bleeds for the unarmed killed, the missing women, the mothers crying for the gone too soon
Don't Shoot
Reconsider
My skin shines when the sun says hello
My fist rises for justice, justice for all, justice for us
My march is united for all people
My words are the weapon used to create spaces
My skin shines when the sun says hello

I felt about an inch tall explaining how I truly hadn't listened to any of the acts and unfortunately, I left the dress rehearsal before hearing Jennifer's poem. I immediately apologized to all of her friends who were now gathered around. They accepted my apology, and we shared a laugh about my ignorance.

Then I thought: *What if she hadn't asked me that question?* They would have never known if I made a racially charged joke or if I was just that stupid. They might have held a grudge against me for the remainder of the semester, or flat out resented me. There are a million different things they might have thought, but I was just so happy they knew the truth. However, knowing the truth in this situation was completely in her hands. Aliaya was the hero of this situation.

While I should have thought before I spoke, I believe there are people who find themselves in just the opposite situation. Those who do not speak up at all, paralyzed in fear of what others will think. If this story teaches us anything, it's that people are far more forgiving than we think, especially in a culture that cancels more easily that it subscribes.

Leaving the union on my way to the cabin, students and staculty went out of their way to say things like, "Awesome job!" and "Laughed hard at your last joke!"

Their only job was to watch the show so if they heard the joke they obviously weren't sleeping. Seeing how people giving their full attention to the show found that joke funny brought me to a crossroads. I knew the diversity of reactions meant that a lot of different people were thinking a lot of different things about me.

Even if we have the best intentions, it's all about how the other person hears your words, not how we say them. I am sure there are folks who believe I was being intentionally racist; however, I was at peace at least knowing Jennifer did not share the same sentiment after pouring her heart out to the shipboard community.

I shared all of this with Zack later in the evening and a lightbulb went off in his head. He offered me two verses of scripture to pray with. James 3:4-5. "Look at the ships also; though they are so great and are driven by strong winds, they are guided by a very small rudder wherever the will of the pilot directs. So the tongue is a little member and boasts of great things. How great a forest is set ablaze by a small fire!"

If our ship had turned its rudder even the slightest degree after leaving Mexico we would have ended up in Australia. Similarly, our tongues have the power to take us to drastically different places *regardless of* if we are aware of the words we are saying. How frightening that realization was for me!

Flexibility—Level One

*"Life is like riding a bicycle.
To keep your balance, you must keep moving."*
—Albert Einstein

THE NIGHT PRIOR to our arrival in Japan, our entire shipboard community was packed in the union like sardines for our very first international pre-port! These gatherings were held the night before docking alongside a new country highlighting safety concerns, basic language tips, and vital cultural knowledge. I agree with my friend Nicole's description as, "some cross between a party and a scolding from your grandma."

The lights slowly dimmed, and the big screen lit up with a map of the world. Our ship was a small blip on the screen starting in Ensenada, Mexico, and then gradually began making its way all the way across the screen to escalating music. The riveting animation grew louder and louder, until reaching its climax when our ship slammed into Kobe, Japan! It was at this moment I began to realize the gravity of what we were doing.

> Day 19 | Jan 23, 2020: The noise from the crowd at pre-port tonight would have been quieter if everyone had just won the lottery. I will not be able to fall asleep tonight. I think my resting heart rate is 120. Tomorrow I will see Asia for the first time.

After that exhilarating introduction, it was time for the moment we had all been waiting for, the winner of our voyage's tagline! The Voice made his way up to the stage as our host for the evening and the crowd went wild. By this point, everyone on board adored him for his corky nature and the hilarious giggles he let out when he slipped up reading over the loudspeaker. When the union was quiet the Voice began, "Wow! There were some terrific submissions, but there was certainly one winner by a landslide! Drumroll, please! The winning tagline of our voyage is… **128, THE WORLD AWAITS** submitted by Johnny Vrba!"

I immediately stood up and waved at everyone in all directions as if I had done it hundreds of times before. The squad who was sitting amongst me were screaming like wild banshees. This was Semester at Sea history! I struggled to pay attention the reminder of our pre-port lecture, but I did walk out knowing one extra Japanese word. *Ohayo!* (Pronounced Ohio) Meaning, *good morning!*

Crawling into bed I felt very accomplished. Slowing down my breathing for the first time all day I felt the waves roll under the ship giving her a gentle massage. I was in love with the motion of the ocean. Lying flat on my back I could feel the slightest rush of blood shift from one side of my body to the other. Being rocked to sleep was one of the most enjoyable perks of life at sea.

Last night's sleep was one of those where you blink and then the sun shines through your window. I set an early alarm this morning to watch Captain Kostas carefully maneuver our campus through a minefield of cargo ships. We were greeted with a beautiful band accompanied with singing and dancing as our ship nestled up alongside our first international port. Kobe, a city located in central Japan, known for its world-famous marbled beef, and soon to be the home of my first Asian encounter.

A few months before the voyage, Jimmy and I jumped for joy from our dorm rooms on opposite sides of the country after we booked a field program titled Bathing Naked in a Japanese Hot Spring. Both of us loved birthdays, and we liked suits even more, so naturally, this was a first-round pick.

We threw on our backpacks, flew open our cabin door, and after about thirty minutes of customs lines I was sitting on my first heated bidet toilet seat. One point for Japan. However, there was no soap dispenser anywhere in sight. Minus one point. I reconnected with Jimmy and a few others I knew had signed up for the program and looked for others we thought might be as crazy as us. Nobody was holding up a sign saying, "Naked bathers" but eventually we found our people.

Our group of twenty loaded onto a bus and headed into downtown Kobe for a bit of shopping before we went nude. Only a few minutes into our drive and I couldn't help but notice the sheer number of people wearing masks in public. We learned that masks were not required and did not indicate that someone was ill, but that they were worn as a preventative measure well before COVID was conceived. For some, wearing a mask was simply part of their everyday wardrobe. I had a good laugh thinking about how everyone looked like a surgeon.

> Japan Day 1 | Day 20 | Jan 24, 2020: When in Japan, do as the Japanese, so I bought a few masks. Wearing one in public is actually kind of a fun sensation!

With an arsenal of masks, carbonated cookies, and crazy KitKat flavors we loaded back onto the bus for the hot springs. As our wheels turned, I pictured us sitting in steaming water amongst mountains with our towels sitting on a rock nearby. Reality struck thirty minutes into the bus ride as we burrowed deeper and deeper into downtown Kobe. The *pssss* sound of our driver releasing the airbrakes confirmed that the mountains would remain a fantasy. Our natural hot spring was adjacent to a shopping center. The men were separated from the women as we walked up a flight of stairs into something similar to a waterpark locker room. Our guide reminded us, "Only one rule, no clothes."

Through a foggy glass door were two crowded pools of dark brown water. We were the only nonlocals in the entire room. Using the handrail I made my first step into the tub and jolted out like I had stepped on a nail. Both tubs were a warm 105 degrees Fahrenheit. The locals had a good chuckle sitting with the water level all the way up to their chin. Ten minutes later I made it into the water and caught my breath. Looking around everyone was sitting a few feet apart, social distancing before it was cool. Being in my birthday suit somehow felt more natural in Japan, even while bathing naked next to fellow students and professors.

Exiting the pool my skin felt like smooth leather. On the opposite side of the room were mop buckets with a hose hooked on the front for us to rinse off. We felt like giants squatting down on our miniature chairs as the cool water steamed off our bodies. Once we were fully clothed, we made our way back down to the lobby and out the door to get some fresh air. Standing in a small circle outside staring into our phones, a murmuring began to spread amongst us. With the chatter growing louder I made out the words *cancel* and *China,* but I didn't have the full picture. Asking for clarification, one of the LLLs in our group read the most recent email from SAS aloud. Turns out, I did have most of the picture: our stay in Shanghai, China had been canceled due to a coronavirus outbreak in Wuhan and our stay in Vietnam was extended one week.

January 24, 2020, was the very first time I had ever heard of the word *coronavirus*.

Every single person in the group reacted with varying levels of frustration. Some, like myself, were just angry enough to stop smiling, others vocalized aloud, but everyone wore the news to some degree in body posture. Overall the group I was with handled the situation with maturity, but I imagined that the other six hundred students could've had different reactions. Once we gathered ourselves, we participated in a collective moan as we mourned our loss of China and the Great Wall.

> Japan Day 1 | Day 20 | Jan 24, 2020: I'm bummed about not seeing China but avoiding the country altogether is the right move because contracting the coronavirus would mean death.

We had no idea what contracting this virus would do to us—as far as we knew, it was as fatal as Ebola. Time continued on as it tends to do and the melancholic air began to blow away. We came to a consensus that it was only China and now we would enjoy the other countries even more, especially the one we were in right now. The value of my time in Japan instantly skyrocketed. I started to enjoy the little annoyances rather than letting them boil up inside. Like how the store clerks annoyingly followed me around their shop. Eventually, I was informed that the vast majority of theft in Japan is from tourists, so it is very common for workers to follow foreign customers around to assure they are not misbehaving. Or how my poor chopstick skills forced me to eat meals at half of my regular BPM (bites per minute).

Only worrying about what I could control (my reaction) made things I couldn't control (coronavirus) unbelievably happier. Victor Frankl came to a similar conclusion after surviving Auschwitz. He writes this in *Man's Search for Meaning*: "When we are no longer able to change a situation, we are challenged to change ourselves."

When I registered for this field program, I stopped reading our itinerary after the title so our post-bath burger was a pleasant surprise. But this was no ordinary burger. Between two toasted buns lie five thinly cut strips of authentic Kobe beef. The meat was so raw it mooed on our plates before we threw it down the hatchet. Day one in Japan was off to a tremendous start and half the day was still before us.

As evening fell and our program was released, I linked up with the squad to go out on the town. Some of the best memories in Japan came after the streetlights turned on. The moment I saw their faces I understood losing China to gain an extra week

Flexibility—Level One

in Vietnam meant an extra week in my friends' company. Jimmy and I had booked our most intense field program of the voyage in China, a five-day, four-night trip, our entire stay in the land of the dragon. Meaning time with my friends would've been slim to none. We had also booked a program to visit Cambodia three of the four days we'd be in Vietnam. Blessed with an additional seven days, I could see Cambodia, Vietnam, and my friends!

Our pace was impressive as the squad poured through every nook and cranny of Kobe trying to find the coolest spot. All of our hard work soon paid off when we climbed an unusually narrow flight of stairs into a tiny shot bar with six stools. Once the man behind the counter had gotten a gauge on the size of our group, he promptly threw out the two locals and introduced himself as "the captain"—how perfect. The bartender quickly put on a captain's hat and insisted we all get comfortable, so like a clown car we packed eleven people around six stools and ordered sake. The captain invited Nic and Maddi to try their hand at bartending as we all cheered them on. In the final minutes of our experience, the captain tossed his hat on Maddi and placed a wet one right on her cheek.

Now we were on the hunt for a karaoke bar. Maddi approached a random Japanese man and started to flail her arms around trying to convey the message that we wanted to sing and dance. The man slowly turned to our group and in perfect English asked, "Is she okay?"

Our knees buckled in laughter—Kate was snorting, Julia couldn't breathe, and Maddi took it like a champ. Suddenly, our new friend jumped on the phone and began speaking Japanese. We knew he wasn't calling the police because he started doing a little jig, swaying his hips side to side, sort of mocking Maddi and, hopefully, confirming he wasn't mad at us. He hung up a few moments later and said, "To dancing, this way!" So we followed him on a fifteen-minute walk across town to a spot called the Rock where he dropped us off like kids at school.

The group was getting settled inside the venue and I was making myself comfortable taking off my coat when I heard a Japanese man scream, "Justin Bieber!" I immediately darted my eyes around the room frantically looking for him until I realized the man was looking directly at me. (I lost a bet with myself two weeks before the voyage that if I did not pass my life and health insurance exam on the first try, I would bleach my hair. It took four attempts and my hair ended up being much more blond than white.) I was certainly spending like Bieber; I was quickly losing any concept of money that I had prior to the trip, and if you ask my mom, it wasn't much to start.

> Japan Day 1 | Day 20 | Jan 24, 2020: I signed a napkin, posed for a photo, and accepted a free drink as the Beibs.

It was at this bar that I heard rumors that there was a group of students who were competing to see who could spend ten thousand dollars the fastest in each country, and thus were initiated into the exclusive 10k club. I was not surprised in the least if it were true.

After about an hour the squad was itching to find one more spot before the night was over, so we bounced and my new Japanese fans were confused to see me leaving without a security detail. The final destination of the evening had much more room to dance. Naturally the entire dance floor—locals and SASers—

Flexibility—Level One

formed a big circle and immediately I was the first to jump in, flailing around like I'd just been electrocuted. Then, I prepared for my signature move by handing off the contents of my pockets before I would jump into the air, arms fully extended, into the worm. I leaped—one arm stuck the landing, the other did not.

CRACK! My chin bone struck the wooden floor as if I didn't use my hands at all. Lying there on the ground I thought I had just been knocked out, but realizing I was thinking I knew I had to be conscious. Ashley ran over to the bar for a bag of ice while I slowly chewed imaginary gum, running my hand along my chin. We determined that it was not broken, just badly bruised. Looking like Buzz Lightyear, I called it a night. To this day, one side of my chin is slightly larger than the other.

Our second day in Japan Jimmy and I began our three-day, overnight field program, touring some of the most famous shrines in Japan. We packed into a charter bus and caught some traffic that made Los Angeles seem livable. I was surprised considering Japan has one of the most advanced infrastructure systems of any nation. Sitting in gridlock traffic, not a single person used their horn. In fact, I do not recall hearing a single car horn in all five days. You can't go more than thirty seconds without hearing one in Chicago, so the silence was refreshing.

Our afternoon was spent exploring the Golden Pavilion and the Imperial Palace. At a few specific spots we were invited to meditate, I prayed to a very different God than the one I was looking at. Then we ditched the bus and took off our shoes to eat at a traditional restaurant in the terminal before catching the bullet train to our hotel in Tokyo. I was in and out of my room faster than you can say *Shibuya* because I was going to meet the squad at the busiest crosswalk in the world. Although none of the squad was on my field program, they were in Tokyo, and I had the afternoons free to travel independently so I was able to hang out with them.

As soon as I arrived, I knew what needed to be done. Since I had flopped literally and figuratively last night, somehow, I needed to regain the confidence to put the worm back in my arsenal of dance moves. The remarkable thing about Shibuya crossing is that once the light turned red, traffic stops in every direction, allowing pedestrians to inundate the entire intersection diagonally. The instant the light turned red I sprinted with all my strength into the middle of the intersection and jumped into the worm. Flopping and spinning simultaneously it was the most glorious worm I have ever preformed. Soon thousands of people scrambled all around me and the squad captured the moment on video.

In the evening, we blew through a few mediocre bars until we ended up at the Womb where we danced into the night to the steady beat of house music. Eventually my phone died, and I needed to Uber back to my hotel to get rest before Jimmy and I's early start the next day. Julia called one off her phone and I left the Womb, walking past half of the ship waiting in line to get in. I was making haste to be sure my ride did not leave without me, because I did not have communication with Julia nor my driver. Speed walking past the line I heard a girl say, "No way, that's Johnny Vrba. He's an icon on the ship!"

My ego kicked around inside like I was pregnant.

Opening the Uber driver's door he asked with a puzzled face, "Julia?"

"That's me!"

Flexibility—Level One

Our third morning, Jimmy and I started our routine again. Breakfast. Shrines. Lunch. Shrines. At breakfast I stood in front of the soft drink machine looking for the button to change the language to English. Finally locating it in the corner of the screen I could now read WATER. As I was walking away, I saw a young Japanese boy go up to the screen and successfully click on the Coke button. I was amazed how, at such a young age, he found the button in English so quickly. It is insane how recognizable Coke's logo is regardless of the language.

Our program took an unexpectedly fun spin when we toured the video game district. The streets looked like Rainbow Road, with blinding lights, and noises in every direction. There were certainly no banana peels on the ground, but there were people racing around the streets in Mario Karts! Maggie and I toured a six-story Sega arcade, where we found locals alongside their gym bags and water bottles using the machines as a workout. Some were even wearing gloves! I did not know Maggie as well as Jimmy did, so it was nice to spend time with a new friend. Right next door was an Animal Café. Each floor housed a different species of animal where people could come in and wind down.

Japan Day 3 | Day 22 | Jan 26, 2020: My life is complete! I pet a hedgehog named Sonic!

Jimmy was working on coordinating dinner plans at a restaurant called Nobu. I had never heard of it before, but he had been raving about it all day. We arrived a few minutes early, and I ordered a sake mojito at the bar. For the next fifteen minutes I watched the bartender make love to my drink then gracefully set it in front of me on what might as well have been a diamond coaster. It was the best thing I had ever sipped in my life. Jimmy and I explained SAS to the bartender and how we only had two more days in Japan.

"Well, you chose the right spot," he exclaimed. "Just grabbing drinks tonight?"

"No, the girls are just a bit late."

"Ah, I see, a double date."

"Yeah, kind of."

"Whadya mean?"

"Well, there's eight girls coming."

"So each of you have four dates?"

"Yeah, I guess."

"So whose paying the four-figure tab?"

The girls strolled through the door with the confidence they had arrived on time. The remainder of the evening would go down as one of the greatest meals of my life. Not being a big fish guy, our waiters (yes that's plural) helped me try all types—raw and cooked—and they were all mouthwatering. Even their grilled chicken was the best I've ever had; I didn't touch my knife a single time. The $120,000 bill was startling until I realized it was in yen. At the time, one dollar equaled 109 yen.

It was now our last day on the field program and our fourth day in Japan. I woke up to news that Kobe Bryant and his daughter Gianna passed away in a helicopter crash. Those who were in Kobe at the time, poured an extra one out. I was pretty shaken up, but our intense schedule didn't blink an eye. Our day began with a tour of the famous Kotoku-in, or the Great Buddha, when Lynn, a LLL, spotted the wheels of a stroller and yelped, "Baby!"

Flexibility—Level One

Japan is home to the oldest population in the world. According to Statista.com, "In 2020, the population aged 65 and older in Japan accounted for approximately 28.4 percent of the total Japanese population." For reference, that's double the percentage of the United States. We were even told in our pre-port lecture that spotting a Japanese baby was rare so to keep our eyes peeled.

The entire group's heads snapped to see Lynn speed walking toward the child. She kindly asked the mother if she could lift her child out of the stroller. After getting the green light, Lynn proceeded to plant dozens of kisses all over the baby's pudgy face. I smiled knowing my mom would have done the exact same thing. We all stood by in amazement watching Lynn love this baby as if it were her own. Everyone gazed into the baby's eyes as if they had never seen one before. By now a line was beginning to form in front of this innocent Japanese family. No wonder nobody wanted a baby, they were like little celebrities. I had great respect for the mother who was patient and more than willing to participate in this spontaneous show-and-tell.

When our bus dropped us back off at the hotel, Jimmy and Maggie wanted to go shopping so I tagged along. After Louis Vuitton, Hermès, and Gucci we arrived at Jimmy's favorite store, Burberry. Like all the others, not a single employee believed Jimmy was a serious customer. This changed when he stuck his arms behind him indicating the worker to slide on one of the several-thousand-dollar trench coats. After several fits and a few turns in the mirror we moved onto a different section of the multistory store. Once Jimmy had placed everything on the countertop, he admired his haul but then he cocked his head. Turning around to a rack behind him he quickly plucked one of the five-hundred-dollar hats and tossed it onto his pile.

> Japan Day 4 | Day 23 | Jan 27, 2020: I'm not sure you'd call what we were doing "shopping"—it was more of a performance. Jimmy put the show in showboat.

My fourth night in Japan was the first time I had gotten more than five hours of sleep. I knew it was not a sustainable schedule, but I only had five days to soak in as much of Japan as possible.

Jimmy wore one of his new designer outfits our fifth and final morning. It seemed as though the fabrics "spoke for themselves." He did look kickass, but then I realized, *don't we all have things in our lives that speak for themselves?* But what happens when they don't? What happens when nobody notices our new outfit, car, or post? And when our incredibly high expectations are shattered... we get a sense of the void that will never be filled by others' approval.

Looking into my own life, I reflected on what was speaking for me. Sitting on a dead-silent bullet train cruising just under two hundred mph, I wondered if it could be myself. Was I always making a scene to show others I am cool, confident, and credible? Did I always have the floor because that's when I felt in control?

The wrestling match in my head abruptly ended when one of the Hermès designer bags fell off the overhead compartment onto my head as our train came to a stop. The great philosopher, Notorious B.I.G., had it right when he said, "Mo money mo problems." We hopped off the train and loaded onto the final bus ride of our trip. Something inside of me yearned to see our ship. Just like I had imagined, the sheer mass of our campus captivated me yet again when we saw her resting alongside the enormous buoys through the bus windows. The glowing string of lights that ran the full length of the ship danced in the wind sending a chill down my spine.

Boarding the ship after Japan was like boarding for the very first time. Once my bags were searched for contraband, I was greeted with the familiar scent of campus as I briskly made my way across the gangway. Picture walking into a well-aged yet extremely clean hotel lobby filled with dark wooden cabinetry, then add a pleasant hint of musk and finish with a note from the sea. I wish I could bottle the smell up and call it "Ecstasea." A much more pleasant aroma than the steamy sewer odor that hovers head high above ASU.

Our homes all have a distinct smell that we rarely notice except when returning from a long vacation because we go nose blind breathing it in every day. The bombardment of foreign smells I experienced traveling around Japan wiped my olfactory palate clean. Every time we boarded the ship was exactly like coming home after a long trip. Recognizing the scent of campus continually reinforced *ship* and *home* as synonyms.

Falling face-first onto my neatly made bed, I reminisced about my adventures in Japan. I'll miss the piping-hot beverages that came out of vending machines, the incredible emphasis on punctuality, and the intentional nonverbal gestures that made you feel appreciated. I reflected on the paradigm of hyper-clean cities, abundance of bidets, and avid mask wearers, despite the nonexistence of soap in public bathrooms. With the largest population of any city in the world, I was shocked at the cleanliness of Tokyo. The streets were so pristine you could eat off them.

Even more amazingly, in all five days I did not see a single homeless person.

Chicago, take notes.

Losing China and the five-day field program I had booked to see some of the most iconic sights in the world had not crossed my mind since it had been announced. I viewed our situation as a legal system of sorts. With China out of the picture, this meant that we had paid our respects to the coronavirus, and now we were poised to experience the rest of the world. Losing one country in an itinerary like ours was just a drop in the bucket of our bucket lists.

~~~~~~

Our enormous 747 took to the skies over South Africa as we soared past Table Mountain. I still couldn't believe I was going home. I was grateful my parents were picking me up because I figured I had forgotten how to drive. Eight hours into my sixteen-hour flight to Newark I slowly lifted my head out of my lap, the brightness of the seat-back screen momentarily blinding me, and my heart suddenly dropped to the floor when I realized our plane was no longer landing in Newark, NJ—our destination was Miami, FL! We must have boarded the wrong flight! I turned around to find my friends' jaws hanging open as they stared at the flight map in front of them.

"*Beep-boop!*" the intercom sounded overhead. Our pilot mumbled, "Hello, everyone, as I am sure you are aware this flight is no longer destined for Newark. Unfortunately, the air traffic controllers monitoring the airspace have contracted COVID. Since we will not have eyes on our bird, we will need to land in Miami before we can continue on to Newark. Thank you for your cooperation."

While the rest of the passengers on our plane reacted as if the captain had issued a mayday, I was comforted to see my friends' faces, seemly unfazed like James Bond in a gunfight. We were just so happy to be together. Taking a deep breath, I lowered my head back into my journal and continued reflecting.

~~~~~~

Twenty-Three Hours and Fifty-Three Minutes

"A man who dares to waste one hour of time has not discovered the value of life."
—Charles Darwin

MY POST-JAPAN reflection session began by expressing our emotions regarding the diversion from China. A few students were still grappling with the news, but the rest of the group was quick to cheer them up. Once everybody said their piece, Dean Gene directed us to share highlights from our time in port. I probably held the floor for too long sharing many of the memories you just read. Eventually others began to share and my attention drifted out to sea.

Twenty-Three Hours and Fifty-Three Minutes

My relationship with the ocean had come a long way since our first stretch from Mexico to Hawaii. Knowing that we could not get anywhere quickly was sort of terrifying but eventually I learned to embrace it. Now I longed for the open ocean. The legs between countries were one long deep breath. I fell in love with the sensation of never being completely still; the ship and I had similar personalities. Both of us also loved to be traveling towards a destination, every ripple from our wake signifying progress. When we were at sea, we were always headed someplace and the idea of the place seemed to always trump the place itself. No matter how bad a day could get at sea, at least we were moving forward.

> Day 25 | Jan 29, 2020: It just hit me that we sailed across the entire Pacific Ocean. The world feels tiny, that with just enough time, I could paddle a kayak from LA to Kobe.

The library computers had now become the busiest spot on campus. A preposterous statement for a cruise ship turned school. Everyone on board flooded the same three desktop computers to book all of their travels in Vietnam because they were the only ones constantly connected to the Internet. It came to a point when the librarian, Holly, implemented a reservation system with fifteen-minute time slots.

The library was littered with grand ideas and travel plans. However, one seemed to preside over all—the famous Ha Long Bay booze cruise. A multiple overnight boozing extravaganza alongside one of the greatest natural wonders our planet has to offer. I was sitting beside Emily, my bus buddy from day one, who fancied a much different idea. In a soft voice, as if she didn't want anyone else to hear, she said, "We've gotta check out Pu Mat, it's literally the hidden gem of Vietnam." Emily and I had not spent much time together after embarkation day, so I was fired up to be included in her plans.

She articulated that our adventures might entail some serious physical exertion so boozing would not be the focal point of our trip. We were both in agreement that we wanted to explore nature *and* remember our experience at the same time. A pretty lofty goal, right? A few clicks later and our adventure in Pu Mat National Park was a go!

Maddi was also in the library and told me about an early morning ab workout led by one of the resident directors, Phil. The excitement of my newly booked travel plans helped me reply yes right away. This was my first time waking up before the sun did—my excuse was that the sunsets every day were so amazing they sufficed on their own. I was wrong. The few brave souls I met on the aft that morning knew exactly what they were doing, and they had been doing it since day one. While the first rays of light shot across the ocean, Maddi and I were on our backs doing figure eights with our legs alongside twenty other sweaty students. I was one of two guys in the class, the other one being Phil, so he pushed me as hard as he could, throwing my legs down to the ground for me to raise them back up again.

"Nineteen! Twenty! Twenty-one! Twenty-two!" he shouted down at me.

Finishing the class I was sore to my core, but our session would not be a valid substitute for the back and bicep workout I had planned. I gave myself a few minute breather before gripping the pull-up bar. After my first set I noticed a girl named Hunter doing her own ab workout. She looked like she knew what she was doing so I challenged her to a plank competition.

The speed in which Hunter accepted the challenge deflated my confidence just as quickly. Down on our forearms side by side on the deck, Hunter started a timer. One minute in I was on top of the world continuing to make small talk, feeling confident about the outcome. Four and a half minutes in I was shuddering and Hunter, in a steady, gentle voice reminded me, "You know, you can quit at any time." Thirty seconds later I fell square on my nose. Hunter remained in position proceeding to hold a perfect plank for five more minutes.

I gave one look at Hunter and determined that I could beat her for numerous reasons: she was a girl, my pride, she was a girl, etc. Our little competition confirmed the cliché that you should never judge a book by its cover, especially this one.

An intense workout in the morning always makes the rest of the day feel far less intimidating, especially when it was time for Dr. Meir Russ's management course. My first class with Dr. Russ twenty-two days ago was a class period that will live in infamy.

My management class was held in the only place on board that would suitably match the sophistication of our course work and its professor, the fancy dining room. Half of the class used their lap as a desk because the tables could not be oriented towards the front as they were bolted down to the floor. On day three of our voyage all twenty students were seated and ready for action with no professor in sight. Ten minutes went by, and our situation began to play out just like Jordi's birthday party, except this time we were not so desperate to go on a man hunt. Twenty minutes later Dr. Russ strolled into class with the grace of a gazelle. Déjà vu.

He immediately proclaimed, "I was lost, but now am found," which jerked a smile muscle on even the grumpiest students' face. Firmly grasping the podium, Dr. Russ went on to deliver one of the most intimidating course introductions in the history of higher education.

"Welcome to class! You are all here because you are brilliant and courageous; you understand we are completely at the mercy of the elements on this ship. My name is Meir Russ, and I have enjoyed learning my entire life. I continue to take MIT classes on the side as a hobby. But don't worry, this is not an MIT class... this is much harder! Firstly, I am the editor of our textbook. I know the material cover to cover, so please do not try to fool me. I will lose absolutely no sleep failing everyone if nobody works, as I will reward proper A's to those who put in the time."

The majority of the class's jaws had migrated toward their chest. Everyone looked around the room in disbelief to see if the same information was being processed. "I am dropping this class," was mumbled out of just about everybody's mouth. I felt like I was drinking through a firehose and Dr. Russ had not even begun teaching.

"I will not be late for the remainder of the semester, and I do not expect any of you to be either. The first thing I want you all to understand is this: humans are slaves to technology."

I felt personally attacked by his statement... which proved his point exactly. Why did it feel like he was talking directly to me? This was not the first time I had heard a statement opposing technology but never in such a blatant manner.

Twenty-Three Hours and Fifty-Three Minutes

Now, just under a month into the voyage Professor Russ's words continued to bounce around in my head. His statement combined with the lack of Internet on board were the first shots fired in a war for my time and energy, my most valuable possessions.

Although our vessel was very easy on the eyes, she did not have easy Internet access. Every voyager had seven free minutes of Wi-Fi every twenty-four hours unless they chose to purchase a package that allowed more time. Jimmy was the only person I knew who purchased it. Most days I wouldn't use any of my seven minutes. Someone could only keep a few Snapchat streaks, scroll through five to ten Instagram posts, or exchange a handful of text messages on WhatsApp before time ran out.

The concept of no Internet was actually something that allured me into sailing on SAS. I remember thinking that being off the grid for the first time since I owned a Razer phone would provide me with a long overdue break. I knew I would become happier as I used my phone less, but I was so used to having my best friend in my pocket all day every day I couldn't imagine life without it. At this point in the voyage I was starting to leave my phone in the cabin when I would leave for the day. Whereas just a few months ago at ASU if I left my room without my phone, I felt naked. By now, I had sailed more than enough to understand the undeniably healthier relationship with technology that our shipboard community was benefiting from.

Let's begin with the classroom. Back at Arizona State, my professors would start class with something along the lines of, "Alrighty, let's put those phones away so we can get this lecture underway." Semester at Sea professors didn't waste a breath with such instructions. There were no longer awkward pauses after a professor asked a question because everyone's heads were buried in their devices. More often than not our classes were excused early because we were able to run through the material so efficiently. Our weakened relationships with our phones was beginning to save us time in places we hadn't known we'd lost it.

In one of my first marketing classes I whispered to Jake, "This must have been what it felt like to go to school when our parents were in college, you know minus the ship."

Jake concurred and wondered, "Totally. How did they ever cheat?"

Not only did the absence of our devices allow for shorter class periods, but it required us to actually absorb and learn the material. Research projects required us to open physical books in the library and if we couldn't find what we were looking for, we would schedule time on a library desktop. The classroom was just the beginning; the real spots making waves were the dining room tables.

Reflecting all the way back to my high school days I thought about where my friends and I spent the most time. My two closest friends were named Kyle and Kyle, convenient right? We hung out all the time outside the confines of our school's walls; however, the vast majority of our time together was actually spent in the exact same place—the lunchroom table. For four years, one hour a day, five days of the week, we would share a meal together. While we slipped onto our phones at the table from time to time, the enormous amount of time spent together at our table yoked us into deep relationship.

Rather than just enjoying one meal each day, SAS allowed us to share three, media free. Every single day spent at sea eating breakfast, lunch, and dinner added up fast with no deductions for distractions. Every table I sat at began their meal with a prayer

Twenty-Three Hours and Fifty-Three Minutes

and quickly burst into a lively crossfire discussion. The silence of our cell phones at the table allowed even the most introverted person to have their voice heard. On a ship with no outside news, it was truly a blessing to dive into real conversation topics rather than focusing on the big headlines and social media trends of the day. What will it take for us to stop drooling over the latest celebrity headlines and become convicted that each other's "normal" lives are intricately woven together and more interesting than anything we could consume through a screen?

The dining halls were truly the breeding grounds for profound friendships and for the first time in our lives, our phones didn't eat first.

> Day 25 | Jan 29, 2020: I've been sharing every meal at sea with the same twelve friends day in and day out. Today I learned that I could predict which dining hall they would eat at based on the weather!

Semester at Sea offered a unique opportunity to develop authentic relationships at a pace that drastically exceeded society's standards. The size of our campus pushed us close both physically and emotionally. There are buildings on Arizona State's campus with more square footage than the area we were allowed to be on our ship. Sure we tried to hide and escape on the Internet, but the *MV World Odyssey* had one goal and she was going to sea it through.

Burberry & Birkenstocks

"I like my money right where I can see it... hanging in my closet."
—Carrie Bradshaw

JUST A FEW DAYS away from Vietnam I was feeling antsy. Maybe because this was our only leg at sea with no ship-wide community events. Regardless, I wanted to spice things up a bit. What creates a great memory, produces uncontrollable laughs, and bonds people together more than a prank?

Crazy enough, Kate had a similar itch. She even had a working prank idea and its recipient in mind: Jimmy, the person I sleep next to every night. I played devil's advocate and warned Kate of the potential backlash this might cause but she would not be convinced otherwise. But deep down, I think we both knew exactly what we were doing.

Burberry & Birkenstocks

While Jimmy was in the early global studies session, I let Kate into my cabin to raid his closet stuffed with all of the Burberry clothes he picked up in Tokyo. She cleaned out every last item, ran down to the fourth deck, and stuffed them all beneath Julia's bed. Now it was a waiting game.

> Day 26 | Jan 30, 2020: I had a feeling shit was gonna hit the fan, and by shit I mean Burberry trench coats.

I passed Jimmy on his way out of the early class as I would be attending the later session. I knew he went straight back to the cabin to change before heading up to the pool deck, so at any moment I wondered if he would storm back into the union or send me a panicked seamail. To my astonishment, he did neither. With a few minutes left in class Julia and I figured he had not gone back to our cabin yet, but this was also not the case. When class finished, we took one step out of the union to greet a cherry red-faced Jimmy.

"I swear, if you guys know where my clothes are tell me right now!" Jimmy screamed.

Rats! Julia and I looked at each other knowing the prank needed to end right away. Instead, Julia slipped away, and I offered a false hint that it might've been our housekeeper, Rommel.

"Oh yeah? The same person who's in our room just as much as us, makes our bed, does our laundry, and even folds miniature towel animals on our beds? Yup, it's gotta be him!" Jimmy shouted.

"Let's go have a look," I said.

So we walked back to our cabin and stared into his vacant closet scratching our heads. I figured his wrath would simmer down as time went on, but he continued to boil over so finally I caved in.

"I knew Kate was up to this!" Jimmy snarled.

And that was the last time I saw Jimmy for three days.

Truly an impressive feat considering our circumstances. He would go to bed after I fell asleep and was gone before I woke. I later found out that Jimmy's daytime hideaway was the spa, booking back-to-back-to-back massage appointments. Obviously, the prank cut far deeper than mere clothing, as we knew it would. What had been the rubbing of two extraordinarily different people climaxed in the shit show that was this morning.

Kate and Jimmy grew up on opposite sides of the country, both very well-to-do, but were raised much differently. When Jimmy told stories of his money, some raised an eyebrow, but Kate was unimpressed. Jimmy's wealth was in your face. Kate's was not. Jimmy's outfits were an extension of his personality. Kate's personality didn't wear designer. Oftentimes, Jimmy's decisions and dispositions irritated the hell out of us, so we took it out on his closet.

A few hours later after a lovely roundtable dinner in Berlin, Nic and I left early to chat in the library. Since the day we met I had been internally competing with Nic to be "the funny guy." I did not like Nic very much because out of all the people on the ship, he was the most similar to me. Confident. Hilarious. Sexy. Humble. Looking back, I wish I could have just owned up to my feelings and said something like, "Why don't I like you?" But I didn't choose the high road. I kept our beef deep in the fryer until one day it would eventually boil over.

Since we both wanted to have a hand in the pranking situation, we had no choice but to work together, and what better way to do so than with another prank? The idea was simple: Nic and I would prank Kate back and call it even. Looking back, I see how unfair it was to be involved in both pranks.

Rather than just pranking Kate, Nic and I went overboard and stole most of the girls' mattresses then stacked them high in Maddi's cabin. Moving them through the tiny cabin doors and narrow hallways was much harder than we anticipated. When the night wound down and the girls were exhausted, crawling into their bed was going to require substantial effort.

The next morning, everyone blamed Jimmy!

Once again, I had not thought very far ahead. This time, I admitted right away that this was not Jimmy's doing and officially retired from pranking for the remainder of the semester.

The idea of our mattresses leaving our cabins inspired Maddi to coordinate a slumber party on the top deck for her twenty-first birthday. Our seamail informed us that we would need to set our clocks backward one hour, which seemed to happen every day now. Getting that notification was a terrific perk of sailing westward.

A few hours after the sun had set, we grabbed all of our bedding and organized a space above the bridge. We wrapped the wooden pool chairs, turning them into beds, and began serenading Maddi with interpretive dancing and singing. At its climax, Jacob and I performed walking handstands in our underpants.

Quickly becoming exhausted, we gazed into the night sky and created our own constellations. We snacked on a few sleeves of Oreos, a precious commodity on board, and before we could finish a sleeve 23:59 was upon us. Our happy birthday song bounced off the deck and rang out into the sea. Then, we set our clocks back and one hour later, with much scratchier voices, we sang to Maddi for the second time. By now, the wind picked up drastically and our wooden chairs proved to be terrible beds, so we made our way back down into the warm belly of the ship.

> Day 28 | Feb 1, 2020: Nights like tonight were what I dreamed school on a ship would look like. I'm a professional expectation setter, so it's pretty cool when they get blown away every once in a GREAT while.

The following day got right back in the rhythm of my routine. Hoping to be efficient, I tried to cut out as much time between events as possible. I'm no triathlete but they've got the right idea. Granted, I would never run a marathon without socks, but I could swap comfort for time to some degree. In the beginning of the voyage, I started wearing my swimsuit to the gym to save time until one day I discovered I could wear my trunks from breakfast until dinner. They were the only article of clothing I could wear to class, gym, and the pool, lowering my transition time to zero. On top of that, I saved money on laundry because I didn't need to wear any underwear.

What about my shoes? Wearing socks to the pool would be an abomination. The solution: rubber Birkenstocks, in my humble opinion one of the greatest inventions of the twenty-first century. They are perfect in class and even better at the pool, but their protection in the gym is nonexistent. However, I could still perform most of my work out to the same athleticism as I would in sneakers. To this day I am seen wearing my rubber Birkenstocks during all hours of the day, even across the graduation stage. They are the most versatile footwear on Earth.

As one can imagine leaving the pool for class was a tough enough transition, but for Meir Russ's class it required extreme discipline. On the twenty-ninth afternoon of our voyage, the pool deck was electric, and I could not find the motivation to leave and *change*. I couldn't wear my trunks to class because I had my first major solo presentation on Patagonia's supply chain issues. I told myself I would run down and change for the presentation ten minutes prior. Two minutes before class it was too late. Unfortunately for me, I had decided to wear the most controversial pair of swim trucks I owned, the detailed bottom half of the statue of David.

Those trunks produced many laughs around the pool, so my classmates couldn't hold themselves together seeing them again as I presented for fifteen minutes. Meir Russ sat in the back and when it came time for questions made no remarks about my less than professional attire. I thought for sure he would reprimand me for this stunt and I knew he wasn't going blind because he had just picked out a misplaced comma from across the room. I guess even Dr. Russ was not immune to the increasingly relaxed attitude of the ship.

Hau Will We Get There?

"I will wait for you."
—*Frank Sinatra*

IT'S THE DAY before Vietnam and Jimmy and I are just beginning to talk again. We made up with the help of Ashley, the great unifier, and right on time because we would be spending a few days together in Cambodia. Jimmy and I struggled to pack wondering how the weather would compare with Japan. Since I perpetually overpacked, I labeled one bag as heads and one as tails, then I flipped a coin to determine which one I would leave behind. (I always put a toothbrush in both bags.)

It always felt good being completely packed before our pre-port meeting. The union was equally electric as it was the night before Japan and our progressive animation continued to be the most engrossing part of the meeting. Shouts of joy rang out with an extra edge to them because we would not have classes for two full weeks. The cancellation of China meant we would be staying an extra week in beautiful Vietnam! This spring break out of left field came as a very pleasant surprise, like the moment you realize the door you just opened has been programmed to hold itself for the person walking a terribly awkwardly distance behind you, saving them from the infamous mini jog when they spill their Starbucks, and you realize it was more of a burden to hold the door open.

Vietnam Day 1 | Day 31 | Feb 4, 2020:
GOOOOOOOOOOOOOOOOOOOOOOOD MORNING VIETNAAAAAAAM!!!

Once again, I woke up a few hours early to watch our ship pull into port. For the first time all semester our ship felt gigantic as Captain Kostas navigated the extremely tight turns of the Saigon River. I was leaning along the railing when a LLL I had not met tapped my shoulder and said, "Hey! You're the surfer boy from Chicago!"

That's a new one!

We began our conversation, but it was violently cut off by the ship's ear-piercing horn blast. There was a tiny fishing boat playing a fatal game of chicken with our ship! The little boat didn't budge, forcing Kostas to deploy our ship's fin stabilizers, which are normally used to reduce rocking at sea, but now assisted the rudder in this aggressive maneuver. The entire ship rolled hard starboard side to avoid a collision, snapped back port side, then continued to sway for several minutes. Come to find out, reaching Ho Chi Minh City was known as one of the greatest maritime challenges in the world.

To make the customs process run as smoothly as possible, our ship was boarded by Vietnamese customs agents via boat as we made our way down the river. Two of the customs officers in full uniform came up to the pool deck, and after politely declining several smoothies, I posed for a photo in my statue of David trunks. I figured we should get on their good side before the fourteen-day bender we were going to throw in their country.

One of the most upsetting and controversial moments of the voyage was that all of the Chinese voyagers were not allowed to disembark in Vietnam due to the virus. Vietnam would not stamp any Chinese passports regardless of when the last time someone was in China. Our hearts went out to those students, but our heads were ready to get what we came for.

The Voice, using his firm important tone, came on overhead and called down the first group to check in. The union was staged as it was on our first day, lined with tables in semicircle fashion. After the last checkpoint I darted up the stairs to the top deck to see our exhaust stacks barely clearing the bridge overhead. City buildings towered over our ship on either side as if we were sailing down Michigan Avenue. The river was at its narrowest point when Kostas brought our campus to a halt. One final maneuver was required to position our ship along the proper dock, a full 360-degree turn. Kostas, with facile grace, spun our ship on a dime leaving just a few feet to spare on either side.

Stuffing the last GoPro battery into my luggage I headed down to the gangway to wait for the rest of the squad. Jake, Jacob, Chris, and Nic were all exactly where we had planned; the girls said they would be ready in five minutes, so we waited. Forty-five minutes later they arrived, and we all entered the line to disembark the ship. By this point all of the guys had fire ants in our pants having watched half the ship run off before us. Bobbing up and down in line I spotted John hauling his luggage down the staircase. We offered John to cut with our group, to which he happily obliged. He stepped up to the counter and handed over his ship ID; I could tell the Filipino crew member treated him extra professionally. As the worker helped guide John and his belongings off the ship, I realized it would be a few days before I saw him again, so I ran ahead and slapped John firmly on the butt. The worker's eyes nearly fell out of his head when John turned around and asked with a straight face, "That hurt your hand?"

Another girl standing behind me in line who saw this play out shouted forward, "You didn't tell me your grandpa was sailing with you!"

"He's not!" I laughed.

Laughs always feel so good, especially when they are a reaction to breaking a cultural norm. Obviously breaking the norm by not leaving a tip in the US or sitting right next to a stranger in an empty movie theater would be less than hilarious, but there are a few norms in the gray area which are fun to play around with. Like how we are supposed to relate with the elderly, or which direction to stand in an elevator.

After waiting close to an hour to get off the ship, the squad finally inhaled the fresh smog of Ho Chi Minh City. Vietnam required us to break many of the most ingrained norms we follow back home, such as avoiding jaywalking, because this was the only way to cross the street in Vietnam. The game of Frogger came to life as hundreds of voyagers slowly made their way across the bustling streets of Ho Chi Minh City with buses and mopeds whizzing by inches on either side.

The only rules when crossing the street was never to run and keep the same pace. Kate found these directions particularly nerve-wracking. Finding the courage, Kate stepped into the street and looking into oncoming traffic, sprinted ahead screaming at the top of her lungs. Stepping up on the curb on the opposite side of the street the squad let go of the breath we had been holding.

Maddi, with worry painted on her face, begged the rest of us to walk slowly and confidently. "No one needs to die this early in Vietnam!" she exclaimed.

By the grace of God the twelve of us safely crossed dozens of streets littered with traffic, and made our way into the Ben Thanh Market, one of the largest in all of Vietnam. The high, vaulted, wooden ceilings trapped the heat inside, so the temperature rose to sauna levels. We pored through the more than six thousand vendors all selling basically the exact same thing. People went crazy racking up as much fake designer as possible. I was not immune to the spending spree, so I bought a few Rolexes and an Audemars Piguet for less than a hundred dollars. I'm sure the ship's security team had a wonderful time going through the thousands of new designer bags, or as they saw them, "places to hide booze." I sported all the watches on my arm like Lil Yachty.

I had already become Iron Man, now it was time to become Tony Stark, and what better way to complete our day than a nightcap at the top of the Stark Tower? The tallest building in Ho Chi Minh City, Bitexco Financial Tower looks exactly like the movie, boasting an enormous helipad that sticks effortlessly out of the fifty-second floor. With the drinking age being eighteen in Vietnam, this was the first time I was legally able to drink in port, because Japan's drinking age was twenty. If I know anything about Mr. Stark, he loves to create a spectacle, so our server lit our drinks on fire before we threw them down.

Over a jaw-dropping view of Ho Chi Minh City Ashley and I talked about our previous jobs and what we hoped to do in the future. Ashley shared that one of her biggest dreams was to do Semester at Sea. I felt guilty having only found the program a year before I would set sail. Meanwhile, she had her eyes set on sailing since she was a girl. I told her that I hoped it would be everything she wants and more.

Tomorrow I would be splitting up from the squad to travel with Zack, Zara, Dylan, Emily, and Eve before our Pu Mat adventure. I was sad we couldn't all be together, but I was excited to travel with a new group of people.

The second morning in Vietnam, Zack and I successfully navigated our first Asian airport and arrived safely in Da Nang. Our only hiccup occurred trying to get a ride to the airport. Whipping out our favorite transportation tool, Uber, we were flustered their services weren't available in Vietnam. Instead, the nation uses a rideshare app called Grab. The difference was that on top of hiring cars, for less than one US dollar, I could make it across town straddling a stranger on a scooter. We opted for the former considering our luggage, but in the back of my head I needed to try the scooter option before we set sail again.

When we walked through the massive front door of our villa, the hectic travel stress melted away. We had more bathtubs than people! Sitting down for dinner we connected to the Wi-Fi, and I found out that the squad was in a sticky situation. The beautiful Airbnb they booked online didn't have a front door and was swarming with mosquitos. This was terrible news but in all honesty, I was delighted because this meant the squad was now headed our way to the villas! When they arrived a few hours later, we celebrated their safety by putting on all of the fancy robes that were in every closet and danced the night away. Da Nang, Vietnam, of all places, was the first and only time all of my closest friends, Dylan, Zack, Zara, Emily, Celeste, Jimmy, and the squad were together off the ship.

> Vietnam Day 3 | Day 33 | Feb 6, 2020: DANG, DA NANG! We rented jet skis and surfboards, played sand volleyball and soccer, scooped our dinner out of fish tanks, and consumed enough pina coladas to raise the GDP of Vietnam.

From the moment I woke up, to the moment I squeezed the throttle on the jet ski approximately four minutes had passed. Today was going to be a great day! Ashley held on for her life as I ran the jet ski off of the waves launching us into the sky. WaveRunner was a good name, but I always thought WaveJumper was much more fitting. I wanted to spend more time in the air but Ashley wanted to spend more time on the water, so we switched positions. We rode until one of the guys from the rental company waved us in, and at this point, every single warning light was lit on the dashboard.

There was something for everyone at the beach that day. If you were a drinker, you were at the pool bar, if you were athletic, you were kicking a ball, if you were an adrenaline junkie you were rippin' jet skis, and if you were Nic Swanger, you were surfing. Jealous of Nic's skillset, I got a board and paddled out until I got tired then turned to face the beach. Half an hour later I had yet to catch a wave and get the board beneath my feet so I quit. Defeated, and in need of a pick me up I cracked open a book titled *Love Does* by Bob Goff, lent to me by a fellow student, Tate. A few days before Vietnam on the pool deck, she excitedly handed me the book, under the presumption that it would change my life—a tall order, especially for a nonreader.

She was right, I couldn't put it down. Admittedly, it was the first book I had ever read voluntarily outside of school. Turning over the last page of the book left me starving for more, launching me into a reading obsession. I wanted to make people feel the way *Love Does* made me feel. The author Bob Goff even left his personal phone number in the back of the book, and he picked up! *Love Does* planted the seed that maybe one day I could share my story. If you consider yourself a nonreader like I did, don't read for yourself, read for everyone who has taken the painstaking effort to construct a book for the benefit of yourself and society.

In the late afternoon of our beach day Ashley and I caught some more time together, once again over a bowl of ice cream. We were both crushing hard on each other, but nothing was official. I was too afraid to ask her to be my girlfriend. There was already so much outside pressure from the group for us to get together I feared the fallout if we didn't work out. All of our friends knew how attracted to her I was because they would snap their fingers in front of my eyes when they caught me staring at the dinner table. I even felt an unhealthy resentment in my gut whenever another guy outside of the squad spoke to her one on one. If there was one thing I knew for sure, it was that I had no idea what I wanted.

Relaxation time was now coming to a close and everyone was itching to get out and explore as many places as possible on our last day in Da Nang. Overwhelmingly the most requested destination among the squad was the Golden Hand Bridge, which is located inside the Ba Na Hills amusement park.

The squad was too large to fit inside one SUV, so we ordered two. The girls—Maddi, Julia, Ashley, Kate, Lauren, Riley, and Jenna—hopped into the first Grab and were on their merry way. A few minutes later, my car arrived and the guys—Jake, Chris, Nic, Jacob, and I—quickly piled in hoping to catch up with the others. The language barrier was severe but thankfully our final destination was already plugged into the app. We were no more than five minutes into our ride when my phone vibrated: "Your Grab has arrived and is waiting."

Since we had gotten into the wrong Grab, we were also going to someone else's destination. I panicked and started to explain the situation to our driver. It didn't take long to recognize that English was about as useful as a glass phone case, so I opened Google Translate and began speaking slowly into my phone:

Johnny: "We are in the wrong Grab ride; would you please take us back to the hotel?"

Grab Driver: "It is okay, we will each cancel ride. I will take you safely."

Johnny: "We are going to the Golden Hand Bridge. Do you know where that is?"

Grab Driver: "Yes, very large, very beautiful, we are going for tickets now."

Johnny: "Can we get the tickets at the amusement park?"

Grab Driver: "Yes, more expensive, I know cheaper option."

We were confident our driver knew our intentions, and we didn't exactly have another option. After twenty more minutes we veered off the highway to what looked like a vacant rundown store. Grabbing all of the cash we had, the five of us in the car ventured into the shop with translators at the ready. A frail woman appeared from behind the counter and pointed to a sign displaying the cost of Ba Na Hills tickets. We organized the money and promptly handed over the correct amount. Sifting through the bills more than half of our cash was handed right back to us.

Johnny: "What is wrong with this money?"

Woman: "Not clean."

We were perplexed. Fortunately for us, confusion transcends borders, so the woman pointed to small stains and tiny tears near the corners of our bills. The money needed to be perfect; it could not have any blemishes. Reaching back into our wallets, we searched for the prettiest dollar bills we had. The woman then inspected them, and this time only rejected a couple. We were running out of money and began to think we wouldn't have enough clean cash to complete the transaction. By some miracle we ended up having the exact amount of clean money to purchase the tickets, leaving us with only "unclean" bills.

A few sentences of translation revealed to us that counterfeit currency is a serious issue in Vietnam. The woman in the store refuses to take any deformed bills, fearing that they will be rejected when she went to deposit them at the bank.

We hit the road again with the Golden Hand Bridge in the

forefront of our minds. For a good portion of the ride we had remained to ourselves, taking in the deep expansive green of the countryside. I was sitting on the edge of my seat and the silence was deafening, so I made some noise into my phone.

Johnny: "Hello, my name is Johnny, what is your name?"
Grab Driver: "Hello, so good to meet you, my name is Hau!"
Johnny: "Nice to meet you, Hau, thank you for driving us!"
Hau: "How long will you spend at park?"
Johnny: "We are not sure, maybe a couple of hours."
Hau: "I will wait for you."

Everyone looked at each other in shock—didn't Hau, pronounced "How"—have other people to pick up? Why would he wait for us? Wouldn't we just call another Grab? We didn't end up asking him any of these questions, but rather decided to take Hau up on his generosity and agreed to ride with him on the way home. I was shaking with excitement as our car pulled into the amusement park. I was so eager to share our wild ride with the girls.

Leaving Hau behind we ventured on to find the bridge with golden hands. We needed to ride a cable car to the park that was perched at the top of a mountain. While standing in line, we were informed that this was the longest and highest cable car ride in the world. Each of us presented our ticket except a flabbergasted Jake whose ticket had mysteriously jumped out of his pocket. Jake was a lot like me, we would both lose our heads if they weren't attached to us.

We ran around for a few minutes searching before one security guard grabbed hold of Jake while another brought up security footage on a computer and went back in time just a few minutes to see Jake at the counter buying his ticket. It was a beautiful and efficient use of technology.

United States, take notes.

Loaded inside the cable car, I felt the same sensation that came over me when I sat on the bus on the very first day. My anticipation grew as we ascended through layers of clouds. Jacob, whose five-pound DSLR never left his side, captured the moment with professional quality. My first glimpse of the hand bridge through the clouds took my breath away. God's hands reached out of the mountainside supporting the bridge ever so delicately as people made their way across. While standing on the bridge was incredible, I'd argue the best view was actually from the cable car.

We knew this park was not merely a one-trick pony, so we decided to walk around and see what else could be in store for us. What we found was quite underwhelming: a super confusing theater production, an array of bizarre sculptures, and hot dogs twice the size of the bun.

On the cable car ride back down I remembered that Hau was waiting for us, and a wave of joy rushed over me. Just like I imagined we found him standing in front of the parking spot we had left him five hours earlier. I shook his hand firmly and thanked him sincerely for his patience.

Hau: "Where are we going now?"

Johnny: "That is a great question, we'd like to go back to the villas, please!"

Hau: "Okay. Yes."

Johnny: "Hau, why are there so many scooters in Vietnam?"

Hau: "This good question. Cars are expensive, streets are small. I am very lucky to have car. I work very hard since I was child to make money for car. First in my family to drive car."

Johnny: "Congratulations! That is an astounding accomplishment. You are very hard working!"

Hau: "Thank you, Johnny. What are you doing later?"

Johnny: "We were planning to check out the Hoi An Lantern Festival."

Hau: "I will wait for you."

What else should we have expected? We showered up as quickly as possible and found Hau waiting out front with open doors and a massive smile. As if his services couldn't get any better, Hau brought along his buddy Ricky who drove the girls in a separate car. And thus, the Grab Convoy feature was born! On our way we learned about the history of the Lantern Festival. A combination of Buddhist tradition that celebrates the full moon, and the cultural significance of lanterns bringing good luck create the event we are about to participate in. The festival only happens once a month, so our timing was impeccable.

WHAM!

Hau's right arm came across my chest as he applied full pressure to the brakes. The streets were poorly lit, and traveling around fifty mph Hau saw his headlights reflect off four eyes in the middle of the road. Letting off the brakes, now moving at about five mph, we drove around two adult cows standing side by side covering an entire lane. We could not believe our eyes—they did not flinch in the slightest.

Hau took us right up to the action in Hoi An, so we didn't have to walk as far. The colored lanterns floating down the river through the center of town were something out of a dream.

Johnny: "I think we will be here for a long time; you do not need to wait for us."

Hau: "Have a meaningful and fun outing. I will wait for you."

Hau Will We Get There?

I gave Hau another handshake, and we were on our way. Walking along the riverside we spotted a few men selling canoe rides, so we whipped out our Dong, and threw on some lifejackets. The lights from town reflected off the water as we lit colorful lanterns and placed them into the steady current of the Thu Bon River.

Back on land we ran into dozens of other students and faculty around town including the Voice; SAS's social media coordinator, Maddie; and a handful of the deans sitting together. We snatched the table just beside them and shared stories of our experiences thus far, then we proposed a toast to our voyage and did cheers with the staculty.

The music blaring from our next stop was equally repetitive as its name, Tiger Tiger. There was not a front door, so the mammoth crowd of people were half in and half out. The walls inside were covered in balloons so I figured it might be someone's birthday. I grabbed one of the balloons off the wall hoping to make my voice squeaky high, but it was slapped out of my grip by one of the workers who insisted that I must pay. *Pay? This thing is worth a few cents,* I thought. I called over another worker to clarify, and he asked if I knew what was inside of the balloons. They were not filled with helium, rather nitrous oxide, aka whippets.

Vietnam Day 4 | Day 34 | Feb 7, 2020: I think I was almost the first person in history to accidentally do whippets.

There was something off about the place. I don't know if it was the wall of whippets or the five-year-old in the SpongeBob shirt breaking a leg in the middle of the dance floor. But the last straw broke when Julia helped herself to a beer from a nearby cooler and seconds later the bartender's hands were around her neck. Meanwhile Jake was going off on one of the workers who chased him out of the bar with a spiked baseball bat. Time time to leave leave Tiger Tiger.

Hau: "Have fun going out?"

Johnny: "Absolutely, a few hiccups but we're okay! Thanks for asking. We are exhausted and ready to go home."

Hau: "What time do you start tomorrow?"

Johnny: "We are trying to get to the airport at nine o'clock."

Hau: "See you tomorrow."

The next morning we found Hau like clockwork; he had been our designated driver for over twenty-four hours now! Nic and I posed in front of our car with Hau, creating a frameable masterpiece. No sentence could be translated to express our gratitude.

On our ride to the airport we realized how wonderfully technology had blessed our relationship. Even when the translator got it wrong, everyone was sure to benefit with a good laugh. The most iconic mistranslation occurred while we were asking Hau and Ricky their favorite part about their culture. They spoke Vietnamese into my device and we heard this come out in English: "A little bit more, I teach you to buy Vietnamese babies."

We were approaching the airport, and I was genuinely sad we would be leaving our new best friend. We couldn't wrap our heads around the fact that we'd built such a terrific relationship with a man who didn't even speak our language. He deserved a hearty tip, so we pulled together a handsome sum. After taking very good care of him I reached for my phone for one final exchange.

Johnny: "Well, this is it! Take care of your family! Thank you so much again for everything, Hau, we will never forget your generosity!"

Hau: "I will wait for you... just kidding. Nice to meet and make friends with you. Have a safe and memorable experience, be in touch, I love you.

Pu Mat

*"In the middle of the journey of our life I found myself within a
dark woods where the straight way was lost."*
—Dante Alighieri

OVER THE PAST few days we had progressively moved further away from bustling Ho Chi Minh City towards smaller less urbanized areas. Most of the squad decided to trek up to do the Ha Long Bay Booze Cruise in Hanoi; however, Kate, Julia, and Ashley decided to join Emily's Pu Mat group consisting of Dylan, Zack, Zara, Eve, Celeste, and myself. I was pumped when I heard they would be joining us and surprised that they separated from the others. The eight of us landed in Vinh on day five in Vietnam and for the first time I felt like I was nowhere near home. Driving to our stay from the airport, we passed through towns so worn down it was as if the buildings would fall over at any second. Our foreheads were pressed against the window; this was real poverty. I realized that I have never had to worry about the integrity of my home. My house was basically indestructible, and no rainstorm or long vacation would change that fact.

Vietnam Day 5 | Day 35 | Feb 8, 2020: I cried, desperately wanting to be fully grateful for all that I had. But was that even possible?

After walking through an ostentatious entrance, our resort looked like the Taj Mahal compared to the surrounding village. Even more striking, the place was as vacant as my tear ducts. How was this beautiful and expensive property staying in business? A few minutes after walking through the door a woman wearing a scrubs-like outfit summoned us down a hallway. Entering a janitor's closet modified to be a doctor's office we sat on a few stools in the corner of the room. None of us had any idea what was going on, but we were all in agreement none of us were going to let her administer a shot. The woman came back into the room with a small tube in her hands and requested that we roll up one of our sleeves.

"Are you giving us a shot?" I said slowly hoping she would understand.

"No... temperature," she replied.

Then she turned to all of us, and we watched her pull out a thermometer from the tube. We assumed this was just the resorts procedure, but it was probably an extra precaution due to the coronavirus. Regardless, nobody asked any questions. Still confused what rolling up our sleeve had to do with our temperature, she lifted up her arm and motioned for us to do the same. None of us had ever had our temperatures taken in our armpit.

Nearly breaking a sweat from the stress, we were certain our armpits would run a fever if we inserted them now, so we sat still for a few minutes to cool down. After everyone's temperature was within the acceptable range, we headed back to the lobby to drink the freshest ginger tea of our lives. I might as well have been eating raw ginger—my throat was scorched after every swallow. I did my best not to disrespect this kind gesture, but I knew my facial expressions had already given me away.

Once our business at the counter was completed, we shuffled into golf carts and were driven to our villas. The sky was pale, and the clouds began to let out a sprinkle of rain. Once everyone found their room we convened in my villa and ordered room service. None of us had realized how hungry we were until the woman on the other side of the phone repeated back our order.

"Are you sure? This is fifteen entrees for ten people?"

Being completely honest we had ordered on the conservative side. An hour later the food arrived, and we decided to toss it all in the center of the table to share. You know when you go into the grocery store hungry, and every single thing looks appetizing? It was the most gluttonous meal of my life. Trying to stuff my fork as full as possible I stabbed something different from each plate and threw it down the hatchet. Pizza, chicken, steak, and fries all in one fell swoop. So much for eating the local cuisine. Not a word was said for twenty minutes before all of the plates were wiped clean. Looking at each other in silence we knew we had to call again.

The second call we asked the woman to bring out another round.

"Fifteen more entrees for ten people? Thirty entrees?!"

"To be fair, we are used to much larger portions back home," we insisted.

Pu Mat

An hour later the food was delivered again, and our rooms were inspected for the extra guests they figured we must have snuck in. After sweeping our villas like Pablo they confirmed the ten of us were only living out our American stereotype. Funny enough after all that food I felt the urge to smoke a cigarette, so carrying out the stereotype to completion Zara helped me light up outside in the rain. A full belly and a cigarette in my hand, all I was missing was an ethnocentric mindset. But I was one of ten Americans in all of Vinh, so we earned a level of respect just by being there, at a pool resort, in the middle of their winter season. Or maybe we just confirmed the biggest stereotype of all. Regardless, we had a gargantuan day ahead of us so we hit the hay so we would be fully charged.

Rolling up to breakfast, we saw one of the workers frantically sprint into the kitchen. No more than fifteen seconds later, the head chef came running out, stared us down, and also ran back into the kitchen. Was the building on fire?

One of the servers jogged over to our table and began, "We were honestly not expecting a single guest this morning. This is the heart of our winter season and you're our only guests on the property."

We ordered about a dozen scrambled eggs as a base for the strange foods we'd consume the remainder of the day. Halfway through our egg massacre we were alerted that our bus had arrived. Stuffing the last remaining morsels in our mouths we made way for the lobby where we met Andy, our lead tour guide; he spoke fluent Vietnamese and fairly decent English. He informed us that the man standing to his side was Jonny Vee, who was also proficient in English, and he would be our cameraman for the day. I immediately burst out in joy and embraced him—he was my Vietnamese doppelgänger in every sense of the word. Everyone was outfitted in bright yellow and blue hats; I'm not sure if Andy thought he'd lose us, but this was a very smart move. We shuffled onto the bus and headed out to our first destination for the day.

Liberally, our bus had four inches of clearance, so we were a bit concerned when our driver pulled off the pavement onto a muddy path. Somehow our wheels continued to turn until we arrived at a small tea farm. Mother Nature began to let out some tears as we paraded through the sweeping rows of green tea. Each of us popped our heads above the bushes posing for an iconic photograph with our new hats. Andy was warming up to us while Jonny and I were practically eloping.

Our next stop, once again, was directly off the main road, however this time we pulled into someone's front yard. Six Vietnamese women were all sitting around a small table constructing something in assembly-line fashion. Andy explained that these little creations were edible and were known as coconut cakes. Mesmerizingly, we watched each woman complete her portion of the cake until the final stage where the treat was wrapped in banana tree leaf. Now, it was our turn to indulge.

Jonny whipped out the camera as we began unwrapping our gifts like Christmas morning. Kate took the first bite and her eyes widened. Was it poison? Delicious? Kate opened her mouth with a big smile revealing that the cake was firmly stuck between her teeth. This was the stickiest substance we had ever consumed. The cakes were delectable but getting them down our throats was a real challenge. Quite the contrary from our desserts back home that seem to slide into our bellies on their own. The locals loved watching us enjoy their homemade desserts. To balance our palate, we were also served fresh green tea. The leaves had just been plucked and placed into a pot of hot water.

Back on the road, the flatulence shortly ensued, and not a single soul was safe from this ambush. Something inside those cakes was not getting along with our insides. Foul smells bother me more than they should, so I offered it up and thought, *blessed are the lips that speak without a tongue.*

Once again, the tarmac didn't last long—our bus was taking a beating, bouncing off small trees and shrubs on either side. The bumps got so big Kate smashed her head into the roof of the bus. The mixture of laughter and fear brewed a strong cup of adrenaline we couldn't wait to chug. We continued off-roading in our van built from LEGOs for about an hour until Andy stood up, grabbed the microphone, and announced our arrival.

No parking lot, no big reveal, just the middle of the jungle and a small trail ahead. Andy provided us with special nonslip sandals so we would not lose traction. A slippery trail of old truck tires led us to a bridge where we finally locked eyes with the eight hundred-foot Khe Kem Waterfall. The mist off the falls was like ice water. Andy, shouting with joy, said, "We are going to make friends with it!"

The group reached a large rocky area where we could set our bags down and orient ourselves. Those who were going to swim to the waterfall needed to start undressing and follow Andy. Dylan, Zack, and I were the only ones who immediately began to move. Andy, in a serious tone for the first time all day, instructed us that we needed to start working out. Andy began repping out sets of push-ups, air squats, and jumping jacks. Contrary to a polar plunge, which recommends its participants to exit the water promptly after entering, we wouldn't be on land for about twenty grueling minutes. The air temperature was sixty, the water was fifty-two, and the sun was hidden behind a thick blanket of clouds; we were nervous. Moments away from our jump we noticed Ashley and Eve running up from behind us. I couldn't believe my eyes.

Andy gave us one final instruction. "Only one rule, don't stop breathing."

Three... two... one... JUMP!

Our bodies slapped the water, my heart skipped a beat, and I held my breath. Andy shouted at us from ahead to keep moving. Five seconds into the water I was already experiencing paralysis in my legs and my breathing was sporadic. Grabbing hold of a rock, Dylan and Zack helped me out of the water to catch my breath. Ashley and Eve were speedily swimming right behind me. Perched on a rock cloaked in slimy algae, I tried to sit as still as possible.

Ahh... ahh... choooo!

My mighty sneeze dislodged my position. I was sliding down the jagged rock at a snail's pace, but I could not stop. I could not secure a hold on any of the rock's surface, so I accepted my fate and braced for impact. Slipping off the edge of the rock, I tore the skin clean off my left shin all the way down to my tibia. Once I had let out a generous amount of unprintable words, I was back on the rock inspecting the damage. I was shocked to have drawn no blood and I couldn't feel any pain. It was as if my body knew I was nowhere near medical attention, so it decided to hold the side effects of my laceration.

We were already across the first pool of water, just one more to go before we would be standing beneath the falls. Jumping into the second pool and inching closer to the falls the roar of the falling water made it impossible to have conversation. We communicated with our hands, and thankfully I just needed one finger to express my feelings to Andy. One final push and we were standing firmly beneath the falls. Each droplet of water felt like a bowling ball. My shorts didn't stay on very long as I fought to hold them up. Jonny was on the spot, flying his drone, hysterically capturing the entire scene as we all screamed at the top of our lungs!

> Vietnam Day 6 | Day 36 | Feb 9, 2020: A few minutes beneath the waterfall and Ashley was turning into Violet from *Willy Wonka*. Too many medical emergencies for one afternoon.

Exiting the falls was a rude awakening. We had been in the water so long that standing up was now the colder option. Andy explained that this was normal and that we needed to dry as soon as possible. We daydreamed of our friends wrapping us into towel burritos. With my arms locked tightly around my blue-toned skin Julia presented me with my clothes, no towel. Damn. I dried myself with the shirt I wore the remainder of the day and held off putting my underwear on till my trunks stopped dripping.

Back on the bus and still shivering violently, I announced, "It's not even noon, and this has been one of the greatest days of my life, and I am—"

My speech was interrupted as my swim trunks were yanked to the ground from behind me. I turned around to punch Dylan and was floored to see Andy gleefully laughing.

Could you imagine a tour guide pulling a prank like that in the States? On paper it was assault, but I felt loved by it.

High on life, we were eager for our next battle against nature. On our way to lunch we picked up a man named Mr. King. Our new friend did not speak a lick of English, but he would assist Andy on our jungle adventures for the remainder of the day. But first, a hearty lunch was waiting for us.

Sitting down at a table on the Laos border, our plates were massive foot-long leaves, and the rice was purple—a quick pinch reassured me I had not fallen asleep on the bus. After mowing down our super healthy lunch we hopped into tiny boats with lawn edgers strapped to the back for motors because the water was less than a foot deep. After shoving off the shore my boat's weed whacker engine immediately gave out. We drifted peacefully down the Giang River until we noticed the water flowing over the dam directly in front of us. Continuing to drift for what felt like ten minutes but was merely a few seconds, our motor decided to work again just a few feet from a very bad day.

The jungle seemed to tower over us like an ant's perspective of a city. The river cut straight through a forest so rich we were convinced money grew on trees. Our picturesque ride ended along a rocky shore; it felt like we were the first humans to stand there. Then out of the blue, Andy shot up and asked us if we wanted to go on a hike. We looked at each other confused because Andy hadn't given us many choices all day. Either he was just being nice, or he was avoiding blame for future chaos. Either way our response was unanimous.

Andy recommended that we put those insanely uncomfortable nonslip sandals back on because the ground would be wet. Half of us obeyed, while the other half started up the hill in sneakers. The air was incredibly thick; drinking and breathing were basically synonymous. The rain and humidity made the grass as slippery as ice and the patches of mud were woefully unforgiving. A few of us fashioned hiking poles from fallen branches for assistance.

Mr. King led the way at the front of the pack as Andy began telling us more about our fearless leader. We were surprised to hear that in Mr. King's sixty-plus years of life, he had never left his home country of Vietnam. He was born and raised in the jungles we were currently trekking through and moved out of the trees when he was old enough to make money and fend for himself. We all listened, fascinated by how anyone could live in such an environment; meanwhile, I complain when my bedroom rises above seventy-five degrees.

About an hour into our ascent, Kate asked Andy to ask Mr. King how far we were from the top. Andy inquired and quickly responded that it was not much farther ahead. Mr. King's attitude had been cavalier the entire time, and we were all dying to know what "it" was; the heights we had climbed already would provide a ridiculous lookout point. We continued onward and upward and ran into two gigantic water buffaloes. As majestic as they were, the neatly swirled piles of steamy poop only added to their sophistication.

Suddenly the group came to a halt, staring at the extremely steep incline ahead of us. Kate and Celeste spoke up, insisting we turn back in fear of how hard it would be to come back down. But Mr. King pressed onward. The ground was so slick we needed to hold on to trees to propel ourselves up the mountain. Connecting hands like a monkey chain we left nobody behind and fortunately, everybody made it up the incline.

We were well over two hours in, and we had yet to experience a jaw-dropping sight. We were all beaten up pretty good so again, we asked Andy to ask Mr. King how far we were from the top. Andy addressed everyone: "This is the part of the hike where we check for leeches." Jokes and instructions were indistinguishable at this point so half laughing and half crying we checked each other's skin. Thankfully, no blood suckers had hitched a ride.

Still hiking vertically, the trail had completely vanished from beneath us. We seriously questioned if we had ever been on a trail in the first place. Mr. King pulled out his twelve-inch machete as if it were a pencil that had been in his pocket and began creating a path of our own. We trusted him and continued forward into what seemed like a never-ending forest, hoping in the back of our minds that we would reach our destination eventually—after all, this was his backyard.

We reached a small opening just wide enough to fit our entire group. Befuddled and beyond disoriented, we'd been ambushed by the forest that had surrounded us the entire time. Turning slowly in every direction, the trail we had squeezed through to get to this point seemed to have grown back behind us. Thoroughly perturbed, we asked Andy to ask Mr. King a final time if we were ever going to make it. Mr. King spoke to Andy in Vietnamese while we waited to hear our fate. Andy took a deep breath and declared, "This is it!"

Standing on our toes waiting for the punchline, Andy insisted that we needed to head back because we were losing daylight. No big reveal, no grand landscape, just the familiar viridescent foliage staring us right in the face.

Pu Mat

Vietnam Day 6 | Day 36 | Feb 9, 2020: I'm not an angry guy, but I wanted to run Mr. King through with his machete. Ok so maybe I am an angry guy.

I was confused and frustrated; we'd just spent hours hiking to come to a dead-end. We could have just hiked for five minutes if we wanted to see this view! Even worse, reality sank in that we would have to make it down those same slippery slopes that we just spent hours crawling up.

Andy, who was as far out of the "know" as we were, reminded us of the extraordinary journey it was to get here, with "here" not being of importance at all.

Disregarding Andy's optimism, I felt a wave of resentment boiling up inside against Mr. King. I figured, if this jungle were truly his backyard, then he certainly should have been able to lead us somewhere better than this!

Taking the first steps back down the mountain I took a rebellious right turn hoping to trailblaze a new path toward a better view. Seeing that no such path existed in that direction, Mr. King handed forward his machete. Never having held a knife this big in my life, I gripped it in my right hand with all my strength. A shot of adrenaline rushed through my veins: finally, I had some sort of *control* over this situation.

Approaching the first branch at an angle about waist high before me, I executed a swift forehand just as I had seen Mr. King do a thousand times. Immediately after making contact the foot-long blade flung clean off its handle deep into the belly of the forest.

My life flashed before my eyes.

I slowly looked over to Mr. King who was grinning ear to

ear. We hadn't exchanged a single word all afternoon, but that didn't matter because his smile shared a story words didn't have the power to tell. We were baffled. Nobody could have known his machete was only good for one more blow. Our situation would have been completely different if we had hiked until the knife broke, then turned around, but we didn't, Mr. King stopped us one swing shy. Throwing the blade off the handle was confirmation we had reached a destination far more breathtaking and meaningful than anything I could've imagined.

Mr. King's oddly timed smile finally made sense—maybe he understood that I would reflect about breaking his machete for years to come. Maybe turning our hike around at that precise location was God's plan. Maybe God was trying to tell me to wake up and smell the roses instead of impatiently waiting for the next lookout point both on the hike and in life.

So there I was, frozen, in front of the pack with a machete handle in my hand. Feeling like a child who just got busted breaking a toy, I gingerly handed the remains back to Mr. King who let out a soft chuckle as he led me over to our original path. Looking down at the steepest part of the trail I knew we were in for it.

SMACK!

Zack's body splatted on the mud behind me like a sack of flour and picked up momentum as he tabletopped Zara. At this moment the attitude of the entire group changed. No more grasping for cleanliness and comfort—it was time to get nasty.

Every few seconds a body would hit the ground, to which we would yell, "Sniper!" Those of us who were still clean knew our time was coming. Walking on our feet was no longer an option, so a few of us submitted to the mountain and slid down on our butts. Those who remained standing had some success sliding on their feet but those falls took a toll on their tailbones. Ashley continued breaking her falls with her hands and I had no idea how her wrists were still intact. Kate was cracking up the entire way down and at one point she slid an impressive ten feet!

My special sandals were coated in mud and my Sparky the Sun Devil socks were crusted to my leg. A few of us reinstated walking sticks to slow our momentum, but they became a serious liability when we fell, so most of us tossed them to the wayside. Mr. King had yet to even sway off balance. For him, this was literally a walk in the park. When we got to a grassier area we had lost so much trust in our feet that we resorted back to our first means of transportation, crawling and rolling. Dylan plotted to tackle Zack who was finally walking confidently on his feet. Like a cheetah hunting a gazelle he leaped on Zack, and they rolled down the mountainside one over the other.

The only person enjoying our falls more than me was Mr. King, who cracked up after every single tumble. Zack was spending so much time on the ground he decided to make a Vietnamese snowball and chuck it at Emily. The brown soggy mudball hit Emily's buttocks dead center. She turned around to reveal the new stain on her white running shorts—she was a great sport and we nearly passed out in hysterics.

We were smelly. We were crusty. We were *out of control*. We were alive.

Trekking up the mountain we kept our heads down, doing our best to stay on our feet and reach the lookout in one piece. But the view had been surrounding us the entire time. All we needed to do was look around. On our descent we stopped and stared out into a landscape we didn't deserve to see. On our left and right the enormous blanket of trees covered the mountains so well that the clouds overhead tinged with green. We had barely beaten the sun by the time we reached our boats. After assessing the damage we turned to see Mr. King taking his final steps of the hike without as much as a speck of dirt on his garments.

A short boat ride and a much longer bus ride took us to our dinner reservation. Our nostrils perked up as we walked into the lavender-scented lobby of another extravagant resort. Waiting for us in the center of a spacious ballroom were two white tables, their chairs draped in white linen. Our entire day had made little sense, so it was logical that dinner would follow suit. Luckily, our food was served before my body odor lofted upward, because it would have annihilated my appetite. Unluckily, leaving our seats revealed an abominable coat of brown filth on the linens.

Then something incredible happened. Before we headed out, I smiled for a photo with Jonny Vee and said, "Zohnayyy" through my teeth. A nickname my friends have been calling me since middle school.

Jonny turned with massive eyes and said, "You're a Zohnay too?"

I screamed, "NO FUCKIN' WAY!" and leapt into his arms.

We jumped up and down celebrating our extraordinary revelation.

> Vietnam Day 6 | Day 36 | Feb 9, 2020: THIS IS INSANE!!! How many Johnny's in the world have the nickname Z O H N A Y?! I guess two, so far!

There was no heat on our bus during our rough ride home, so we cuddled up next to each other. Our wet windbreakers turned out to be poor substitutes for blankets. Shivering periodically and in and out of sleep, we were miserable until we felt our bus finally lurch forward to a stop. But our hopes were zapped as we sat upright to find ourselves in the middle of nowhere on the side of the road. Everyone let out a breath large enough to fog their entire window realizing we had forgotten about Mr. King's stop. Wishing him well, we passed money up to the front of the bus and watched him disappear into the darkness.

Unfortunately, letting out Mr. King let in a bone-chilling gust of wind. Zack took matters into his hands by peeing into an empty water bottle and cuddling it, then Zara cuddled Zack creating a most fascinating chain of warmth.

By the time we were tucked into our beds our body batteries were well below zero percent. We hadn't just burned both ends of the candlestick; we'd chucked the entire candle into the fire. It was the type of day I will retell to my grandchildren in detail from the rocking chair of my front porch. You know it's been a fantastic day when the thought of sharing it decades down the road brings butterflies. Even if I forgot a detail, I could re-watch our adventures in Pu Mat because Jonny was going to make a video edit!

Everyone who has made a travel video knows how gray the line between filming the moment and living in it can sometimes be, but when you're not the one filming two brilliant things happen.

1. You live in the moment
2. You're actually in the video

Every time I re-watch Jonny's video I catch something new, but there is one thing I am reminded of every single time. Journey > Destination.

Ponderings, Poops, and a Spider

"I have a terrifying long list of fears. Literally everything— diseases, spiders... and people getting tired of me."
—Taylor Swift

EVERYONE EXCEPT OUR group was wearing a mask in the Vinh airport. Parents even covered their newborns' mouths with masks, which was an adorably horrifying sight. We figured if everyone else was protected, then so were we.

In foreign airports especially, food and time took on an entirely different meaning. Meals were whenever they were available, and time was whenever the plane was ready. Touching back down in Ho Chi Minh City the effects of our mammoth day were starting to hit us. Arriving at security, the group before us had just been busted with a dozen vodka shooters, so we needed

Ponderings, Poops, and a Spider

to dump out *everything*. This was the first time I had my hair gel and toothpaste inspected. Opening my cabin door around dinner time, I unpacked half my bag, laid down on my bed, and woke up past breakfast the following morning.

> Vietnam Day 8 | Day 38 | Feb 11, 2020: I slept thirteen hours last night. I re-upped on candlesticks so hard I had a full candelabra.

Jimmy and I had our three-day Cambodia field program tomorrow which required a visa photo I had yet to acquire. The picture must have the proper background and dimensions to be accepted, so I needed to get to a store and have it done professionally.

I ran over to Berlin, the home of exhilarating epiphanies and sensational stories, to grab a bite to eat before hitting the town when I saw John serving himself in the buffet line.

"You're sittin' with me today," John said.

"Gladly," I replied.

We sat down in the middle of the dining room in the heat of the lunch rush. From the get-go John's tone was different from normal, almost like he was being serious. Naturally, I mirrored his attitude and tried to dial back a few notches. We were just chatting on the surface when John executed one of his famous pivots, diving into his first question. "Do you enjoy our conversations?"

"Yes, of course!" I promptly responded.

We had only shared a couple of conversations thus far, but they were always chock-full of wisdom.

John continued with another question, "If this table were

to be filled with people, would our conversation continue as it was?"

I looked down and thought for a brief moment. "Well, no."

"You're right, the conversation we are about to have could not continue in the same manner. Therefore, I want you to say a proper *no* to anyone who invites themselves to sit at our table."

"What... why can't we just talk somewhere private?"

"Because, Johnny, I've got a hunch you don't say the word *no* all too often, and I know it's rarely said to you."

ZINGER! John was right on the money. Sitting still with my arms crossed, he pulled out a napkin and a pen, then slid the materials over to me.

"I want you to write down the schedule of your typical day at ASU hour by hour."

Taking my time to carefully remember what my day-to-day looked like, I wondered if John was testing my memory to see if the things I was up to were of any value. Regardless, while I started filling in the time slots John stepped onto his soapbox.

"You know in my day we used to seek out distractions, not vice versa. And one would think that as technology improves, our efficiency should follow a similar path. So why are our parents and professors recommending you to put your smartphone in a separate room when you are working? There was once a time when it was more helpful to have our tools in the same room as our work."

I chuckled as I jotted down my last task in a typical day. I tried to write as legibly as possible, but the napkin started ripping in a few small spots.

"Done."

"Hand 'er over."

Ponderings, Poops, and a Spider

Putting his readers on, Johns eyes ran down the napkin and within seconds barked back, "Wrong!"

"Wrong? What do you mean?"

Starting to get flustered I snatched the napkin from his hands and reviewed my day. Maybe I had a brain fart. Looking down at my fully booked schedule beginning around 7:30 a.m. and ending at 10:00 p.m. John asked, "Now where do you squeeze in those three hours on social media?"

Silence.

"There's no way I spend that much time," I said shakily.

"Let's find out!" John replied.

John knew all about the screen time feature and honestly, I was scared to check; I had looked in the past but my stats didn't exactly encourage me to look again. Scrolling across to December 2019, one month prior to the voyage, I was spending more time than John predicted! Three and a half hours to be exact.

John whipped out his phone's calculator and started chugging away. "So if you're awake for fifteen hours, that's over twenty-three percent of your day consuming media. If you're alive for eighty years, that's just under fifteen percent of your life spent scrolling, or roughly eleven years staring into your screen, and that's only counting social media!"

There's a reason iPhone's screen time feature only depicts up to our weekly usage. Those of us who grew up playing video games know of the feature that showed our total time in game, and it was always startling. "I have been playing GTA V for two weeks of my life?!"

I wonder what our total screen time would be starting when we powered on our first smartphone. Days, weeks, and months carry weight, but years pack a punch.

Before John and I left the lunch table that day he made one final remark that will stick with me for the rest of my life: "Every hour that you spend scrolling, your goals realize one hour later."

I was ready to run through a wall, but I needed to run into town and get this silly visa photo for my Cambodia trip tomorrow. I grabbed my backpack from my cabin and headed down to the gangway when I overheard a lifelong learner named Lynn explaining how nervous she was that she wouldn't get the right size photo. This thought was also top of my mind, so I apologized for eavesdropping, and it turned out she was on my exact same field program.

Lynn was a shorter woman, but you'd never know by her walking pace. Almost every day I watched her and her friends speed walking around the top deck for exercise. They executed an impressive number of laps, always with bright smiles on their faces. Pumping our arms across Ho Chi Minh City, I was not surprised at how easily Lynn crossed the roads considering how high she held her chin.

Making our way to the photo shop we began conversation by sharing a bit about our families and backgrounds. All of Lynn's grandchildren called her by the nickname Wabster, and she wished for me to do the same. Wabster's lovely soft tone of voice kept me calm as we asked some strangers if we were headed in the right direction. They pointed directly across the street as if the place had just fallen out of the sky.

Within a few minutes we had our photos taken and were standing back outside the store wondering how it could've been that easy—nothing was ever that easy. Sure enough, it was. Grateful for the speedy service, Wabster treated me to a few balls of chocolate mochi which were amazeballs. I was elated that my

Ponderings, Poops, and a Spider

absurd sensitivity to strange textures did not hinder my enjoyment of the rice flour-coated ice cream.

Wabster and I skipped across the dock like children joining the back of the security line when a student said, "Oh my gosh! You didn't tell me your grandma was meeting you in Vietnam!"

Before I could even open my mouth, Wabster butted in, "Yes! I am so lucky to have him as my grandson."

Neither of us could keep a straight face all the way onto the ship—it was a tremendous compliment for both of us. Sticking my visa in the multizipper travel pouch that hung around my neck, I triple checked my bags had everything I needed for Cambodia. Tomorrow we would rise at an ungodly hour.

Our ninth morning in Vietnam Jimmy and I were off the ship by 04:30, and the cold apple I ate for breakfast stung like a bee in my stomach. Since I had just traveled independently for the last week in Vietnam, I was happy I wouldn't have to worry about my plans day to day because our entire trip had already been scheduled minute by minute. However it wasn't all peaches and cream as you imagine traveling internationally with a group of thirty—ages nine to sixty-nine—might be. Our only rule was not to check a bag because we would only be there for three days, and our strict schedule did not allow us all to wait around the baggage claim. Entering the security line I noticed my dance professor throwing her bag onto the scale. Even the nine-year-old held onto their luggage.

Our plane slammed into Phnom Penh as the sun was just beginning to rise. Our landing might have been smoother if we had just slid in on the belly of the plane. Our touchdown was so egregious we applauded when our bird came to a stop. I had my passport and visa photo at the ready as I exited the plane. Pulling up to the first checkpoint I placed all of my documents beneath the window and the agent immediately slid back my visa photo.

"Don't you need this?"

The agent shook his head as he passed back my passport. "Next!"

Soon we loaded onto a large coach bus and Mr. T, our guide, laid out our agenda for the day. He announced our plans as if we had the entire day ahead of us. *Surely, it's close to noon,* I thought. It was 09:00! I was honestly intimidated by the full day we had ahead of us and then I pondered a question.

Why did I always consider travel days to be throwaway days?

Any time I stepped foot on a plane, in my head I would always say, "Well, this day is shot." I always thought planes made me tired but technically I've got better air circulating sitting in that tube than anywhere else on Earth.

While something inside of me still wanted to put my stuff in its place and relax, I realized that two out of our three days in Cambodia would involve a plane ride. If we didn't actually travel after those flights, we would be left with just one day to explore. Thus, I became very grateful for our loaded itinerary because traveling independently I might have thrown in the towel on forty-eight hours of adventure.

After touring an Angkor Wat museum and having lunch at a local restaurant, we stood in front of the largest religious structure in the world by land area. This was the first time I had gone to a museum and the real thing in the same day. Mr. T was thorough. Pondering that it was built almost a thousand years ago left me baffled. Angkor Wat was originally built as a temple for the

Ponderings, Poops, and a Spider

Hindu gods, but it's now used for Buddhist worship. Halfway through the day, a couple of monks wearing orange and yellow robes, the youngest roughly fourteen and the oldest probably sixty, led us up a wooden staircase into an open room. Our entire group sat on the floor facing the monks as they began to chant while throwing spices, flowers, and water on us. I would have probably started to giggle if my attention had not been redirected to the puddle of sweat forming beneath our sweltering bodies. It seemed we had no choice but to stay and receive this Buddhist blessing ceremony, so I prayed for the monks in my head.

When we were finished and started to walk out, I couldn't help but think of the app Temple Run when the kids in our group darted around the corners of the structure. Late in the afternoon, now drenched in sweat, the cotton shirt that rested against my skin so delicately on the airplane was now suffocating me. In the hottest part of the day, the stench from the mud patches lofted into the air while the temple walls guarded the funk from escaping.

Leaving Angkor Wat, our entire group was running on fumes. From afar it looked like there was a swarm of children around our bus, and as we got closer this was exactly the case. Dozens of kids aged six to thirteen were giving their pitch, attempting to sell ten postcards for a dollar. They were professionals at utilizing their age and innocence, but their selling point was fanning out the cards and showing how well they could count to ten in English. My heart was full when I saw our bus littered with hundreds of postcards. We stayed in a local hotel the first night, but we were stoked for tomorrow when we would sleep off the grid.

Our second morning in Cambodia we set out to see the reason I signed up for this field program but first we stopped at a local school to drop off toys and supplies. The children's smiles were radiant. I knew they were giving me much more than we could ever give them. It resembled an American elementary classroom with a blackboard in the front, posters, multiplication tables, and the alphabet taped to every inch of the walls. Some of the differences were two students shared each desk, there was no playground, and half the year the kids took canoes to school.

We made a couple drawings, taught them how to throw a Frisbee, then hopped back on the bus for Kampong Khleang. Jimmy chose to stay behind on the bus, but I'll cut him some slack. This whole poverty thing was new to him. I was proud he was even on the field program in the first place. Who's to say he couldn't be equally impacted watching us interact with the kids as he would playing himself?

The roads we were now driving on were normally covered by over ten feet of water during the wet season. To combat the monster monsoon season, the Kampong Khleang village is permanently stilted thirty feet above the ground. When the monsoon season hits, scooters and wagons are substituted for small boats which are sitting right outside or underneath their homes. All of the houses were made from wood so we were baffled to see villagers cooking inside on open fires. We loaded onto boats very similar to those in Pu Mat, because the muddy water that flowed through town was only a few feet deep. Our captain was fourteen years old, and his copilot was nine. When our boat stuck to the bottom our copilot would pull out a big stick and push us along. The locals were the only ones who gave tours of their community, so the money stayed within the village.

It felt a bit strange taking pictures of their neighborhood but

I'm sure the locals would've done the same if I had driven them through mine. As we winded our way down a branch of the Mekong river, other tourists boats passed on the opposite side and their faces mirrored ours. About an hour into the ride, the congested and shallow waterway opened up into the largest freshwater lake in Southeast Asia, Tonle Sap. Burping along one of the most productive and diverse ecosystems in the world, I could not distinguish houses from boats. The Tonle Sap floodplain is home to more than three million people and supports two thirds of Cambodia's protein intake worth two billion dollars.

On our way back inland, we passed tiny fishing boats operated entirely by kids. One little girl who was throwing a fishing net could not have been older than five years old. But perhaps the most difficult information to swallow was the most common cause of death. It wasn't famine, it was falling, and it wasn't a balanced demographic, it was the curious babies who crawled over the edge of their homes. And if they didn't die on impact they were drowned in a few inches of muddy water.

> Cambodia Day 2 | Day 40 | Feb 13, 2020: Leaving the floating village today there was a pterodactyl inside of me that wanted to burst out and tell the world what I just saw.

I hardly had an appetite for lunch, but I needed to eat because Mr. T had a full afternoon of temples to guide us through. The first being Beng Mealea whose grounds were surrounded by a minefield. Not every bomb had been defused in the area, so they suggested we didn't step off the trail. This was a rule I could follow, but not without tossing a few rocks first.

By the end of the day all of the temples were starting to blend together, sort of like what happened in Japan. After making sticky rice and maple sugar candies with a few locals we were back on the bus headed toward our homestay. It was a spacious property with a large wooden barnlike structure in the middle. The entire building was elevated a few feet above the ground so that critters wouldn't join our slumber party. The space was filled wall to wall with thirty razor-thin mattresses on the floor and respective mosquito nets neatly hung above.

In front of the sleeping quarters was a very long and skinny pool about fifty meters in length and one lane wide. Jimmy and I were pleasantly surprised; we immediately stripped down to our undies and dove in. We found out the best place to escape the humidity was underwater, but it was too bad nobody had a straw. A few others in our group joined us until we were called out for dinner.

The dinner table took the same shape as the pool and turning my head side to side I had not eaten one meal with so many people in my life. Regrettably, I could not remember the name of the traditional Cambodian dish we ate, but it tasted much better than it looked. Following supper, the entire group participated in Khmer-style dancing, and we all took turns playing the drums and tambourine.

When the festivities were over, a few of us climbed a spiral staircase leading to a free-standing deck a few stories above the property below. In the center of the platform, was a small table dressed in white linens ready for two romantic lovers. If I hadn't already proposed in Hawaii this would've been the spot. Jimmy, Nicole, and I shared a glass of wine while Nicole shared her comedy sketch that was censored out of the talent show. "I'm a Jew,

Ponderings, Poops, and a Spider

so I can say that," Nicole added as she punched her final punch line.

The eagles nest swayed as we came down, but it could've been the wine, or our equilibrium. It was getting late, so the only noises at this point in the night were crickets, zippers, and the sound of water making its way into the human body. Jimmy said he felt like a princess with the bright pink mosquito net hanging around his bed. I asked him if Burberry had come out with one yet. They have not.

"But if they did, it would keep out more than mosquitos... liberals too."

"You have a problem keeping liberals out of your bed?"

Crickets, zippers, gulping, and now our conversation pierced the silent room. If there was any night that Jimmy was going to need his Burberry mosquito net, tonight was the night.

Cambodia Day 3 | Day 41 | Feb 14, 2020: It was 01:00 in the morning when I was rudely awakened by the worst abdominal pain of my life.

Inside the area just beneath my bellybutton a war was commencing. Beads of sweat fell off my forehead as I lifted the mosquito net over myself and stepped over a sound asleep Jimmy. Slipping on my Birkenstocks I walked down a few stairs and into a wooden shack labeled BATHROOM. Squatting down, my dinner broke the sound barrier as it left my body. I thought the shed was leaking overhead, but it was drops of sweat hitting my cold feet. Suddenly a wave of panic came over me when I realized I had not checked if there was toilet paper. I snapped my head to the left and found myself looking directly into the eight sparkling eyes of a Cambodian wolf spider. (Google this thing right now.) If the military manufactured lightweight camouflage precision killing spiders, Mr. Wolf would be top of class.

As a lifelong arachnophobe, my life was basically over. I had barely conquered the daddy longlegs in the corners of my suburban Illinois basement. My body froze; I couldn't swivel my head to check the other side for toilet paper in fear I'd lose sight of Mr. Wolf. Shakily taking three deep breaths, I snapped my head to the right and discovered a completely full roll of single-ply toilet paper. Thank God! Once I finished my business, I sprinted back up the stairs, tiptoed over Jimmy, and fell down into my bed. My entire body radiated heat, so I tossed my sheets onto the floor beside me. Lying there in my boxers I used my forearm to wipe the sweat from my head. Luckily, the pain had subsided, I just needed to fall back asleep. Turning over and over like a cement truck I could not find a comfortable position.

I was asleep for one minute before the white-hot pain was back enough for me to let out an audible cry. Again, I lifted the net, jumped over Jimmy, and plopped down on the toilet with nanoseconds to spare—the barbarians at the gate must have reached Mach two. It was not long before I remembered my good pal Mr. Wolf. Once again, I was in a staring contest a few inches away from the most horrifying creature I had ever seen. After rolling out half of the toilet paper I said goodbye to my bathroom buddy for the second time.

It's past 02:00 and I am wide awake lying atop my covers. Outraged at my situation, I flipped over and screamed into my pillow. I would have been more comfortable lying down on a knife. This was the point when I entertained concerns of pancreatitis or kidney stones, but the pain was in the wrong places.

Ponderings, Poops, and a Spider

Walking over to one of the professor's beds, I stood over him and saw his children cuddled alongside; I simply couldn't bring myself to lift their mosquito net and wake them up.

Skipping the Birkenstocks this time I darted outside and with tears in my eyes I greeted Mr. Wolf for the third time. He looked back at me blankly, almost empathetically, because we both knew the toilet paper was on its last few rotations. We shared a special moment together as Mr. Wolf watched me give birth to my first son, Joe... Sloppy Joe.

Feeling completely defeated and vulnerable, I confessed to Mr. Wolf that I had been afraid of his kind my entire life and vowed never to be scared again. I watched in amazement as Mr. Wolf's tiny little mouth opened and in a pitch shockingly lower than I expected he said, "If I wanted to kill you, you'd be dead already." This comforted me greatly considering the image that came into my mind when we first met. When I first noticed Mr. Wolf, I knew we both had the power to kill each other, but I worried that as I brought my fist around Mr. Wolf would see it in slow motion, jump onto my face, pluck out one of my eyeballs, wrap it, and gift it to one of his friends.

At this point I had lost several pounds, and I was beyond dehydrated. Walking back upstairs I located the fridge in the pitch black and my heart sank as I tugged the door and heard the clank of chain and lock. Collapsing into my bed for the third time I was confused if I was trying to sleep or die.

I made three more trips to Mr. Wolf's office that night. Eventually catching one hour of sleep from 05:00 to 06:00. Waking up for the seventh time to sees unlight bleeding through the door my body was filled with relief so great I could almost taste it. I leapt out of bed and inhaled my water bottle, which hid from me the entire night.

I felt 100 percent better, other than the fact that the bags under my eyes could hold a week's worth of groceries. I began reflecting on the agonizing past seven hours of my existence when I remembered Mr. Wolf. Did he even exist? Could I have been hallucinating? Jimmy, who was standing beside me, asked, "Who are you talking to?" as I repeated these questions aloud. I disappeared faster than a cartoon, jumped the entire staircase, and flung open the bathroom door. Mr. Wolf was nowhere in sight.

A shock of disappointment rang through my body like a gong—this was the first time I actually wanted to see a spider. I scoured every surface looking for my hairy little friend. The sight of the bare brown toilet paper roll made me acutely aware of my baboon-red tushy. But when I leaned down over the roll, I couldn't believe my eyes.

> Cambodia Day 3 | Day 41 | Feb 14, 2020: Mr. Wolf's love language was gift giving! He left me a masterpiece, decorating either side of the toilet paper roll with the most intricately designed web I'd ever seen!

It was in that moment I realized my fears don't want me to be scared of them.

Pocket God

"Faith is taking the first step even when you don't see the whole staircase."
—Martin Luther King Jr.

LANDING BACK IN Ho Chi Minh City we had one last day before we would set sail for Malaysia. In the morning I visited the American War Museum. As I worked my way up the three-story building, the displays gradually grew more explicit. On the top floor I saw conjoined fetuses in a liquid tank, eviscerated bodies, curb-stomped jaws, and pictures of people so deformed they lost all resemblance of a human being. Many were consequences of the Agent Orange chemical the US sprayed across Vietnam's agricultural landscape. When I made it to the gift shop I took a deep breath, happy I had seen all the museum had to offer but happy I was finished. Then I saw a man, born without eyes, playing the piano in the corner of the shop. I was destroyed when I found out Agent Orange's effects will be present for generations to come. I have never visited a Vietnam War museum in the US, but I imagined it couldn't have looked anything like what I saw that day.

After the museum it was time to go pick up the matching bright purple suits Dylan and I had purchased our first day in port. The reason we chose purple was different for both of us: it was my mom's favorite color, and Dylan's school color was purple. As our tailor, Minh, made a few last-minute adjustments I darted my eyes around for a bathroom. There was no sign in sight, so I asked Minh if she had one in the store. Setting down the measuring tape, she proceeded to push away one of the shelves like it was magic but there was no trickery involved.

I took one step off the pristine white tile into the dark, leaking pit that was Minh's home. I instantly forgot what the comfort of her air-conditioned store felt like as my shirt grabbed ahold of my skin. Stepping over buckets and fans I walked past her bedroom where some of her family were still sleeping then past the kitchen filled with broken plastic chairs and a makeshift table. A very wrinkled woman who must have been her mother pointed across the room. Their bathroom was in horrendous condition, yet I felt terrible using it. Taking extra time to clean up after myself, I stepped back into the store and the air conditioning slapped me across the face.

After taking good care of Minh, I couldn't stop thinking about how that experience was an analogy for my life. I was blown away that she so willingly invited me into her house, and I wanted to do the same. How often do I hide the mess of my life with an extravagant facade. I'd let anyone walk into my pristine store, but I would never let someone use my bathroom.

Dylan and I took one last run through the black market. By this time we were master negotiators. We knew the locals used the principal of anchoring—asking an unreasonably high price to skew the rest of the negotiation—to their advantage. We slashed the first price we heard by 90 percent. They made the face like we just stabbed them, then we started walking away, to which the store owner would run and pull us back. Even then, we were still getting a terrible deal.

I said goodbye to Dylan and ordered a Grab. Pulling up to the dock the total was 78.00 dong, so I handed him a 100.00 and told him to keep the change. He looked at me like I was crazy. I felt good about it.

There was a coffee shop with free Wi-Fi conveniently located on the dock just before the security lines began that many of my shipmates would frequent. I had not been there before, and since this was my last afternoon in Vietnam, I decided to take a load off.

Just after plugging in my phone at the coffee shop I was yanked up out of my chair by a police officer telling me I had not paid my driver properly. I explained how I gave him over the proper amount and the officer handed me the 10.00 dong I had given to my driver.

Oops!

I jogged back over to my Grab and handed him 200.00 for all his trouble. He looked at me like I was crazy. I felt good about it.

Plopping down at the café for the second time, a few of my friends walked by and invited me into town for one final adventure. I decided to hang back and spend some time catching up with everyone back home. By the time I picked up my head the afternoon was behind me, and a gigantic line was already forming to board the ship for Malaysia. The queue was longer than usual because medical personal were temperature checking all voyagers. In line there were rumors stirring that Malaysia and India were going to be cancelled. How did they have any idea? Some of their parents were watching our situation closely from afar, and other parents were travel agents so their predictions might have legs.

On board the conversation was more of the same; those walking around with drooping heads had heard the news, while others with upright posture had not. Soon everyone had heard some variation of the rumor. What right did they have bringing down everyone's mood? Nothing was official yet. Why didn't we just relax until it was a fact? But at the root of all my frustration was myself.

The thought that two more countries were in jeopardy infuriated me with how I spent the last half of my day in Vietnam. They say it's not about how you start, but how you finish, and I didn't come in with enough speed to even break the tape. The truth was, I wasn't catching up with my friends back home, I was stalking them. Embarrassingly, I didn't communicate with a single person in all four hours of "reconnecting." I devoured my friends' content like a ravenous beast, but I was not able to satisfy my hunger. When I scrolled for the last time, I couldn't recall a single thing I'd learned about my friends. The last hour of my digital date was spent perfecting my own post.

The past two weeks had produced some of the best images in my entire camera roll and everyone needed to know. Toward the end of our time in Vietnam the urge was stronger than ever to share the multitude of photos I deemed "Instagram worthy." The way a photograph earned this title was based on its potential for comments and likes. So, what gets the most activity? While on the beaches of Da Nang I took a photo with a rice hat covering my crotch. Following the formula, less clothes = more likes, it was easy to select this as my first photo in a series of ten. I wanted to share this photo the second it was taken, but I had no Wi-Fi. This was the moment I realized just how badly I wanted to post, and the lengths that I would go to make it happen.

In the United States, I am fortunate enough to have an unlimited data plan. I can throw up a post anywhere from the Illinois River to the South Rim of the Grand Canyon. In Vietnam, I could only use the Internet when I had Wi-Fi. I had the option to purchase a SIM card and utilize the country's local Internet, but having someone open up my phone that didn't speak English scared me off.

The fact that I don't drink coffee made using a coffee shop's Wi-Fi without my friends even more miserable. The point where this issue crossed the line was when the memories I was creating in real time became secondary to posting them.

Having a much better grasp on the situation I thought to myself, *My time is so precious in Vietnam, I may never return again in my life! Why did I spend all that time obsessing over what my friends were doing, especially because what I am doing is so much cooler?*

That repulsive thought led me to beg much better questions: What if all my time was as valuable as it was on the last day of Vietnam? Why was that yucky feeling of going down the rabbit hole now somehow amplified ten times?

Simply because I had placed a tremendous amount of value and importance on my time in Vietnam, but the truth is, my time is equally as valuable whether I am on the other side of the world or sitting on my couch after a long day of classes.

Out to sea I was already experiencing real freedom, but it's drastically easier to avoid the Internet when it's not available. But why couldn't I hold myself from indulging when I had an afternoon of free time and Wi-Fi? I curiously went to check my screen time again. I had spent more time on my phone the last day in Vietnam than the combination of the thirteen days prior. I scrolled left to check out my stats from our time at sea: an average of twenty-five minutes a day. Roughly seven of those were used to contact home, fifteen were used at the gym to change songs already pre-downloaded, and the rest were spent taking pictures. Adding up all thirty days at sea that came before Vietnam added up to twelve and a half hours, which is the amount of screen time accumulated in just two days back home.

Even if it was only a few hours, I was disgusted. I made a commitment to both myself and my friends in Japan to live presently and I had just gone back on my word.

Vietnam Day 9 | Day 42 | Feb 15, 2020: Today I deleted my social media apps for the rest of the voyage.

The thought of deleting all my accounts crossed my mind but there was no way I could do that. At least not having the option to click on the app would prevent a situation like this from happening for the remainder of the voyage. Even though my phone lives in my pocket, I wear the pants.

Flexibility—Level Two

> *"To reach a port we must set sail –Sail, not tie at anchor. Sail, not drift."*
> —*Franklin D. Roosevelt*

WHEN I OPENED my eyes this morning, I was jubilant to be back out to sea. I sprung out of bed like I'd been cured from a disease. I could hardly wait to look out the window.

> Day 43 | Feb 16, 2020: Moving the curtains away from my porthole to reveal the peaceful glistening ocean I was startled to be staring into the bustling streets of Ho Chi Minh City.

Beep-boop! "As you might be aware, we are not in the middle of the ocean. Please monitor your seamail for more information to come."

The plan was to leave port in the middle of the night and

begin making waves toward Malaysia. I was sick to my stomach wondering what had gone wrong, although I knew it could only mean one thing. On my way to the gym to let off steam, I passed a group of tear-filled lifelong learners. Standing on the steps between the seventh and eighth deck the itinerary update was read aloud to me as it was in Japan. Malaysia and India rejected us from porting fearing we were one of the disease-carrying ships desperately looking for a place to dock. We were desperate but not diseased. Instead, we added one of the honeymoon capitals of the world, the Seychelles, an archipelago of 115 islands off East Africa.

Getting back in the gym for the first time in over two weeks was charitable to my spirits. I believed if I didn't work out six days a week, I would lose the muscle I gained, but this was not the case. Finishing a set on the bench press, I noticed someone weeping over the same handrail where I had heard the news a few minutes earlier. Just after they left, someone else came down the steps, on the phone. We were still in port, so some people were able to get cell service from the starboard side. Since the steps on the staircases all around the ship were abnormally narrow, most people slid their hand along the rails just in case. About halfway down the student's hand hydroplaned right over the tears forcing him to stumble over the second half of the staircase.

After a quick shower, I joined several conversations around the ship. One girl had plans to meet up with her family and boyfriend in Malaysia. Raj lived in India, so he had only packed a few outfits expecting to grab the rest when he got back home. However, these instances were the overwhelming minority.

Our post-Vietnam session was rather unusual considering Vietnam was still just outside. Nevertheless, our group rendez-

Flexibility—Level Two

voused in our usual meeting spot in the back of the union. Our reflection session after Japan had been inspiring but now it was infuriating. Right off the bat, students began firing away at Dean Gene asking, "How does Seychelles culture replace India and Malaysia?", "When are we going to be compensated for our losses?" This may have been the first time in history people were let down about getting to spend time on one of the most beautiful islands on Earth. Everyone was itching to place the blame for these diversions on somebody's shoulders. Dean Gene was looking forward to Malaysia and India just like the rest of us and I could not sit there listening to any more unanswerable questions so I entered the conversation.

"Hey! We're lucky we got an additional country at all! And if our dean had decided to dock our ship in Shanghai our entire voyage would have been terminated three weeks ago. We never planned to spend two weeks in any single port, and we all had the time of our lives in Vietnam, didn't we?"

With that, the bombardment of questions seized, and Dean Gene explained he had zero control over our itinerary. With no other questions, and everyone's tempers simmered, we were released early from our session. Angela hastily approached me as everyone packed up their belongings. She asked me how I could possibly remain so positive in such an ambiguous and frustrating situation. I explained to her how my friends and I were preparing for a semester like this after we lost China by treating every single second of this voyage as if it were our last. I told her how our ship's community would be brought closer than any voyage in history. All we needed to do was wake up and smell the roses. After all, we were receiving college credits on a cruise ship. Some of us may have sailed for free with the help of family or scholarship, while others may have forked up astronomical money. I ended by saying that those who had undertaken enormous personal debt and remained focused on the joys of our voyage were mentally invincible.

Walking out of the union I was famished, so I made my way to Berlin for lunch where I hoped to find the squad. The volume in the dining room was at a disturbingly low level compared to the normal noise pollution. Peering over the buffet area I was giddy to see Kate's water bottle at a corner table; she was standing across the room in the soup line. Grabbing some chicken I plopped down across from Kate as she salted her soup with tears. I had seen her laugh so many times I was surprised she even knew how to frown.

She was royally pissed off we wouldn't see the Taj and bought the most common lie that all the time and money spent on this semester was going to nothing. I nodded my head and rephrased what I had just told Angela. No amount of money could ever have taught us the virtue that is *flexibility*. Plus, none of these itinerary changes have taken any time away from each other, they've just changed *where*. Kate concurred and together we renewed our vow to make the most of our time at sea.

The tears continued throughout the day, and they fell off more than just students. Right before dinner our ship's hull slowly released its kiss with the buoys along the shore. We were in motion once again making our way down the tightest body of water we'd sail in all semester.

By evening I was desperate for some fun, so I found myself in Zack's cabin brainstorming some activities. Zara strolled in and Zack smacked her across the face with a pillow. Game on! Zara came back with force, a pillow in each hand, smacking both of us at the same time. We made enough noise for our neighbors to hear so they busted through the door and joined the war. Three minutes later, breathing heavily and sweating, everybody raised their little white flag. Assessing the damage we were surprised to discover welts the size of a baseball. Apparently, pillows were scarce, so in the heat of the action TV remotes and shoes were substituted.

Before I fell asleep, I prayed aloud, "God, the coronavirus seems to be just one step ahead of us. She has already cost us three countries. If it is your will, could you trip her?"

The next morning I got my first haircut on the ship, and I was extremely pleased. My natural brown hair now showed beneath my fake blond locks creating something a class above frosted tips. I was eating lunch outside on the top deck when one of the ship kids, Finn, ran over pointing at a massive wall of storm clouds behind our ship. Soon everyone's conversation shifted to the storm, and they picked up their belongings and went inside. Finn and I stuck our ground, the storm chaser in us leaping with joy until we realized the storm was chasing us. We continued staring at the clouds until rain pelted the sea about a hundred yards off the aft. There wasn't a single soul outside when the rain hit the deck. The downpour was so extreme we could barely see each other ten feet away, then the wind came spinning us around like ballerinas. Our uvulas took a few punches as we screamed into the sky. With our clothes sopping wet we ripped off our shirts and twirled them around. To those watching through the window I'm sure we looked ridiculous, but to Finn and me, executing the rain dance was the only logical response.

Prancing around the deck I couldn't understand why I felt

so free. Oh to be nine again! But I was ten years older, and I still acted like Finn and maybe even more rambunctiously in that moment. Why do we lose this freedom as we get older? Well, what would be a test of freedom? Can you do a spontaneous cartwheel in the grocery store, or are party tricks reserved for parties? It's not a question of who can act out the most, rather who is acting when they're out. Acting is much more than just playing someone you're not, but holding back someone you are, in fear you might embarrass your friends. Or maybe you're constantly acting out trying to earn attention from your friends, because I'm with you on that one. Regardless of which side of the spectrum you fall, if you can't dance in the rain, you're not free.

Tomorrow I would need to perform a much more elaborate dance for the lip sync event in the Sea Olympics and we had procrastinated practicing till the night before. I reached out to my team, the Adriatic Sea, to find someone to help us get started. One of the students on our team, Miles, stepped up to the plate and volunteered to choreograph and teach twelve of us a dance. He was relentless with our execution and did not settle for any mediocrity, we couldn't believe he pulled this entire thing out of his head.

> Day 44 | Feb 17, 2020: Five hours, three room changes, four noise complaints, and a bucket of sweat later we had perfected our five-minute lip sync dance and "Truth Hurts" by Lizzo is now my least favorite song of all time.

It was past 01:00 by the time I went to bed and tomorrow was one of the biggest days of the semester. And for some terrible reason tonight we needed to set our clocks *ahead* one hour. ADRIATIC, PURPLE RAIN, WE ABOUT TO WIN THIS THANG!

~~~~~~

A few hours before landing in Miami, I collected the elephant-themed gifts I had gotten Ashley for her birthday and put them in a brown paper bag. It was the only bag I had. I figured it would be better than dumping all the little gifts on her lap. I wanted to be the first to wish her happy birthday, but I felt bad waking her up. After a few groans she was conscious, and I handed her the bag. There was no one else awake on the plane, so it was a pretty sweet moment to share.

Just before touchdown our pilot informed us that we would need to deboard and go through customs and security, before reboarding the exact same plane. Exiting the aircraft I needed to book a flight straight home to Chicago rather than reboarding and continuing onto Newark. I opened a tab on my phone for every airline that could take me to Chicago. United was the only airline with open seats available. I clicked CONFIRM… and black.

I didn't want to waste precious time attempting to find an outlet and charge my phone, so I sprinted over to the counter.

"Wait!" Ashley shouted.

I would need to say the first of the goodbyes I had been planning in my head the entire voyage. My throat closed as I said goodbye to Jake, Ashley, Nic, and Weston because they would be continuing onto Newark. Tears fell on each other's shoulders exactly how I had pictured it. Even the pressure of the hugs was on point. I didn't say goodbye to Kate, Maddi, and Lauren because I would be joining them on the flight to Chicago.

With the first set of goodbyes behind me, I sprinted across the terminal over to the counter in an attempt to change my flight from Newark to Chicago. Standing in line at the counter I waited no more than three minutes before Jake, Ashley, Nic, and Weston were standing directly behind me in line. Awkward...this was definitely not how I pictured it. Apparently, this was the same counter that they needed to check in for their flight to Newark.

When I reached the counter, the woman told me if I would have arrived thirty seconds earlier she could have booked me on the flight to Chicago. It took all of the effort in the world to hold in a full-blown temper tantrum. Instead, with my friends still behind me, I channeled my inner Bob Ross and decided that this happy accident would make for a great story.

A moment later, I realized I said goodbye to the friends I was still with and nothing to Kate, Maddi, and Lauren on the flight to Chicago. Major bummer! Jake, Ashley, Nic, Weston and I boarded the exact same aircraft two hours later, *ideally* on our way to Newark. An additional three-hour delay on the tarmac allowed the crew ample time to clean and repack the airplane. Weston taught Ashley and I about lift and how these massive metal machines actually take flight. We were completely captivated. He is my favorite kind of bird nerd.

The winding of the jet engines was music to our ears as we took to the skies for the second time. With twenty-three hours of travel under my belt, I took two massive deep breaths and lowered my head back into my journal.

~~~~~~

The Twelfth Man

"Extreme Ownership. Leaders must own everything in their world. There is no one else to blame."
—Jocko Willink

THE SEA OLYMPICS were one of the most iconic ship-wide community events on Semester at Sea. Our ship was divided into eight eighty-person teams or seas. The events were chosen by the sea captains who were voted in by their sea at the beginning of the semester. I was a sea captain for the Adriatic Sea and our color was purple. A perfect coincidence considering I just bought a purple suit.

The 128th Sea Olympics events included: synchronized swimming, frozen t-shirt, bite the bag, limbo, backwards spelling bee, crab soccer, knockout basketball, coin dive, relay race, eating challenge, Minute to Win It, musical chairs, trivia, Cross-Fit, ping-pong, volleyball, gaga ball, water balloon dodgeball, mathlete competition, and chess. Events were happening in all different areas of the ship during all hours of the day. Naturally, I wanted to be a part of as many competitions as possible, but I had to miss some events due to the overlap.

The most important part of the competition was the lip sync dance which started off every Sea Olympics. Taking the stage, the twelve of us hit every single move synced perfectly with the music all with big smiles on our face. When we finished the union erupted. That was going to be hard to beat. I speedily changed out of my purple suit and slid on my rubber Birkenstocks for the CrossFit competition. My team encouraged me to wear sneakers, but I rejected, for the same reason you don't take an exam in a different desk on test day.

When I arrived at the gym there were four people there to spectate. My expectations were shattered—I had envisioned a massive crowd screaming my name, and Ashley sitting in the front row. I went back to my room to recalibrate and catch a break from the heat and when I returned those four people had multiplied filling the entire deck, staircase, and railing above. Ashley sat front and center. Nobody could stop me now.

Each team had one representative complete ten strict pull-ups, thirty push-ups, fifteen burpees, and seventy-five sit-ups as fast as possible with proper form.

> Day 45 | Feb 18, 2020: The second I jumped up to the pull-up bar I harnessed all the energy from every individual in the crowd and 2:06 seconds later it was all over.

My body was so hot I could have cooked an egg on my stomach. The temperature outside was close to a hundred degrees with the humidity. Nic and Zack competed against me in this event, and I cheered both of them on as they raced to beat my time. After everyone had finished, it was announced that the Adriatic Sea had won! I cared much less about our team victory and more about the fact that I beat Nic who was stronger than me, I just had less weight to throw around.

The Adriatic Sea was off to a record-setting start taking home gold in nearly every event in the morning. After an ice-cold shower I was back out on the deck to watch the frozen T-shirt contest, coin dive, and bite the bag. Hopping from event to event a fellow sea captain reminded me that I was scheduled to referee volleyball. This event was held on the sports court, which is the highest level of the ship non-crew members are allowed to be. Just a few feet behind the pool a single flight of stairs leads up to half a basketball court covered with netting on all sides.

While refereeing the game I was simultaneously watching synchronized swimming down below. I was blown away by how in sync the teams were in the water. The lifts and twirls were quite the spectacle. What's more, we were sailing around Singapore so the famous Marina Bay Sands resort (the three towers with a boat-looking structure on top) was clearly visible just off in the distance. By the time Singapore was out of sight, events on the top deck were wrapping up so I went to check out the indoor competitions.

Waltzing into a dead-silent Lido lounge I spotted Dylan plugging away at his calculator!

Bewildered I said, "No way, you're smart?"

Dylan nodded his head as he continued solving a problem.

I yelped, "Math! Math! Math!" cheering him along when the

facilitators ran over to kick me out. "This is the only event you can't cheer for."

After chanting and banging on the glass a few more times outside I headed over to the ping-pong table for the final event I would compete in. I was most excited for this one because the winner would have the chance to play Captain Kostas. I had played almost every day leading up to the games, so I felt very prepared. I accounted for the waves, wind, lighting, even the number of stars on the ball. But the only thing I did not account for was the extra ninety eyeballs watching me play. Just a few hours earlier the crowd had spiked my adrenaline enough to blow through the CrossFit competition but now the pressure was floundering my technicality and focus. I was eliminated in the first game, but I was at least happy my opponent went on to win the gold.

Once again, my lack of sleep was beginning to catch up to me, but I just needed to make it through the awards ceremony. I saw a few others in purple gathered in the very front of the union, so I knew they felt as confident as I did. We didn't want to walk all the way from the back of the room to accept the trophy. The lights dimmed, and we prepared ourselves for a primal scream. Sensing the ship was exhausted, they cut straight to the chase starting with the last place sea.

"And eighth place goes to... the Adriatic Sea!"

We turned to each other laughing that they had read the list backward, but then they continued with seventh place. Surely, they must have miscounted. A few members of our sea stood up and interrupted the awards to ask if they had made a mistake. They had not. Stupefied, we continued looking at each other, some on the brink of tears, others already past. When the ceremony finished, we were made known that our sea had been deducted

The Twelfth Man

points for multiple unsportsmanlike incidences throughout the day.

I did my very best to attend every single event, so I was puzzled how I did not witness a single one of these altercations. Learning about the situations, it was confirmed that I was not present for any of them, and I was livid. However, one stood out above the rest as particularly infuriating. During water balloon dodgeball, while I was playing ping-pong, one of our players decided to pick on one of the smaller guys on the other team, Weston. Harping on him for his height then shoving him backwards.

> Day 45 | Feb 18, 2020: How the fuck does a game of water balloon dodgeball on the sports court of a cruise ship sailing past Singapore get to the point of picking on someone's height?

Somehow, it happened, and as the leader of the team at fault an apology was in order. Running down to my cabin I opened my laptop and wrote Weston via seamail:

> Weston,
>
> It has come to my attention that there was an altercation between yourself and one of the Adriatic Sea players during the water balloon dodgeball competition on the sports court earlier today. Out of all the places where unsportsmanlike conduct might have occurred, I am embarrassed that it happened during this event. I would like to apologize and take responsibility for my team and our actions. I am truly sorry for what transpired today. See you around the ship!
>
> Johnny Vrba
> Adriatic Sea Captain

Weston responded shortly after and accepted my apology on behalf of my sea. Then I had a thought. *It's kind of scary when you're responsible for people because you have absolutely no control over them.* I know fraternity presidents understand this fear, some facing jail time for other brothers' actions. In the most extreme case of former Navy SEAL Jocko Willink, an error caused by his team means life or death, and as their leader he is responsible for their lives. If I want to be a leader, I need to seize accountability, not avoid it. When I find myself pointing my finger, I know I've got three pointed right back at me.

The days following the Sea Olympics Weston and I continued our conversation in person. Sitting down for the very first time with him, I was saddened that it took forty days for us to connect. It didn't take long to know Weston was the type of guy to call and wish your dog a happy birthday. What surprised me at first, and most attractive about Weston, was his boldness to call me to a higher standard, particularly in my speech.

When Weston and I were together and I'd say something crass or use the Lord's name in vain he would not hesitate to shake his head saying, "Come on, man!" in his rich Georgia accent. Weston understood that my speech was a reflection of my soul. In those moments I was livid—who are you to tell me what to say? But the more I thought about it the more I realized how much he truly cared. I wish he could have been there before I tasted half of the Purell hand soap flavors back in middle school. My relationship with Weston was edifying, and when I needed it, he showed me tough love, the type of love that I so desperately needed. Our conversations rarely stuck to things of this world, so I invited him to join my Bible study group, to which he happily accepted.

The Twelfth Man

A few evenings had passed since the debacle that was the Sea Olympics and a Bible study meeting was commencing. After praying, we gave Weston an opportunity to share about his story with Christ. Five minutes later we were brought to tears. Weston's father had tragically passed away when he was in high school. How could someone suffer such a catastrophic loss and be so rooted in faith? How could someone who was partially robbed of his boyhood grow up to become a zealous man? That doesn't happen by chance. Weston was no accident. He wore his heart on his sleeve and everybody knew what wasn't going to fly when he was around. The more time I spent with Weston the better man I became.

The squad was equally excited when Weston graced us with his presence—the quality of our conversations skyrocketed. I know the guys in the group were stoked about his presence because excluding me we were outnumbered seven to four by the girls. Weston was our twelfth man.

Wanderlist

*"Whimsy doesn't care if you are the driver or the passenger;
all that matters is that you are on your way."*
—*Bob Goff*

IN ORDER TO MAKE the trek across the Indian Ocean to the Seychelles, our ship would burn approximately half a million gallons of fuel, therefore, a proper fuel stop was necessary. Since we already had a reservation in Malaysia, we decided to dine and dash. While our ship guzzled enough fuel to run Jarvis, my Jeep Wrangler, for 450 years, we gazed out into land thinking *what could have been*. No one was allowed to disembark until we reached the Seychelles.

Classes proceeded and people talked; there was not a single soul on board who did not feel teased by our situation. We were ported in a brand-new country, stuck on the vessel that was designed to give us freedom. The alluring glow of the countryside invoked a sense of FOMO, but this time everyone was missing out.

Day 46 | Feb 19, 2020: I must have heard the question, "Does this count?" a gazillion times today.

It's the same mental gymnastics we perform in our heads during a layover in a new place. Technically, I am physically in a new location, but I haven't even left the airport, therefore, I have not experienced the culture, so in conclusion, it does not count. But there are more complex examples. Someone enjoys baseball; in the back of their head they think it would be a cool idea to visit every MLB park in America. If they happen to be in Chicago for the weekend but don't have the time to sit through an entire Cubs game, sure they could only catch one inning or just drive by the park because technically they did see it, but it wouldn't feel right. Some folks may count a single inning, others would need to stay for the entire game.

In short, the question, "Does this count?" was entirely flawed.

The first time I heard this question in the morning of our Malaysian refueling, I thought nothing of it. But as the day progressed, every conversation in every room seemed to be centered around those three words. Primarily in a joking manner, people were kicking the question around like a hacky sack. The frequency assured me that in some way it was on everyone's mind, but what was at the root? It's safe to say that those who begged the question also operated in a destination-oriented mindset, and they have every right to do so. We all signed on the dotted line to explore a dozen countries, and we were losing more and more every week—this was not a positive situation.

Thinking all the way back to my discernment of Semester at Sea, the sheer number of destinations was at the core of my decision to pursue SAS; the ship was simply a means to an end. Knowing this, I thought back to when we lost China. Shouldn't I have been more upset? When the next curveball was thrown and the virus stole Malaysia and India from us, I should've been livid, right? If I would have known a coronavirus was even an option before committing to SAS of course I still would have sailed. No one ever thinks it's going to happen to them. Prior to SAS I never could have envisioned what ship life could look like no matter how many YouTube videos I binged. My main motive for choosing Semester at Sea was changing with each day especially as the fruit from my relationships was becoming super succulent. Being on the ship was no longer a means to an end; being on the ship meant more time with the most inspiring people in the world.

Now, the majority of the people affected by our voyage weren't even on board. They were the thousands of friends and family back home. Trying to continue living their lives while simultaneously being worried sick for their child/friend abroad was a tall order. I can picture parents sitting on their couches, white-knuckling their phones desperately trying to grab some sense of control. I like to think that our fans back home were always rooting for us but in some cases I'm afraid they were rotting us.

My mom played an invaluable role in my happiness on board the ship from the opposite side of the globe. Through seamail and the occasional phone call in port she wouldn't remind me of the physical losses I was suffering, rather the incredible story I would be able to tell. Oftentimes, she would even request that I only email when I had free time as to not take away from my experience. Our conversations rarely mentioned the virus because our ship was already diverting from any potential threats. She was the Pippen to my Jordan, but unfortunately that wasn't everybody's luck.

I was disheartened when I heard some of the things parents were saying on Facebook, group chats, etc. There seemed to be two camps of parents. The first was glued in front of the TV back home, relaying information to their children, creating a Godzilla monster out of the virus. They believed using the scare tactic would cause their children to be more cautious and hygienic, just like the repulsive images on their cigarette packs stop them from smoking. Ya, right.

The second, I'm afraid, were a far more destructive force. They were shooting their best shot to discredit our on-ship time as anything but enjoyable, productive, or valuable. Even going as far to say that the rest of our voyage would be a waste of time. From an outsider's point of view, our voyage might have looked miserable. And yes, each diversion technically made our voyage less successful. But this immense pressure from parents who judged our ship life from land didn't just hinder their kids' experience, they took full chunks out of it. Now, not only were students hoping to visit countries for their own enjoyment, but they also depended on the realization of each country knowing folks back home were convinced more ports equaled more happiness. Even if a student was able to overcome their grief of a diversion, it would only be temporary before they contacted home and their optimistic mindset was sabotaged. A lose-lose situation. How could anyone be optimistic when their biggest cheerleaders were dropping the pom-poms? The only way to understand the joys of ship life was to be on the ship. Period.

In the afternoon of our Malaysian refueling, I was talking about this dilemma in Lido with my friend Kat who also happened to live in the cabin next door. Kat explained how one of her friends on board was seriously considering flying home wherever our next port may be. This friend discovered Semester at Sea by following someone on Instagram who had sailed in the fall of 2018. Falling head over heels after seeing all the incredible content constantly being pumped out, she decided to apply, intending to do the same. By the time our voyage had arrived in Vietnam, only our second country, she was through. Kat's friend explained to her that our experience was nothing like she had seen on Instagram. As the coronavirus began to reveal its hideous face and water proved to be the slowest form of travel, her instant gratification needs were not met. Was she genuinely upset because she did not get to experience a new culture? Or was it because her next Instagram was deleted before it was ever posted? The visual stimulant from a colorful feed led her on an adventure her head was in, but her heart was not.

> Day 46 | Feb 19, 2020: The *MV World Odyssey* sounds a lot like *Envy World Oughta See*. And I think some people boarded the latter.

So, there were quite a few different pressure points pushing for Malaysia "to count." But there was still one more thing nudging us to beg this question, and most of us brought one on

Wanderlist

board: a scratch-off world map.

After stepping foot onto new soil, we would scratch off the thin black film revealing the brightly colored country beneath. Intimidated by the dullness of our maps and itching to scratch off a new place, the sensation of scratching off Malaysia to reveal a new color would be a refreshing hit of dopamine. But, most of our Malaysia's remained unscratched; the itch, however, remained.

Frustrated by this dilemma but still encouraged to use the map I started scratching off the countries and states where I had made friends. Suddenly the world lit up before my eyes displaying a much more accurate representation of our voyage's success.

When I was surfing the web to find my scratch-off map prior to the voyage, I fell on the term *wanderlust*. The word originated from the German word *wander* (to hike) and *lust* (desire). However, in modern times, the word has been extrapolated to "having a strong desire to travel." But there is also an aspect of impulsivity, a spin-the-globe-and-go type of feeling. The idea of traveling with the destination being secondary. We were all consumed by wanderlust when we first applied for Semester at Sea, in a very positive way. Sort of like the opposite of homesickness, we felt the urge to venture out and explore new lands. "Cover the Earth before it covers you" mentality. We didn't necessarily need to go anywhere in particular, so long as to not stay in one place.

Similarly to how good things only need the slightest twist to become bad, our innocent wanderlust sold just one vowel, morphing into *wanderlist*. Wanderlist is a made-up term, and it's also an oxymoron like deafening silence or meaningful hookup. Wandering with a list doesn't make sense, so why should we travel with one? The world is my oyster, not a checklist.

Out to See

*"Chemistry can be a good and bad thing.
Chemistry is good when you make love with it.
Chemistry is bad when you make crack with it."*
—Adam Sandler

APPROACHING FIFTY DAYS into our Semester at Sea everyone had their "spot" to work. All of the dining rooms had ample space, especially between meals, however there were far too many distractions for me to focus, which was also the problem with the library. My cabin turned out to be a poor option because my fifteen-inch laptop barely fit onto our tiny desk. And so, I found my spot on the seventh deck at a round table in the shade where I could hear the ocean. However, this was not my first choice.

Although studying outside to the sound of waves was a dream, I was annoyed when the wind turned my pages prematurely. Also on the seventh deck there was a random desk situated in the corner of the hallway where foot traffic was light. It was conveniently located in the middle of the ship so finding the action was just one door away in every direction. The only ones who passed through this area were voyagers who lived nearby or Curious Georges like myself. This hidden gem was occupied by Dr. Russ nearly every hour his class was not in session. I was frustrated at first that Dr. Russ had beaten me to the spot, but in hindsight it was awesome, because we probably went through the same thought process and great minds think alike.

After a productive study session in my breezy spot, I took a detour through Dr. Russ's lair to say hello. He was excited to have a visitor, and not the least bit surprised that I was without a shirt.

"Johnny, my wife and I have a question to ask you."

This was probably the type of conversation that required a shirt.

Dr. Russ continued, "We know how good you are with kids. Would you facilitate a dance party for them later today?"

I laughed out loud, as did my expectations!

Later in the afternoon I blew through the union doors fully clothed and ready for the greatest darty (day party) of my life. I was relieved to see the one they call Madz, a fellow student and massive personality, starting to rally the kids at center stage. Finn was my sidekick, and it turned out Madz had her own, Tara. Tara was a brilliant young girl with the swagger of a nine-year-old, the sass of a sixteen-year-old, and the confidence of a twenty-five-year-old. Madz knew as well as I did that the kids were itching to expel energy—hitting play on the music was like dropping Mentos in Coke. So rather than blowing a hole through the ship we decided the kids needed to dance to their own music. Peeking behind the stage curtain we were lucky to find an assortment of drums. Although the sound was deafening, I was happy they were beating the drums and not me. The kids' performance was brilliant, but the highlight was the smiles on the faces of their parents in the audience.

One of the moms came up to me afterward, and noticing the fraternity letters on my shirt asked, "Could my six-year-old rush your frat?"

Laughing, I joked, "Of course! At least he'll remain a boy forever!"

"Are *you* really in a frat?" she genuinely inquired.

I confirmed my membership by reciting our creed, The True Gentleman.

> "The True Gentleman is the man whose conduct proceeds from good will and an acute sense of propriety, and whose self-control is equal to all emergencies; who does not make the poor man conscious of his poverty, the obscure man of his obscurity, or any man of his inferiority or deformity; who is himself humbled if necessity compels him to humble another; who does not flatter wealth, cringe before power, or boast of his own possessions or achievements; who speaks with frankness but always with sincerity and sympathy; whose deed follows his word; who thinks of the rights and feelings of others, rather than his own; and who appears well in any company, a man with whom honor is sacred and virtue safe.
>
> —John Walter Wayland"

Out to See

I was shocked at how shocked she was!

I said, "Can you imagine if our fraternity followed this creed? We would be a Saint making factory!"

"Why don't they?" she replied.

"If only doing good were as easy as knowing it."

She inquired more seriously, "Would you let your son rush in college?"

"Absolutely! But only if he knows why he's rushing. Without answering that question he risks joining the statistic of floaters who join Greek life without a purpose. The only thing worse than a brother who does not pay dues is a brother who *only* pays dues."

Late in the afternoon I bumped into Ashley who informed me of the legendary sunset commencing outside. We bolted out the nearest door on the fifth deck and leaned over the railing toward the fiery reflection on the water.

> Day 47 | Feb 20, 2020: I was staring into the sunset when my peripherals detected movement... DOLPHINS! A POD OF DOLPHINS WAS SWIMMING ALONGSIDE OUR SHIP!

I was nearly moved to tears—this moment called for one of my dad's famous phrases, so taking in a deep breath I exhaled, "This doesn't suck!"

Ashley concurred, the ruby-colored rays reflected off her face adding the finishing touch to her already sun-kissed cheeks. I wanted to kiss her, but I was so nervous, like my lips would slide clean off my face. I imagined apologizing as I grabbed a net and scooped them out of the sea then dried them off with my shirt. The moment was already perfect. *I'll wait for a better opportunity* I thought. *Wait, can it get better than perfect?* But before I could have a coherent thought Ashley suggested that we head up to the pool deck and see what the squad was up to.

By the time we ascended four decks it was pitch black outside, as if the sun had not shown for the past year. We heard shouts of joy ring out around the ship and soon found our squad playing an intense game of spoons as if it determined who enjoyed unrationed meals, if it got to that point. Spoons. Quick movements. Loud noises. I was made for this. After the first few rounds Jake left early to order from the poolside grill, where most people ordered when they were tired of pasta and chicken from the dining rooms. The only item that the ship never got sick of was the famous dinner rolls—they were the only item that saw the bottom of a purse and toilet in the same night. I rarely found room to complain about the food considering I hadn't the slightest clue how to make it. A few minutes later Jake came back with a pizza, three orders of fries, and some Skittles: a well-balanced meal.

I couldn't focus on the spoons because hordes of people passed by our table on their way to the front of the ship, so I grabbed one last slice and joined them. The bow, which was normally a very well-lit area of campus, was now pitch black. Stepping over bodies sprawled out on the deck floor I shined my phone's light on Madz and Tara who made room for me to lie down. Professor Denning, aka Scott, was the only person standing as he passed around a couple of his five-hundred-dollar pairs of binoculars for us to try out. By now, many of our relationships with the professors on board allowed us to drop the titles of doctor or professor. Handling the binoculars with extreme care we saw stars so clearly, we could have reached out and touched them. Scott informed us that some of the light we were seeing was more than two million years old. We were even able to see the tiny gleam from the International Space Station as it soared across the sky. Our entire voyage was centered around seeing new places yet we found ourselves captivated by the same specks of light we see every night. Granted, being in the middle of the ocean with no light pollution allowed many more specks of light to reveal themselves.

Lying on the deck the stars rocked smoothly back and forth. I wondered how often hundreds of college students voluntarily showed up to a late-night lecture and found themselves thoroughly entertained. Then all of a sudden the stars disappeared as the bridge crew arrived and turned the lights back on. We all grumbled and begged for more time, but having the lights off on the deck for any duration of time was a privilege because no lighting was technically violating ship code. Discombobulated, we slowly rose to our feet and went to sleep.

The following morning I pulled apart the blinds from my porthole and the glass was warm to the touch. For the next week, the UV (ultraviolet radiation) index hovered between twelve and fourteen as we sailed along the equator to make the trek from Malaysia to the Seychelles, creating some sort of unspoken tanning competition. The EPA doesn't recommend going outside in anything above a UV of ten. With a UV of fourteen it would take a fair-skinned person less than a minute to burn in direct sunlight. The Sicilians turned black, the Germans burned, and the pool deck was uninhabitable for the Irish. Finding a chair on the top deck was now much more difficult than simply showing up. First thing in the morning students claimed their chairs and often occupied them the entire day.

The scorching sun all day left me with a burning appetite, so the Spaghetti and meatballs called for thirds in Berlin. After dinner our Bible study group got together and reflected on God's mercy and forgiveness. We started to dig into sin and repentance, and as we talked, many of my shortcomings rose to the top of my mind. Most were in a hurry to get there, as if the lead weight pinning them down on the ocean floor was removed. It was now clear to me that my personality and character were in disagreement. I could be Johnny Catholic on the outside by saying all the right things, but behind closed doors I was King Nimrod. I lacked integrity. I had plenty of wonderful ideas of how I wished to change but they didn't have a spine.

Towards the end of our meeting we talked about the sacraments, and particularly reconciliation. I learned from protestants that in the early Catholic Church, communities would gather together to perform public confessions. *It's hard enough sharing sins with a priest,* I thought. I went to confession for the first time since middle school at the ASU Newman Center three months before the voyage.

> Day 48 | Feb 21, 2020: Everyone always knows the good we're doing. I wonder if sharing the bad would bring us closer together.

This thought resurfaced the animosity between Nic and I. If you asked the rest of the squad, they wouldn't believe it existed, but inside my head it was all out war. I wondered if Nic was even aware of the tension. I wondered if keeping a mental score was a sin, even if it wasn't affecting anyone else. I knew I couldn't stay in this imaginary competition forever. I knew I needed to just confront Nic and reconcile. But my ego was just too big, and the game continued.

After another full day of sunburns and school, Tara and I stuffed our faces with ice-cream cake on the pool deck in celebration of one of her friend's birthdays. Lance, my marketing professor, walked by and I asked Tara if he could join the party. He lit up when we invited him into our celebration; the cake was just a bonus. Lance's family decided to stay back home, so he was taking this voyage on by himself. I'm pretty sure Lance mentioned they stayed back because his daughter wanted to go to prom. I couldn't fathom anybody making such a decision.

After an hour I said my goodbyes and headed for the gym because I had yet to get in my workout. Tara and the other kids grabbed my arm and insisted that they tag along. Looking over to their parents who gave the nod of approval, Finn led us all to the gym—I guess the only thing better than a workout partner is seven, so we hit the weights!

I gave brief instructions on how the equipment can be used to work out all types of muscle groups and the children were amazed. Frankly, their excitement gave me an opportunity to stop and think how cool working out really is. Think about it: there's nothing we can think inside our heads to make us physically stronger but working out grows our bodies and our minds!

Some of the parents watching us from the deck above yelped

down, "They will have you there for hours!"

"I've got all night!" I shouted back.

I told myself I would not stop until the kids were completely drained. Very slowly the volume of their voices began to decrease as more and more energy drained from their tanks. Soon the kids requested breaks, and longer they became until eventually Finn set the weights down for the final time.

"Can we be done now?" he said.

"You led me here... you were the one leading this workout the whole time!" I replied.

"But... how did I... " Finn sputtered.

"Can you do one more push-up?" I asked.

Placing both of his hands shoulder-width apart and body parallel to the deck, Finn began to lower his chest and fell flat on his face.

"We can be done now," he exclaimed through an exhausted smile.

Beep-boop! "Good morning! I come bearing some very exciting news. Voyage One Twenty-Eight will host Semester at Sea's first ever fashion show tomorrow night in the union!"

Well aware of this unexpectedly long passage across the Indian Ocean, the leadership team got creative to make the most of our time at sea. The fashion show was strategically placed after Vietnam, and everyone had purchased some sort of flamboyant outfit, whether it was fake designer, real designer, banana print, elephant pants, custom suits, etc.

Upon hearing the news, Dylan and I immediately got together to devise a game plan. Obviously, we would enter the competition with our matching purple suits, but we needed to choreograph our walk. We also needed to submit witty answers to the boring questions, "What do you want to be when you're older?" and "What are you wearing tonight?" which the MC would read off as we strutted our stuff. Dylan and I got to work in the back of the union and walked a mile in spurts of ten steps. On top of our walk, Dylan and I practiced holding a completely straight face while the other told jokes.

> Day 50 | Feb 23, 2020: Déjà vu. I found myself sweating in a suit behind the union's stage curtain. At least this time I had no lines and someone else was wearing the exact same outfit.

When our names were called, we broke through the curtains side by side and as planned, mid-stage I swiftly rotated 180 degrees on my toes for Dylan to execute a firm slap on my butt. Then we crossed paths walking with perfect posture to opposite sides of the stage when the host read our answer to the first question.

"When Johnny and Dylan get older...they want to be your husbands!" She laughed into the microphone.

It was nearly impossible to keep a straight face but miraculously neither of us broke as we turned from our corners to meet center stage for our final pose. Dylan got down on one knee and I stood directly behind him with my hand on his shoulder. Turning our heads once in each direction with the steadiness of a robot, the second question was answered.

"When we asked them what they were wearing tonight they said, "Clothes... for once."

They liked that one even more. Dylan slowly stood up, we turned away from the crowd, and the second we passed through the curtain we let out every laugh we'd held in for the past two minutes. Then we tore off our layers and found some seats near the front to watch the rest of the show. There was a table of judges who scored the overall performance and we felt like we'd clinched it until four guys busted out their all-white suits calling themselves "the Seamen." How did I not think of that?

While the judges were tabulating their scores, Dylan was putting his suit back on. After seeing the rest of the show, I told him there was no chance we would place in the top three, so I didn't bother fussing with mine, to which Dylan said smartly, "Suit yourself!"

Third place was announced, and not hearing our names, I sank back into my chair satisfied that we gave it our best shot.

"Second place goes to Johnny and Dylan!"

Dylan and I leaped out of our seats and into each other's arms. I told him I didn't deserve to go up on stage for my lack of confidence, but he suited me up anyway. We were shocked and overjoyed to hear the Seamen had not taken first place. The winner was Alicia whose hips swayed away across the stage with no delay. She displayed, and we wanted a replay. Even with a wobbling runway, the fashion show replenished life in the community as we prepared to tackle whatever the virus might throw our way. Tomorrow was Neptune Day, and we were instructed not to set our alarms. I liked the sound of that already!

Still Out to See

"The unexamined life is not worth living."
—*Socrates*

"YOU HEAR THAT?" I grumbled to Jimmy from under my covers after being awoken out of a dead sleep.

"Yeah, what the hell is goin' on out there? It's six a.m."

"It sounds like the Energizer bunny found the kitchen." I laughed, coughing up some morning phlegm.

I sprinted to the door in my boxers and swung it open to see a dozen crew members dressed in funky green outfits banging pots and pans together with all their might on a mission to wake up the entire ship. I spun into my swimsuit like Wonder Woman and bolted up one deck to breakfast in Berlin where I could hear the ruckus vibrating through the floor and ceiling. I had never seen so many people show up to breakfast in their bathing suits. A sure sign this was going to be a fantastic day!

Beep-boop! "This is King Neptune! I hope everyone is having a peaceful morning. Please report to the pool deck immediately for the opening ceremony." It was Captain Kostas using his booming voice. All the staircases seemed to shrink as the entire ship made their way to the top deck. I arrived just in time to see Captain Kostas coated in green paint from head to toe as King Neptune, and Dean Sue dressed as the goddess Minerva splitting the crowd in two. The fact that they had sold out for this event inspired us to do the same.

Neptune and Minerva took their position directly across from the pool and reminded us why we were all gathered this day. We were all currently slimy pollywogs and by participating in this time-honored tradition of Neptune Day as we crossed the equator, we would earn the trusty shellback designation. The series of tasks to officially earn the title of shellback were as follows:

1. Bucket of green slime dumped over our heads
2. Enter the pool and swim across to King Neptune and Minerva
3. Exit pool and kiss a dead fish and Neptune's ring
4. Take a knee to be sworn in by the sword
5. Shave head (optional)

By the time I could process the series of events that were about to unfold the music cranked up, the lines formed, and the slime was already running down spines.

> Day 51 | Feb 24, 2020: There were fish guts in the slime and it felt nasty running over my face. This was not the Nickelodeon recipe!

Swimming on my back across the pool, I prepared myself

for the coldest kiss of my life. I successfully locked lips with a dead cobia and proceeded to lay one on Neptune's ring. Finally, I locked eyes with Kathy with a sword in hand and a maniacal smile. Needing to complete the fourth step to earn shellback status, I took a knee and felt the blade touch both my shoulders. Surprised that my head was still attached, I erupted in a victory cry!

The day was still young and most of the squad had not even been slimed yet. Kathy pointed me portside where a crowd was gathering for head shaving, but I was only interested in spectating. The crowd was so tight I had to walk all the way around from the starboard side to catch a glimpse of Holly, the librarian, whose luscious locks were falling to the deck! Shrieks of joy rang back and forth between the crowd and the newly bald.

Stepping up onto a chair I finally got a view of the entire scene. I'm not sure who I expected to be shaving heads—maybe one of the hairdressers from the spa—but surely, I thought they could find someone more qualified than John! That's right, somebody actually thought it would be a good idea to give Kathy a sword and John an electric razor for the entire day! Quite honestly, it couldn't have been a more perfect job for John; he was right in the middle of the action. While everyone watching this madness might have aged in the process, I am certain John gained a few extra years.

Weaving my way through the crowd for a closer look, John was holding up a massive clump of long blonde hair in his left with the razor in his right. Waving my hands high I finally caught his attention, simultaneously doing the same with Zack. I turned to acknowledge Zack and by the time I looked back at John he had disappeared from his station. Rotating in a 360 I spotted

John coming up on me from the side until he stood next to me with hair and razor still in hand. There were two girls watching the newly shaved admire their egg heads in front of me, one of whom happened to have long blonde hair. John gave me the look, flicked on the electric razor, and proceeded to run it past this girl's neck without cutting her hair. She squealed and snapped her head around to see John holding up a clump of long blonde hair. The poor girl threw both her hands around the back of her head and let out a sigh of relief when she felt her hair still in place.

Surprisingly, John did not get slapped. I'm certain my face would have looked equally horrified if he had done the same to me. I had just gotten a haircut a few days ago, and for the first time, it was one I really jived with. Out of nowhere, my thoughts were brutally interrupted when Zack started chanting my name. John immediately joined him and soon the entire deck followed suit. "JOHNNY! JOHNNY! JOHNNY!" My insides were boiling, the crowd continued, and the pressure was insurmountable so I turned around and booked it in the opposite direction. When I caught my breath, I was surprised to find I wasn't harboring any resentment towards Zack but I was actually upset with myself. Somewhere in my heart I felt like I needed to shave my head, but I couldn't put a finger on why.

Back near the pool with all my hair I watched the last few voyagers stand under the slime bucket. People here and there would ask me, "So when are you shaving your head?" as if it were a scheduled event.

I replied, "I'm not!"

I had already put myself in the limelight so many times throughout the voyage I started to concur with their rebuttal. "It just seemed like a thing Johnny would do."

Still Out to See

In similar circumstances in the past, crowds had a perfect record getting exactly what they want when they say my name more than five times in a row. So did I really like the way I looked that much? Was my twenty-dollar haircut holding me back? It was not about the money but all about my appearance. I simply didn't want to look like an egg... but why?

If I looked like an egg, I would have less confidence.

That's truly what it came down to. I was less than excited to find out so much of my confidence was wrapped up in my appearance. As I went back and forth in my head the sound of the action thundered port side and there I was cowardly standing on the starboard. I timidly made my way back over to the shaving station and stood as far in the back as possible when a large arm wrapped around from behind. It was John's roommate, Herbert. He knew something was off instantly, like when I came home from high school and my mom shouted, "What's wrong honey?" before I even took off my shoes.

I started to explain my predicament, then Herbert began, "Why don't you want to shave your head?"

"Because I look better with hair!" I replied.

"Who are you trying to impress?"

"Her," I said, pointing at Ashley.

"You know deep inside you want to do this, but it comes at a price. Or does it? I think you've forgotten to ask one person."

"WHO?!"

"Have you asked Jesus if he cares what you look like?"

I had no idea Herbert knew Jesus, maybe he didn't, but it didn't matter. A switch inside flipped and a light turned on that allowed me to see that this was something I needed to do. Just before John made contact with my head, I grabbed his arm and made a special request. I pointed to Ashley, who stood right in front of me with the rest of the squad and told John the job was hers. While John demonstrated how to make the passes over my head, I could feel the adrenaline boiling inside me.

> Day 51 | Feb 24, 2020: When Ashley brought down the razor, I let out the loudest scream I have ever produced.

I could feel her tiny hand shaking as she gave me a reverse mohawk. The locks of blond and brown hair falling onto my lap were fully documented by everyone in sight. A few minutes later, I was without my voice and my hair, but I was a very happy egg!

It was only a matter of hours before I became aware of how much hair protected my scalp. With a palm full of sunscreen, I could hardly muster the courage to plop it down on my head. Eventually, I made contact, and the sensation was more bizarre than I had anticipated. At first, my head felt sort of fuzzy from the thick liquid sinking into my burning scalp, but thankfully this only lasted a few minutes.

Walking around the ship seeing so many other bald heads was encouraging—we were like a club. Every conversation I entered started with something along the lines of, "Wow! You actually look great!" or "Of course, you can pull off a shaved head!" But as these types of compliments continued to rain in I became very uneasy. You see, this was the first time I had not done something for attention all semester.

By the end of the day I felt like I was carrying around a lion on my back so I tried to get to bed early but I could not fall asleep. This was a predicament I had never faced. I even tried repeating my nightly routine—shower, brush teeth, fluff my hamburger pillow, but to no avail. I decided to go for a walk and ended up venturing into the union where I found Jake, Jacob, and Chris editing away at their Vietnam footage. As soon as I walked in, they knew something was up. I explained to them how I was getting too much attention, but they couldn't comprehend why I would not be ecstatic. Starting to break down, I tried painting them a picture.

"I know everyone's compliments are totally innocent and sincere, so this is not their problem, it's mine. When my motivation for doing something is attention, and I am flattered, I am content. But when my motivation is outside myself, and I am flattered, I am disturbed. This is the first time flattery has left me disturbed, which can only mean one thing... this was also the first time my motivation has extended outside myself."

This was the part when I figured they would slowly begin repeating, "It's not your fault, It's not your fault," like Robin Williams to Matt Damon in *Good Will Hunting*, but this was not the case. They couldn't formulate a response before the dams to my tear ducts burst wide open. I am sure this made as little sense to them as it did to me. They had not seen me in this state all semester, and neither had I. Through tears I tried to push out an explanation for what motivation outside myself really meant.

"My motivation to take on the razor was like a death to self. And partially so I'm not constantly using my phone's reflection to adjust my hair all the time. But that's exactly the point, I was so obsessed with how I looked I wouldn't even give into a mob of people chanting my name! When Herbert brought up how Jesus looked at me, I knew he saw far beyond my physical appearance. Neptune Day was the perfect opportunity to take on a less than flattering look, breaking my reliance on my appearance for confidence."

This situation was comparable to the way finding a pimple on my face in the morning seems to deplete not only my confidence but all my expectations for the day before I even step out the door. I laugh now knowing I had bought the lie: "I am going to be less successful today because I have a blemish on my face." To me, losing my fresh new haircut was equally debilitating to my confidence as waking up with Mount Everest on my nose. But unlike a pimple, I had a choice.

So, why did being flattered after doing something motivated by something outside myself result in my discomfort? Well, simply because death to self and flattery do not go hand in hand.

It seemed like everything I did warranted some kind of praise. Whether I was telling an inappropriate joke on stage or going bald, I was flattered no matter what I did. I wondered if I had sought out attention to such an extreme that I had conditioned my fellow voyagers to compliment me on anything I had done recently. It had gotten to the point when someone said to me in passing, "You're the most interesting person I have ever met in my life," which I'm sure was just a nice way of saying, "You're a walking personality disorder."

This was why Weston's tough love struck a chord in me because he was not in the business of flattery. His words pierced right through all of the fluff that was constantly being stuffed around my precious ego. If complimenting my scalp was adding a cotton ball, a comment like the one above tossed in a Six Flags sized cotton candy cone. Aware of how much cushioning was built up around my ego, Weston wasted no time ripping the stuffing out of me like a Build-a-Bear Workshop session played back in reverse.

Venting all of this to the guys, they remained silent and listened intently as I concluded my thoughts.

"So regardless of if my head actually looks nice bald, or if people think everything I do elicits praise, both are beside the point. My confidence and motivation need to come from something, someone, outside myself. I've lived my entire life with attention as my driving motivator and we all know I am very good at getting it. If my motivation in life comes from myself, I'll continue being content the rest of my life, but I'm not content with contentment. I want excellence!"

With this, I hobbled out of the union a bit lighter than when I walked in. I was grateful for Jake, Jacob, and Chris's interruptibility, who set down what they were doing and listened without trying to find the right thing to say. I reflected on the moment after I turned away from the crowd chanting my name when I felt that almost indiscernible desire to go bald. I now understand that to have been God whispering, "Your heads getting too big, shave it."

Flexibility—Level Three

"I'm so sick of the water."
—Michael Phelps

IT HAD ALWAYS been the case that my exams at ASU managed to fall at the least opportune times, and the curse continued with our ship-wide global studies midterm. Neptune Day and the fashion show had taken up all of my mental real estate the past few days, so I left all my studying until the day of. I had never been one to procrastinate, especially schoolwork, so feeling woefully unprepared for a big test was more than unnerving. Thankfully, the "Three Ds" (three doctors) as we called them, were sympathetic and offered to entertain questions in various spots around the ship all afternoon.

By noon I had sat down with Drs. Scott and Michael, but I had yet to find Dr. Sue. It was important to catch some time with

Flexibility—Level Three

all of the Ds because they each added a piece to the puzzle that was our exam. Walking into Berlin for lunch I spotted a gathering in the middle of the room. Sue was at the center patiently answering questions while her nine-year-old impatiently danced around her chair. At one point in our Q&A, a student brought up an error made on one of Sue's study guides to which she replied, "Eh, fuck it," forgetting her little boy was with her at office hours. She turned to him and apologized. Moments like these took pressure off an exam encompassing everything from oceanology to sustainability.

Studying all day left me famished by dinnertime so I was elated to see everyone scooping spaghetti and meatballs on their plate. We celebrated Julia's twenty-first birthday with an iconic ice-cream cake before heading to our designated testing place. Every room on the ship was staffed with proctors because some six hundred students would be taking the exam at the same time. My testing location was the Adler Lounge, which shared a wall with the gym.

Out of all the potential staculty and LLLs, one of the three proctors in my room was John! Since I had walked into the room a bit late, the lead proctor was reading off directions mainly harping on the no loud noises rule. Despite their instruction, John picked up a metal folding chair and slammed it open in front of me to sit down. Some of the students in the room had already begun the exam due to an accommodation when John announced that the first answer was C, forcing the proctors to break their silence and intervene. I couldn't contain myself in my desk, so I bit my fist and tried to hold it together while John was escorted out the door for the second time of the semester.

The mental space that I was normally transported to when

I began an exam was a slum compared to the utopia I was in now. I always believed the tension in the room before big exams was so tight that it tripped up well-studied students on its own. John's shenanigans snapped any points of tension allowing me to not only learn while taking the test but also enjoy the process. I promise that John did not pay me to write this. Plus I'm not sure why he would have any incentive to promote the educational process.

After checking my work twice and making sure I didn't spell "went" with an "h" on the short answer portion I handed in my exam to the proctor with a smile and whispered, "Sorry about the old man, but cut him some slack. Testing rooms probably looked a little different in the eighteen hundreds."

The head proctor was either a stone-cold killer, or the lights were on and nobody was home. Either way I don't know how "We tried to separate family for the exam, guess it wasn't bulletproof," was a proper response to my joke.

The second the door closed behind me I realized that finishing my global studies midterm meant our voyage was halfway over. Reminiscing on the first fifty-two days, I headed back to my cabin and opened my laptop to start sorting through some of my camera footage. Taking a quick break in the process, I refreshed my seamail and a new message populated.

> Day 52 | Feb 25, 2020: When I read the subject line of Kyra's email—"Worship Night in Kino"—I laughed. That was the absolute last thing I wanted to do right now.
>
> Tonight was drink night, and I wanted to celebrate finishing

Flexibility—Level Three

the exam with some red wine and a sea breeze on the pool deck. Plus, the air-conditioning in Kino, a mid-sized theater room located in the middle of the ship with no windows, had broken. My only exposure to worshipping God in this manner was with the Saint Paul's Outreach men two months prior to the voyage. In the back of my head I thought, *What if nobody goes?* Then I read the last sentence of Kyra's email, "No pressure to come. I've just been really missing worship so I'll be praising Jesus regardless of attendance." I wanted to support Kyra more than I wanted to praise the Lord, so I found Weston whose priorities were probably just the opposite and together the stuffy air smacked us across the face. I could tell Weston was super jazzed I was there, and I had a feeling God was too. Although it took everything inside me to do so much as raise my hands, I looked down at my crucifix and realized how small this sacrifice was compared to His.

The fifty-third day of our voyage we'd cover the last distance at sea before reaching the Seychelles after traveling over three thousand nautical miles. The tiny blip of our ship was approaching an equally small land mass on the monitor in our cabin. This was our third major stretch of ocean this semester. First, from Mexico to Hawaii, then from Hawaii to Japan, and now from Malaysia to the Seychelles.

During this leg of our journey, everyone had ample time to use the library computers for booking plans in the Seychelles. However, the more time people spent researching the Seychelles, the less exciting the island seemed to be. Comments resurfaced like, "The Seychelles does not have enough culture," and "Nobody's going on a honeymoon." It was puzzling how badly everyone wanted to step foot on sturdy ground again, but apparently *this* ground did not make the cut.

Just before our Seychelles pre-port meeting, Riley requested my presence in Berlin to help out with a project for her religion class. Before sharing a meal together, students representing all different religions were to offer a prayer. Riley had selected me as the Christian delegate.

I am Catholic so I started my prayer with, "In the name of the Father, and of the Son, and of the Holy Spirit," then continued, "Lord, thank you for this community of people You have brought together this evening. Bless our conversation, and let Your will be done the remainder of our voyage. I ask that You keep us safe and healthy from the coronavirus. Amen."

Then we sat down and made sure different religions were evenly distributed between tables. I shared a table with an atheist, Muslim, and a Buddhist. I was shocked when the atheist commented, "I really enjoyed the simplicity of your prayer."

The remainder of our conversation was so rich and healthy I couldn't help but think what our world would look like if varying opinions could get along so well. Not a single voice was raised, and everyone's faith or lack thereof was proclaimed—quite the opposite of the incendiary rhetoric I was accustomed to. This was the first time the scripture 1 Peter 3:15 came to life, "Always be prepared to make a defense to anyone who calls you to account for the hope that is in you, yet do it with gentleness and reverence."

However, I wasn't of great faith. In fact, once again I thought: *You are not qualified to lead a Bible study and you're certainly not qualified to defend Christianity; you're hardly a Christian.* Yet there I was defending Christianity. I sloppily scattered

Flexibility—Level Three

seeds of truth around the table and only God knows if they fell on fertile soil.

The very end of our dinner conversation was cut short as rumors about Seychelles began buzzing around the room like a swarm of bees. Pre-port was just a few hours away, and I heard someone say, "The Seychelles is cancelled!" and "I'm one hundred percent sure our voyage is going to end!" I checked my sea-mail immediately and found no official itinerary update. There was some truth to the rumors before our last itinerary change, so I tried to take them with a grain of salt. Then, the commotion across the ship was silenced at the sound *beep-boop!* The Voice began with a long exhale, "We will now be holding our pre-port meeting in thirty minutes."

In the blink of an eye, those thirty minutes had expired, and a hoard of angry faces stormed into the union. Captain Kostas was standing on stage wearing black pants (which we didn't know he owned) with Dean Sue at his side. They attempted to begin the meeting by quieting the crowd, but this proved to be a great struggle. Students from the balcony would not stop their conversations and I was cringing so hard my contacts were gluing onto my eyeballs. I was losing my faith in humanity that had been restored over dinner.

When the union quieted, Dean Sue began and wasted no time as she read word for word from the email chain with the Seychellean government. "The *MV World Odyssey* has been denied port from the Seychelles and Mauritius is now in question."

There are not many words capable of describing the emotions in the room, much less people's reactions. The place went bonkers, and everybody's hand shot into the air, so it was a full-on screaming match to try and ask a question. People shouted,

"Balcony! Balcony!" as if it was on fire to bring attention to themselves. Out of the blue a student in the front row jumped up and began berating the leadership team onstage. I couldn't contain myself any longer, so I jumped on top of my chair. Crazy enough Nic burst out of his seat simultaneously, and together we yelled, "SIT. THE. FUCK. DOWN!" in perfect unison.

This may have been the first time we were in agreement all semester. Our word choice was poor, but this situation called for immediate support from the crowd. It was six hundred against two. Sitting back down Nic and I reconvened. The same folks who didn't want to visit the Seychelles were now abhorred that we were diverting away!

> Day 53 | Feb 26, 2020: Nobody seems to understand that Captain Kostas is literally in the same boat as us!

The people who were pissed about the countries our ship was or wasn't going were now face to face with the person behind the wheel. Kostas showed up to the meeting to inform and encourage us about our situation but instead he was ruthlessly bullied. I would compare chewing out our captain that night to yelling at the architect of a house that burst apart during Hurricane Katrina. Kostas was doing everything in his power to keep our voyage afloat.

After a few eons of time spent answering unanswerable questions, the union finally settled to a level where one could hear themselves think. Dean Sue started again by laying out the harsh reality of our semester: "We are over halfway through our voyage. We have visited two countries and cancelled five. How-

Flexibility—Level Three

ever, our voyage is undoubtedly the craziest, rarest edition of Semester at Sea to ever set sail!"

A few spontaneous shouts and moans rang out from the peanut gallery.

"When we lost Malaysia and India we gained the Seychelles, so now that we have lost the Seychelles, we have a new surprise in our crosshairs... Maputo, Mozambique!"

Half the room went ballistic while the other reverted into a fetal position. "Is that even safe?" many people questioned. Mozambique is in southeast Africa along the coastline that shares its northern border with Tanzania and its southern with South Africa. I couldn't help but think we were in a real-life game of spin the globe. I had no plans of ever traveling to Mozambique in my life, so I was fired up. Other folks had no plans of ever traveling to Mozambique in their life, so they were derailed. After a few more loaded questions were fired, it was obvious many still had full magazines. Regardless, the meeting was terminated, and my fellow shipmates had to carry their machine guns to bed. There is not a dollar amount you could have paid me to stand in the leadership's shoes that night.

Talk about an adventure—most voyages have their itineraries planned out and solidified years in advance while we are taking on new countries just days before arrival. Although Mauritius was in question, there was a berth with our ship's name on it and we would travel there until instructed otherwise.

After our meeting, the chaos mobilized into the library as hundreds of people flocked to three computers in an attempt to get refunds for their plans in the Seychelles. Many of us were able to get some sort of refund either partial or in full, but there were plenty who didn't have such luck. And more valuable than the money were all those precious hours spent creating an itinerary flushed right down the drain. Knowing a last-minute cancellation was a real possibility, very few people decided to pre-book independent travel plans for Mauritius.

In desperate need of a pick-me-up, the squad rendezvoused in Maddi's cabin. The only person who might have been remotely excited to turn away from the equator was Jake. The trek across the Indian Ocean had burnt him to a crisp forming boils all over his body which were now oozing out beneath his clothes. Chris reported that Jake was so delirious he would stand in front of one of the paintings in their cabin, moaning, while running his fingers over the bumpy canvas.

Jake was explaining how this was the greatest physical pain of his life when he was interrupted by a knock at the door. One of the guys on the ship, Josh, known for his spontaneous backflips and no-handed headstands, brought over his Nintendo Switch to play Mario Kart. Fidgeting around with the remote we clicked through different input settings. Pressing the button very impatiently, we skipped past the screen displaying our live route. Those who happened to be looking at the screen shrieked and yelled, "Go back!" We had made a ninety-degree turn away from the Seychelles. While we waged all-out war in the union, Captain Kostas's crew were busy turning our ship around. We were so close to the Seychelles some of us had cellphone reception, and I thought our Malaysian tease was bad! There was a brief moment of silence before we all looked at each other and let out one of those belly laughs that make your abs sore. Tear ducts dried out and frown muscles exhausted left laughter as our only option.

We had gone through the stages of grief (denial, anger, bargaining, depression, acceptance) so many times that by now

Flexibility—Level Three

we skipped straight to acceptance, which explained how some of us were able to poke fun at our situation so quickly. I think that everyone on board skipped stages of this process to some extent. Oftentimes, it seemed that people tried to make the great leap but landed just shy, in the depression stage. Walking out of Maddi's cabin at the end of the night was startling; the ship had turned into a post-apocalyptic zombie land. Pale faces attached to hunched over bodies lurked around lifelessly. Some had serious anxiety attacks, questioning if we would ever see land again.

Maybe we weren't all on the same boat.

On the fifty-fourth morning of the voyage I sat alone in the corner of Berlin and watched the *Passion of the Christ* over breakfast. To this day I am not sure what prompted me to watch Mel Gibson's masterpiece that morning, but I am certain I did not finish my eggs. Some of my friends had downloaded hundreds of movies for the semester. I had three, and a rather peculiar bunch: *Mean Girls, Casablanca, and The Passion of the Christ*. All of the crucifixes I had ever gazed upon only depicted drops of blood coming from Jesus's hands, feet, head, and side, but I never imagined Jesus's execution to be as gruesome as *The Passion* portrayed. Then, realizing that the real thing had to have been more brutal than a movie, I cried.

I had not diverted my eyes from my phone the entire duration of the movie, so I was startled to find that I was the only one left in the dining room. I blew my nose, tossed some cold water on my face, and left the room in a peaceful somber reflection. I didn't make it more than a few steps out of Berlin before my peace was disturbed by a thumping bass echoing from three decks above. As I climbed the staircase the music and commotion grew louder and my steps faster. I threw open the side door to the pool deck, and I was immediately transported back to a Saturday afternoon at Arizona State, minus the copious amount of alcohol.

Recognizing the ship's distress, the leadership team orchestrated a spontaneous community day. A fellow student, Ryan, was DJing the pool party and LLLs were running the yard games scattered around the deck. Where Ryan found a professional DJ deck in the middle of the ocean remains one of the great mysteries of our voyage. While some of the flashbacks came on unwelcomely, I was happy to see many of those pale faces brighten after hours of beat drops in the blistering sun.

As night fell, many of the unsunscreened souls around the ship were in great agony. I overheard a few newly burned ask each other, "Why don't we ever feel it before it's too late?"

For me, I am always far too engrossed in the action to take thirty seconds and apply sunscreen. The newly burned's question provoked a number of thoughts, which I brought to the squad at the dinner table.

"Why don't we remember driving on the road?" I asked. Sometimes I feel like I only remember getting in the car and getting out, no matter if it's ten minutes or ten hours in between. The squad nodded their heads and agreed. "We can only see so far up the road, but we just continue driving and trust that the pavement is going to continue. Our voyage was no different: we can only see so far in front of the ship and yet we've made it halfway around the world. After one of these waves we will see land.

"Okay guys," Kate said excitedly, leaning into the table, "would you rather ride in a car Captain Kostas was driving, or a ship he was steering?"

"Car, for sure," Riley replied.

"Why's that Ri?" Maddi asked knowing her answer.

"Closer to the cap!"

"I'd say car too," Jake added.

"So I was right about you!" Nic said holding in a laugh.

"Definitely ride in the car with Cap," Jenna and Lauren agreed.

"Y'all trippin'. I'd say ship," Chris announced.

"No Cap?" Kate asked.

"No, with the cap," Chris replied.

At this moment Nic and I detected a very rare sight in the Berlin dining hall, Captain Kostas, makings his rounds greeting the people.

Nic seized the opportunity and shouted, "Stop the cap!" then waved the captain over and the squad twisted around in their chairs to find Kostas standing over our table.

"We were just debating if we would rather be passengers of a car or a ship that you were steering," Nic said, giving Kate the eye.

Slightly flattered, the captain responded, "Well, I am a bit biased, but there's more room for activities on a ship."

"What sorts of activities, Captain?" I inquired raising my eyebrows.

"Oh, like ping-pong of course!"

"Of course! Of course!" We all exhaled in laugher.

The captain left the table after reassuring us that we would see land soon, and sooner if he went back up to the bridge to take the wheel from the chef, and he already had enough on his plate, worrying we wouldn't have enough on ours. The *MV World*

Odyssey had enough food to stay at sea for a maximum of approximately thirty days. However, taking our stress eating into account I'm sure we took a few days off that number. By the time we reach Mauritius we will have been at sea for ten days, so in the event that we are rejected we would have twenty more before we ran out of food. The squad agreed how ironic it was that we were so uncomfortable sailing on a vessel solely designed for comfort. Sometimes, I think that I mistook life for a German love boat.

Just before bed I received a seamail from my hometown best friend, Kyle, who was just checking in. This was my first connection with any of my friends outside the ship all semester. I tried to be concise, catching him up to the craziness that was our voyage. It was amazing that we didn't communicate for months and were able to pick up right where we left off.

> Day 55 | Feb 28, 2020: This morning came with some terrific news: tomorrow we would step onto land for the first time in thirteen days!

Mauritius was no longer in question; it was the answer! In my elation, I scheduled a spa pamper session for all the guys tomorrow night so we could unwind after running around the smallest nation in Africa all day.

By this point in the semester global studies had turned into an infectious diseases course. Jake and I couldn't believe some of the slides being presented in class. One of the bullet points read, "It is highly encouraged not to hook up with any strangers nor animals in Mauritius so as to avoid contracting the coronavirus." Nobody on board had shown symptoms of the virus yet so we were confident this statement would hold true after Mauritius,

Flexibility—Level Three

considering its distance from Wuhan.

After class I headed over to the library to take a load off. Its centralized location made it a great place to people watch. There are no solid walls on either side of the room, just fancy open paneling that many people felt awfully comfortable about based on the nature of their conversations. Sitting alone, I began to hear a faint conversation involving a few high-pitched voices. I closed my eyes hoping to hear better but jerked them open when I felt a tiny hand on my shoulder. It was Tara, and she was not holding her head as high as usual. Before I could speak, she sniffled. "I have to go home."

"What! Why?"

"My daddy said so. We're flying home from Mauritius."

She sat down across from me and explained how her dad, Nick, would take her home while her mom stayed back on the ship to finish teaching. I played ping-pong with Nick on a number of occasions; his biggest fear was our ship going into quarantine like other cruise liners around the world. Getting Tara home safe was his number-one priority and who could blame him? Sadly, Tara's heartbreaking situation was not unique. Other students were also forced home by their parents upon arrival to Mauritius. No questions asked. I was so grateful my family back home trusted Semester at Sea to fulfill their number-one priority, the safety of their most precious cargo.

Before our Mauritius pre-port meeting Tara's parents held a small goodbye party on the top deck. Watching Tara's closest girlfriend, Alex, cry her heart out and squeeze the life out of Tara made me wonder if my goodbyes would look the same. The *MV World Odyssey* was not ageist when it came to bonding its passengers. I laughed thinking how many times Tara and her friends were going to ask for their parents' phones to keep in contact, something us big kids will take for granted.

When the party was over, we headed down to the union for pre-port. The same animation projected on the big screen showing our ship sailing from Malaysia across the Indian Ocean. We all shared in a collective laugh when our little blip sharply turned south just pixels before reaching the Seychelles and then plowing into Mauritius.

The leadership team announced there was a chance we would be able to stay extra time in Mauritius which was unanimously accepted as a good thing. The plan was rather odd: we would reembark after our full day on land tomorrow, then circle around the island for two days before returning again for five bonus days. As ridiculous as this sounded, nothing was off the table. We kept our expectations low, but not too low, because tomorrow we would finally touch Africa!

~~~~~~

We finally landed in Newark just over ten hours behind schedule, meaning that the people on my connecting flight to Chicago had already unpacked their bags at home. Lightheaded and over hungry I said goodbye to Jake, Ashley, and Nic for yet another "final" time; we kept this one much more casual just in case. Weston and I were the only ones with a third flight ahead of us. Staring up at the big screens I could hardly make out the numbers. My contacts felt like fiberglass. The last two flights of the day to Chicago were in five minutes and one and a half hours. I let out a massive

Flexibility—Level Three

gasp of relief. Weston on the other hand gazed upward as if he'd just seen the boogeyman. The last flight to Atlanta had just taken off. Weston assured me he would figure it out and told me I needed to leave him behind. We embraced, and I took off like a rocket for the baggage claim.

Waiting anxiously at the baggage claim, I ran into Jake! We shared a good laugh as I helped him take his baggage off the carousel. I remember watching him walk out of the airport still convinced I'd run into him again. Sitting on the unforgiving airport tile waiting for my bag the unthinkable came across my mind. Ten minutes, no bag. Twenty minutes, no bag. Thirty-three minutes, I broke down. I jogged over to one of the counters to inquire. My eyes lit up when the lady informed me that my checked bag just took off for Chicago. I guess it doesn't matter who gets there first. "There's just one seat left on the last flight to O'Hare, and it's yours, John."

At this precise moment the overhead intercom mumbled something about Chicago that I couldn't comprehend.

"Run!" the agent yelped.

Sprinting like a cheetah my energy was depleting rapidly. I was only able to run in stints before I would need to stop and catch my breath. It felt like the weight of my backpack and carry-on had tripled since my first flight.

Arriving at the very end of a lengthy security line, the thought that I would end up like Weston and have to stay overnight crossed my mind. I just wanted to be home! This thought motivated me to ask person after person if they would be willing to let me skip them in line. Begging over and over, I was able to jump at least twenty people.

Completely drained after security, I glanced at my phone's

clock: my flight was scheduled to leave five minutes ago and my gate was the farthest away, which always seemed to be the case. Turning corners like a downhill skier, all of a sudden I knew exactly where I was. I passed the gate I had deboarded over an hour ago and found Weston still in line at customer service! Weston, being the seasoned traveler and commercial-rated pilot he is, devised a plan to Uber to a different airport where there was still one flight remaining to Atlanta. I hugged him one last time, and I was gone faster than a toupee in a hurricane. By the time I reached my gate, they were holding the plane just for me. A flight attendant slammed the door closed after I stepped onto the plane; making my way to the back row I was greeted with dozens of scrunched eyebrows.

I was now alone.

Sinking into my seat on my third and God willing my final flight home, a deep and uncomfortable loneliness crept through my body. At this point I had been traveling home for thirty hours and nothing more than water had entered my body in thirteen. My tummy grumbles were so loud they woke up the person sitting next to me. I was officially bottoming out. In my last attempt for sanity, I tapped a passing flight attendant and alerted her that I was in dire straits. She comforted me and with the softest smile in the world, kindly informed me that all food had been destroyed. My heart fell to the floor—none of my neighbors had any food or snacks on them, merely a stick of gum. On the verge of a panic attack and slowly filling with rage, I asked the flight attendant, "Whose idea was it to get rid of all the food?"

She responded, "That's well above my pay grade, honey."

There I was, sitting inside a metal tube with wings trying to understand the logic behind that decision. Out loud I said to my-

Flexibility—Level Three

self, "There must be a formula. Hmmm, let's see here. Pandemic + Destroying Food = Safety. That makes sense!" Nobody had a never-ending gobstopper, so I settled for yet another lukewarm bottle of water. I was so peeved I remember complaining about being handed Dasani and not Ice Mountain. Our engines finally began to spin, and I took three massive deep breaths before lowering my head into my journal for the last time.

~~~~~~

Johnny's Quiet

> *"Most people do not listen with the intent to understand;*
> *they listen with the intent to reply."*
> —Stephen R. Covey

WHEN I WAS A KID, I used to army crawl with my brother to the edge of our upstairs banister on Christmas morning to see if we had gotten any presents because we both knew we had been lousy little shits all year who didn't even deserve coal. So rather than conceitedly running down the stairs to our presents, we approached the railing humbly on our bellies. Then without fail, we would slowly raise our heads and peek over the banister to see presents exploding from beneath our tree. We were spoiled, but not rotten.

Walking out onto the deck to find our ship docked along Port Louis, Mauritius was a very similar experience, only I was a much bigger little shit. I crept up to the railing with my hat pulled down over my eyes until my feet were over the edge. I took off my cap and slowly began lifting my gaze to see something I did not deserve. The colossal mountains were not simply the backdrop of Port Louis, they were fully in the picture, towering directly over the city buildings. Every single seat both inside and outside of Lido was taken, so I soaked in the views standing up with my breakfast. My Mom always told me I would get indigestion from standing up while eating, but she had never eaten breakfast in Mauritius.

Imagine, hundreds of wildly exhilarated college students unload from a ship having been at sea for over two weeks with absolutely no plans. As of now, we only had one day in port so rather than just taking on the town, we took on the entire country. Everyone disembarked the ship with just their day packs; the lack of luggage made our exit much smoother, but Mauritius's infrastructure had different plans.

We could see Port Louis off in the distance, but it was still a few miles away. There was only one road that led to and from the dock and since there were no taxis in sight everyone just started walking. The girls took too long to get ready, so the guys disembarked without them and found ourselves at the very front of the pack. We walked backwards down the street looking at the mass of people covering both lanes, hoping we were going the right way. After a ten-minute walk there came a fork in the road.

"Right?" I shouted back to the crowd. The right road seemed less abandoned than the left so I figured we should see a car any second. Just then, an unmarked sedan turned the corner a football field away, zooming quickly toward us. I ran up to the car, and the man rolled down his window.

"Are we going the right way?" I asked out of breath.

"Yeah," he replied shortly.

And with that, he rolled up his window and parted the crowd behind us. At this point I had a terrible feeling in my gut that we were leading everyone into oblivion until another car came zooming down the road, this time, with a yellow taxi sticker on the side. A group behind us jogged ahead and stuffed in like a clown car. Before we could process a course of action, we were no longer in the front of the pack. A few moments passed before a flood of taxis turned the corner—it was a complete free-for-all to hail one down. Rather than the traditional method of standing on the sidewalk and waving an arm, we sprinted ahead of the mob and jumped in front of one of the taxis.

After the five of us piled in the car, our tires screamed as we drifted around corners approaching Port Louis at unfathomable speeds. Our suspension didn't have time to react to the speed bumps, so we hardly felt them. Coming to a stop our driver rushed us out of the car and we threw all the rupees we had at him. When the door slammed shut, he drifted a 180 and headed directly back for the sea of people like a whale shark trying to catch as many krill as possible. It was a feeding frenzy, and our ship was going to employ every cab driver on the island.

We walked around downtown and found another taxi who would be our driver for the rest of the day. We took turns taking shotgun on each leg of our journey because the other four of us had to squeeze into the back seat. With the audacious goal of seeing an entire country in one day, I'd say we were quite successful.

> Mauritius Day 1 | Day 56 | Feb 29, 2020: With our precious time on one of the most remote islands in the world we snorkeled at Flic en Flac beach,

Johnny's Quiet

drove past the world-famous underwater waterfall, walked through the Seven Colored Earth Geopark, watched 150-year-old Aldabra tortoises make love, paid a few locals to cliff jump off the Maconde viewpoint, drank homemade tequila, and made it back to Flic en Flac by sunset where we ran into the girls.

But we couldn't hang out for too long because I had reserved the entire spa for the guys in a few hours. I connected to some nearby Wi-Fi and refreshed my WhatsApp before going dark for the next two days. Jonny Vee texted me that our Pu Mat video was uploaded on YouTube!

I grabbed Ashley, Julia, and Kate and we relived our gargantuan adventure for the second time. It brought tears to our eyes. But the most extraordinary realization came after watching the second time and renaming the cast: our hike in the jungles of Pu Mat was analogous to our voyage.

> The Squad = The Squad
> Andy = Captain Kostas
> Mr. King = Coronavirus
> Jungle = Ship

Our day in Pu Mat began without a hitch. We ate and drank new foods, and met new people. Then, as time progressed, we seemed to seamlessly slip into a situation completely beyond our control. As we ventured deeper and deeper into the trek, we lost a few points of contact and fell time and time again. We seemed to be crawling along blindfolded, making fresh tracks through uncharted terrain with no sign of a lookout point in sight. Andy merely translated important information as Mr. King took over the wheel. The world was only as big as the things we could see in front of us, and we had no idea how to get home. We swung and missed on the route we wished to travel, Mr. King got his way, and laughed at us all the way back to safety.

Drawing this analogy in my head gave me plenty to think about as we walked through the dark, snail covered streets connecting the city of Port Louis to our ship. Reflecting on our voyage in this way also helped me not to dwell on the unsettling *crunch* sound when someone misplaced a step, exploding a snail beneath their shoe, splattering juice out either side. We did our best to avoid them, but their slimy army numbered more than one thousand.

Back on the ship after our stupendous day in Mauritius, I flung open my cabin door to find Jimmy passed out fully dressed on his bed and a ping-pong paddle with a message written in Sharpie on mine.

> Dear Johnny,
> My daddy no longer has use for his paddle, so he wanted me to give it to you. We couldn't find you last night, so we broke into your cabin. I hope you have an awesome time in Mauritius! Please visit us soon in Australia!
> Your best friend,
> Tara

My heart was so full as I shed a tear and held the paddle tightly. Once I found a safe place for it, I shook Jimmy and sent a

Johnny's Quiet

seamail reminder to the guys that our long-awaited pamper session was just an hour away. Before leaving for the spa I refreshed my inbox one last time hoping to find out whether we would be welcomed back to Mauritius or not. Nothing.

Nic, Jake, Weston, Chris, Dylan, Zack, Kyle, Jacob, Luca, Jimmy, and I rendezvoused in front of the spa; we couldn't believe that fifty-six days into the voyage it was finally happening. Like something out of a dream, three massage therapists opened the double doors revealing a fully nude statue of a man. His entire body was a dark green copper except for his penis, which was solid gold. We were instructed to touch it for good luck before continuing on with our session. For the next two hours we sat in the steam room together, received massages on the heated stone beds, jumped in the indoor heated pool, and some of us even drew a bath, all while jamming to our favorite tunes.

Every so often we would request an update, and someone would check their seamail but nothing had come through. While we were in the pool the masseuses issued our fifteen-minute warning. What were the final songs we were going to play? Weston wanted Kenny Chesney, Jake wanted Odesza, I wanted rap, but our conversation seized at the sound *beep-boop!*

"Good evening, voyagers!"

Right off the bat the Voice's tone was elevated, but we stayed true to our abhorrently low expectations.

"The *MV World Odyssey* has been granted five extra days in Mauritius!"

We blew up, splashing all of the water out of the pool, flooding the ship from the inside! Our voyage of discovery was truly transforming into a voyage of immersion. We made history with the longest stay in Vietnam and now we were staying six times longer than any other voyage in Mauritius! Everyone was exultant—this was the first time we had a confirmed itinerary for the next five days in over a month. Oh, how we love certainty! Mozambique was thrown out the window like a piece of gum and nobody batted an eyelash. Whatever happened after Mauritius would take care of itself then; we were just thrilled to get back on that island.

Transitioning from school to Africa to school proved to be more than just an unorthodox learning environment. It was bloody impossible! While we were in class Captain Kostas was having the time of his life on the bridge. I'm sure this news also came as a pleasant surprise for him because he had the opportunity to manually steer his ship around the island rather than just autopiloting across endless horizons of ocean.

In between classes I found myself reading starboard side but being able to see cars whizzing around the island was distracting so I moved portside to face the ocean.

Beep-boop!

What the heck could this be? This was a very unusual time for an announcement. The speaker began by clearing his throat and I knew right away it was not the Voice. Hopefully we had not been pirated!

"Attention. There are two whales spotted portside, repeat, two whales portside. Thank you."

It was Captain Kostas! I lifted my gaze just a hair higher over my book and laid eyes on the magnificent beasts, effortlessly cruising along the surface of the water. In a matter of seconds, doors burst open, and the entire ship was pressed up against the railing pointing in the same direction. I felt awful for anyone sitting on the toilet. I also wondered if the rapid shift of weight swayed the ship at all, but only the captain's instruments would be able to detect such a thing.

Our second and last day at sea before porting again, Kostas anchored us a good distance off the coast. In the middle of class, I felt the vibration of our ten-ton anchor being pulled up from the ocean floor. After class I ran into John and asked if I could check out his cabin. I knew he had a balcony view on the eighth deck, and I wanted to see it for myself. Besides the ability to enjoy the sea breeze in private, fresh air at night, a full-size TV, ample storage, and more wall outlets, our cabins weren't much different.

We talked about insurance and personal assistants then made our way down to Berlin to grab lunch. This time others were allowed to sit at our table so when Herbert and Wabster strolled in John waved them over prompting me to bring back a phrase from middle school, "This table is stacked!"

We began dreaming of how we might like to spend our extra time in Mauritius and then our conversation drastically changed course. Reading my journal entry over and over from this day I am still dumbfounded how we went from travel plans to love so quickly.

John began the conversation by addressing the elephant in the room: everyone sitting at the table had lost their significant other to cancer. So John posed a question for the table: Can someone fall in love again?

Wabster leaped out of her seat with an enthusiastic yes! She was explaining how she had recently begun to fall in love again, when Herbert jumped in and shared that he was in a very similar situation. Acknowledging that someone could fall in love again and to the same degree as their late spouse, Herbert asked the table, "How do you know you're in love?"

Almost unanimously all three of them responded, "If you have to ask, you're not in love."

Then John took the floor and clarified that the feeling of love I was referring to does not last forever. He expressed his disappointment with people who think their relationship must no longer continue because it doesn't feel good. John had some choice words about decisions based on feelings alone. He basically reiterated a quote from Mark Manson: "Decision-making based on emotional intuition, without the aid of reason to keep it in line, pretty much always sucks. You know who bases their entire lives on their emotions? Three-year-old kids. And dogs. You know what else three-year-olds and dogs do? Shit on the carpet." Emotions are neither good nor bad but they must not take the driver's seat of our lives.

In my head, I reflected back on the rush I received when I flew to visit Arizona State, and drooled down the airplane window when I saw the football stadium wedged between a mountain. I still get the chills to this day, but over the course of four years the thrill wore off. However, now I have acquired a much greater love and appreciation for the campus and have discovered innumerable qualities which I couldn't have seen from an airplane.

John said that love hit him when he was least looking for it. His late wife was first and foremost his best friend. John argued that focusing on physical attraction alone was the sinkhole in the foundation that leads to a broken marriage. Of course, a person's

Johnny's Quiet

beauty is the spark plug that ignites the engine of the relationship, but it is certainly not the fuel it runs on. We're all familiar with the saying, "You wouldn't buy a car without taking it for a test drive," relating to dating. Well what happens when the car gets old, are you going to get a younger one?

John believed that deciding who you marry was the most important decision of your life, and it should be treated as such. The entire table agreed there is no better time to start working on your marriage than before you're married.

Understanding the feeling of love from a very high level, and recognizing that a widow could fall in love again, John posed a final question.

"So then, which spouse was your soulmate?"

Silence fell upon the table for the first time, and I sat patiently, eagerly awaiting their response. Nobody answered the question.

John broke the silence by saying, "That's right, because there is no such thing as 'the one.'"

I remained quiet as John spewed his wisdom all over the table. How small are we to think of God that he's placed just one individual for us to find? That is, if our vocation is marriage. If "the one" existed, then finding him/her out of eight billion people would result in an exponentially higher worldwide divorce rate than we have now. The truth is there is not one person who is capable of being a lifelong companion, there are thousands.

Having been silent thus far John said, "Johnny's quiet. I'm shocked you haven't said a word this whole time. Come to think of it, 'Johnny's quiet' is a great oxymoron."

HAHA...haha...haaa...ha.

I let one of those laughs that die off when you realize a joke was terrifyingly accurate. Then John executed one of his famous pivots, swapping the topic of love for listening. It was striking how similar the two were. You ask any married couple how they are doing it and they will tell you three things: Communicate. Communicate. Communicate. While every school has some type of speech class John lamented how there was no "listening" class. What would that look like? John believed there was nothing more valuable than a great listener and no better feeling than being listened to.

> Day 58 | Mar 2, 2020: John ended our incredible conversation with this golden nugget: "You've got two ears and one mouth. You think God did that on accident?"

Since I had sat down for lunch over two hours had passed and I needed to start packing for Mauritius, the sequel. I thanked John, Herbert, and Wabster before heading to my cabin. I had never felt like such a part of a conversation without saying a word in my life. I had nothing to add, but everything to gain.

Moreitius

> *"Mauritius was made first and then heaven;
> and heaven was copied after Mauritius."*
> —Mark Twain

FLOODING THE STREETS of Mauritius for the second time, we turned our pace up a few notches leaving uncertainty in the dust. This time around, Weston, Jake, Chris, Jacob, and I secured a van, so we didn't have to sit on top of each other. Aiming not to waste a second on land we started to prioritize our agenda. Mauritius was known for having one of the largest giant sea turtle populations in the world, which clinched our number one spot.

After sputtering out to sea for fifteen minutes on an old shore boat, we arrived at the site and quickly realized that we weren't the only ones to hear about the turtles. There were a few dozen boats surrounding about four turtles so each one had its own mob of paparazzi bobbing up and down with their GoPros. Tourism is obviously critical to the world's economy, especially in Mauritius, but sometimes it just doesn't feel right.

Needing a breather from humans, Chris and I were dying to SCUBA dive. We held the same belief that since the majority of the world was covered by ocean, a world traveler ought to have a scuba certification. The rest of the guys were not certified so unfortunately, we had to leave them behind. Chris and I went back to our beachside villa, refilled on water and snacks, then took a short drive to the dive shop. We literally had to step through a hole in the wall to enter the place. Extremely skeptical but starving to breathe in some tanked oxygen, Chris and I walked over to the counter. The head dive master introduced himself as Koul, pronounced "cool."

I instantly thought of our last foreign friend Hau, pronounced "how."

HAU KOUL!

Koul gave us the rundown on the different dives around the island and we were sold. A few signatures later, Chris and I were lugging our tanks down the street and into our boat. On all my previous SCUBA trips, the boat was always packed to the brim, and the equipment was strewn everywhere. Chris and I had Koul and his neatly ordered boat all to ourselves. An hour later we were back in our happy place as we slowly sank into the open ocean. One would think an activity with limited oxygen, extremely slow movements, and fifty pounds strapped tightly to your back would induce feelings of confinement, but diving was the most liberating sensation I have ever known.

As we descended deeper and deeper, the red accents on our gear lost their color, consumed by the rich blue of the sea. Continuing to equalize, the eerie darkness of a shipwreck began to appear below. Once we reached the wreck, I checked my dive computer for the first time, 102 feet. This was the deepest I had ever dove, so I hyper focused on my breathing and remained calm. While we often take it for granted above water, breathing is the greatest superpower of a diver. Using only my breath to control my buoyancy, I inhaled when I wanted to rise over the railing of the ship and exhaled to come back down.

Thirty minutes beneath the surface we had already turned the dive and begun to slowly make our ascent. Koul had been leading us the entire time with Chris and I staggered just behind on either side. Both of us had our arms crossed effortlessly flutter kicking along when we heard a loud quacking noise. Jerking up our heads at the same time we saw Koul pointing both of his hands at our eleven o'clock.

> Mauritius Day 2 | Day 59 | Mar 3, 2020: Out of the blue the fins of a giant sea turtle came into view, and I nearly forgot to breathe!

We stopped kicking and just stared as the turtle approached us with intimate proximity and then effortlessly glided past us seeming to wave goodbye. The second our heads shot through the surface we ripped our regulators out and shouted for joy. Our dive was starkly juxtaposed with snorkeling off the beach just a few hours earlier! The slow nature of SCUBA not only put our new friend at ease, but it also made him curious enough to approach us.

Chris and I knew the rest of the guys couldn't miss out, so we begged Koul to let them dive with us tomorrow. We looked over Koul's beginner course packet, but we didn't want the other guys to *waste* any time *learning*. We wanted them to see what we saw ASAP! Koul put on his thinking face, scratched his head, then grabbed a sharpie and added "rapid" to the course title. Koul beans! The instant Chris and I reunited with the guys we gave them the spiel and they gave a resounding, "YES!"

Like clockwork, Chris, Jake, Jacob, Weston, and I stepped through the wall of Koul's shop, filled out the paperwork, and hopped on the boat. This time around, Koul took us along the coast to the northernmost point of the country to a tiny uninhabited island covered in lush greenery known as Gunners Quoin. Colossal black cliffs surrounded the island on all sides preventing any humans from setting foot on its immaculate soil. Since there were no beaches, Koul nestled our boat right inside a stunning inlet and tossed the anchor. The contrast between the green grass and turquoise water looked photoshopped and the white boobies flying overhead completed the picture.

> Mauritius Day 3 | Day 60 | Mar 4, 2020: Once Koul killed the engine, Jake whipped out his drone and captured what he claimed to be one of the greatest shots in his portfolio. Even David Attenborough would've been speechless!

When I finished my four-day SCUBA certification course two years prior, the first thing I said was, "Wow! I wish I could do this with all my friends." And here I was about to do just that! The guys would not earn a certification after taking Koul's rapid course, they just needed enough knowledge to stay alive. Once they had mastered the "okay" and "out of air" signs they had tanks on their backs ready to hit the water. The first time I took a breath underwater in pool training in the spring of 2017, it took hours before I was comfortable to stay under for more than a minute, so I was pretty nervous at least one of the guys wasn't going to make it down.

All of us were sitting on the edge of the boat with our tanks facing the water ready to fall back on Koul's signal. We looked like a Seal Team squad and our black gear was hot to the touch reflecting the Mauritius sun. I feared the guys might pass out and fall into the water, but Koul wanted to make sure our breathing was in control before we entered. Getting hotter by the second Koul finally began a countdown and on zero our tanks slapped the ocean. For a beginner SCUBA diver, there is not a more disorienting feeling than performing a back roll water entry. The impact of hitting the water might knock your regulator out, you could roll a second time backwards in the water filling your mask, and you're completely blind for a few seconds from the explosion of bubbles.

The boys' entries were executed flawlessly.

Koul counted our heads and gave the thumbs down meaning "all clear to descend." Seeing the looks on the guys faces I'm not sure training got that far. Once the last of our hairs fell below the surface, we all looked around with wide eyes and gave slow-mo high fives. The newbies floated around in every direction like astronauts making me laugh out loud into my regulator. Their buoyancy control was deplorable, and the drift current didn't help their cause. Chris showed off his mastery by rising up and down with his breath in the genie pose. The visibility was the best in the world, so I wasn't worried we would lose anyone. I was more worried that someone would try to exert themselves and run out of oxygen because new divers already breathe much faster. Everyone moved around relatively slow except for Jacob who darted around the reef like Nemo.

Sharing one of my favorite activities on Earth filled my heart with joy, and, based on the hootin' and hollerin' when we popped out of the water, the feelings were mutual. Back on the boat we cruised over to Flat Island where we ate chicken and rice Koul had made on one of the most pristine beaches in all of Africa. Post-lunch I posed in the surf line like a model and Jake snapped away, capturing some hysterical blackmail. Then all the guys lined up with our buns in the sun for a photo we would later gift to Kate as a birthday present. On our way back to the mainland, Koul poured a shot of rum down my snorkel tube to the cheers of the guys. When we got back to our stay, I packed my things and headed back to the ship because I had signed up for a field program the following day titled Canyoning Tamarind Falls.

The following morning, on our way to canyon the Tamarind Falls (I honestly didn't know what that meant when I signed up, I figured something cool with a harness) our bus stopped at a local antique shop. The former house turned workshop was filled with everything from airplane models to gigantic handmade ships. It only took a few minutes before everyone saw the price tags, took a few photos, and loaded back onto the bus, but I had my eyes locked on the coolest penholder of all time. Its dark wooden base supported a sturdy curved stand that suspended a foot-long solid metal F-16 fighter jet, beneath which a single pen could be placed. The remarkable attention to detail and intricate design of the model for the sole purpose of holding a single pen captivated me. I figured a man's pen holder ought to be as brilliant as the man holding the pen; therefore, this hunk of beauty was bound for my father's desk.

I loaded back onto the bus with my massive box, and everyone freaked out.

"No way! You actually got something?"

"A penholder," I replied.

They were irrationally frustrated that I did not take it out of the box, but it was packaged together with the intent of making it home to the opposite side of the world. In fact, at 11,310 miles away, Port Louis was literally the farthest city away from Phoenix on Planet Earth. So after running into every post office on the island, I understood how difficult it was going to be to ship my seven-pound box to its farthest possible destination. I could either sell one of my kidneys or somehow stuff this terribly awkward penholder into my luggage, so I chose the latter.

Thirty minutes later our twenty-person group was properly harnessed up in a gravel parking lot. *Cool, so there are harnesses,* I thought. Once our kit was double checked, we took a fifteen-minute hike through very thick, slippery jungle, which gave me flashbacks of Pu Mat, but it was much less fun falling down every other step without my friends. The jungle eventually opened up to a rocky river where our guide, Joseph, briefed us on our task: abseil down the 120-foot waterfall behind us. *Very cool, I liked waterfalls.*

Since we were already standing at the top of the falls, Joseph encouraged us to take a peek over the edge. Inching up to the edge in army crawl position, our stomachs curled as we stuck our heads out and looked down at the rush of water smacking the earth below. I was shocked Joseph had this much trust in us.

It would all make sense in a few moments because what was to come would require an insane amount of trust in him.

When it was my turn, I walked toward the waterfall, this time on my feet, and watched Joseph carefully clip me into the rope. Facing away from the falls, I took baby steps backwards until I had no more real estate and performed a trust fall into the harness. With my weight fully back I began steadily walking down the waterfall. As focused on the present as I needed to be abseiling down slippery jagged rock with water gushing over my face, I was not. Not even a quarter way down the waterfall, I couldn't stop thinking about what my friends were doing. It didn't matter what they were up to, I just wanted to be with them.

> Mauritius Day 4 | Day 61 | Mar 5, 2020: I cannot believe I am writing this, but I would rather sit in a coffee shop with my best friends than abseil down a 120-foot waterfall without them.

All of a sudden a wave of guilt came over me, "How are you not having fun doing this extreme activity, you love those!" When I signed up for this field program months prior to the voyage, I was elated. But now, I understood many of the friends I would make along the voyage did not sign up for the same programs that I did. However, I figured leaving them behind to do something incredible wouldn't be a problem. But there I was, forty feet down a waterfall, pouting in my harness like a dog.

Just two days ago I purposely left the other guys in the dust when Chris and I ran off to SCUBA dive. My thought process went something like: *Ugh, these commoners think kicking turtles in the head while treading water is fun. I'm going to utilize my open water certification and have the entire ocean to myself.* Why didn't we all just go dive? Koul would have still done the rapid course and we would've had a whole extra day to dive together.

On our bus ride back to the ship I kept writing the same phrase over again on the blackboard of my brain. "It's better to do nothing with friends, than everything without them." Sure it was just one day, but once our voyage passed the halfway point, I cared deeply about every second.

When I plopped my box containing my F-16 fighter jet on the security table before boarding the ship I said frustratedly, "It's just a penholder... do I really have to take it out?"

"HA! That's a good one," the agent replied.

So carefully undoing all of the tape and Styrofoam, I unveiled the magnificent piece of art to the awe of everyone in line behind me and the confusion of the agent.

"All of this just for that little gray pen, huh?"

"Heck, yeah!" I said pridefully.

Confronting Lions

"It is because I wanted to be the big noise at the party that I am so annoyed at someone else being the big noise."
—C. S. Lewis

TWENTY PERCENT OF our grade in every course we take on the ship excluding global studies was attending a field class. We already sailed past all of my other field classes, but marketing was rescheduled for day five in Mauritius. Our class loaded onto a bus, Lance took roll, and we were on our way. Pulling into the parking lot nothing seemed out of the ordinary. But as we unloaded a man dressed as a blue elephant came out to greet us. By the time I got off the bus the park's mascot was bear hugging Lance.

If a zoo and an amusement park had a child that was the place we visited. We rode carts down a mountain that felt like they would snap off at any second and touched almost every animal on the property. We started off by hand-feeding carrots to giant tortoises, then we worked our way up to giraffes, until we were jerking our heads back to feed the ostriches. The animals we were interacting with were not getting bigger each time, rather more aggressive.

Checking to make sure we had all our fingers, we followed our guide through the park until we arrived at the big cats section. This was the first time in my life I was upset not to see a No Touch sign, anywhere. *There's no way we're really doing this, are we?* Our guide handed us each a wooden mop pole and told us not to use it, whatever that meant! Leading us slowly into the lion's cage our only instructions were no loud noises and absolutely no quick movements. Very unfortunate considering 99 percent of my waking hours were spent doing one of those things. Turning my head around like an owl, there was not one, but five kitties in the cage with us. Approaching one of the lionesses lying down, our guide instructed me to kneel and give her a good back scrubbing. Following his orders, she let out a deep moan and yawned. My mind was racing with potential escape routes if this lion got angry. But she remained calm, so I carefully rose to my feet and let the next person show some love.

Mauritius Day 5 | Day 62 | Mar 6, 2020: I cannot believe I pet a lion! Mom is not getting those photos!

At the break of dawn of our sixth and final day in Mauritius, Ashley knocked on my door and asked if I wanted to swim with dolphins.

"Why, yes, Ashley, perhaps I could go for a swim with dolphins this morning."

I mean, come on! Is this real life?

The squad took on the island the last time with a man named Govind, who had been the girls' faithful driver since day one. The island native extended his services from driver to captain, taking us out on his boat in search of a pod of dolphins. We hung our legs off the side in position to jump whenever Govind gave us the greenlight. "There!" Govind shouted and a dozen bodies hit the water swimming full speed toward the fins. We only caught a glimpse of the dolphins before they passed us by and were out of sight. Even the strongest of us couldn't keep up for more than a few seconds before hopping back into the boat. As I laid exhausted on the deck, I decided I would stick to SCUBA diving and let the wildlife just come to me.

The extreme ebbs and flows of the morning left us pooped. When we reached shore, I found myself in "the position" as my mom calls it. Fair warning, I'm about to get pretty vulnerable. I was considering leaving it out of the book altogether but then you'd be left thinking, "Why the hell is he holding it in?"

The position is standing with my legs crossed and my jaw clenched down looking like I'm constipated... because I am. My habit dates back to fourth grade when I left recess to go number two. When I returned, the entire playground was in hysterics because Timmy sank the most unbelievable trick shot the world had ever seen and so I vowed never to miss another moment again.

But gradually, my case of FOMO extended far beyond the playground. I held it in class so I didn't fall behind and stuck in front of the screen watching movies with my friends even though the bathroom might have been just a few steps away. I was so engrossed with my current activity, I began to extrapolate

Confronting Lions

my hatred for pooping to other important activities such as eating and showering because I believed real life took place outside those monotonous tasks. Holding my poop helped me to live in the moment and seize the day. I'm laughing out loud as I write this now.

When the initial urge came on, I of course battened down the hatch and squeezed it back up. The second time it came a bit harder, but I knew I had a few more squeezes left in me. Eventually *the* urge would come, and I knew it was time to go. But oftentimes, I wouldn't make it, resulting in a code brown.

The most scarring memory of my childhood was playing basketball in Mrs. Nothnagel's sixth grade PE class. I was cross-legged, standing courtside, after mysteriously checking out of the game for hamstring pain. Clenching tight with all my might I was either going to pop a blood vessel or shit myself. Or both! I released the pressure for but a moment to take in a breath and three small separate lumps like slightly melted M&Ms dropped through my AND1 basketball shorts and slapped the squeaky-clean wooden court. Immediately receiving tunnel vision, I spotted a few other kids running my way for a water break and I nearly went into shock. If they found out about my accident, I would need to relocate my family, my father's job would be in jeopardy, and they would take my mother in for counseling. So after going number two three times next to the bench, I played it cool like I had dropped some candy out of my pants, swiftly bent over, picked them all up, put them in my pocket, and walked to the bathroom, hands in my pockets, like I had gotten away with murder.

You'd think I would have lived in the bathroom for the rest of my life after such a horror scene, but this was not the case. I continued to hold for longer and longer stretches until the stool living inside of me was hard as a rock and the doctors declared it impacted. I have medical proof that my poop impacted me, so I hope it's impacting you! Lying on my belly on the ice-cold ER table, the Really Rocky Road was scooped out of me.

I quickly understood that holding my poop was correlated more closely to death than life, so I retired "the position."

But there I was, standing in "the position" on a beach in Mauritius at nineteen years old having not gone to the bathroom in four days. Our voyage seemed to be on its last waves, our time on land was limited, and God forbid I *waste* any of it on the toilet!

> Mauritius Day 6 | Day 63 | Mar 7, 2020: I thought I wiped myself clean of my constipation complex but somehow Mauritius reverted me back to my deadly habit.

The bathrooms that were cleaned daily in my middle school looked dreamy compared to the public restrooms of Mauritius. At this point I couldn't care less because I was approaching code brown, but Govind said the nearest bathroom was a short drive away. I couldn't make it. I was in dire straits.

The emergency sirens were wailing in my head, so I pulled Weston over to create a game plan. While everyone dried off and checked out some of the GoPro footage with Govind, I wobbled down the beach like a penguin. With no protection to squat anywhere on shore I was completely out of luck, but there wasn't a soul in the water.

Standing in front of Weston with my jaw clenched, his eyes

lit up. "Have you ever executed the notorious aqua dump?"

"A what?!"

"Everyone pees in the ocean. Number two is the same—it's all feeding the fish."

Hobbling into the water as fast as I could I yelled, "Don't look at me!"

"I never thought I'd hear you say those words!" he shouted back.

After expelling a few demons while laughing at Weston's remark I felt a hundred percent better. Then I thought: *Could that have actually been the first time I said those words?* Control F-ing the files of my brain those four words had never been arranged in such a manner. But before I had adequate time to address the rush of thoughts coming to my head, the clouds finally let go of the weeks' worth of rain they had been holding in for us. Govind dropped all of us off back at the ship and we shared a heartfelt goodbye. It's strange, exploring Mauritius day one without an itinerary we felt spontaneous, and should I dare say free? Now, reembarking after our sixth day, still without an itinerary, we felt trapped.

> Mauritius Day 6 | Day 63 | Mar 7, 2020: Are we voyagers, tourists, or captives of a ship pirated by the coronavirus?

The rumors running rampant certainly didn't help everyone's uncertainty. Some claimed we would never reboard the ship again. Others said our voyage was going to reach Europe. No one had any clue how much time we had left, we just knew it wasn't long enough.

Jimmy wasn't in the cabin, so I plopped down on my bed and attempted to address Weston's response—"I never thought I'd hear you say those words!"—which was still echoing in my head. Most things I hear tend to go in one ear and out the other, but this time it felt like someone stuck their hand out and stopped those nine words between my ears, so I dropped my head into my lap to think it though.

I anticipated a barrage of distractions but instead two different memories came to mind. The first was at the dinner table in my early high school years. I had earned enough negative attention that day to cash in the biggest prize at Chuck E. Cheese but instead of tickets funneling out of my mom's mouth she said, "The day your brother was born was the worst day of your life, because you no longer had our full attention."

The second was a statement made by my freshman-year suitemate, also named Jimmy, at the end of our first year at ASU: "It's strange, when we met at Camp Carey in August, I was an extrovert like you, but after all this time together, somehow you've turned me into an introvert."

I always wanted to be the biggest noise, no matter the cost. My mentality was simple: walk into a room and own it—that's how I was raised. At ASU, campus is half indoors half outdoors so I would "turn it on" so to speak just before entering a room on campus. But what happens when campus is just a floating nine-story building consisting of a conglomerate of rooms? Nobody hung out in the hallways; everyone was always making their way from room to room like a game of Clue. The flux of my shipmates meant I rarely "turned off" after leaving a room which led to working on owning outdoor spaces like the pool deck, which I previously respected as a demilitarized zone. Nobody realizes they are being a ball hog until watching film after the game, so I only realized this when reflecting post-voyage.

I scanned every room I walked into, producing a mental radar of any other sharks so I could devour them before they won any sort of approval from others. Most of the time my confidence was intimidating enough to push over the fencers who didn't know if they should try to be the funny guy or not. Since a partnership was outside of my vocabulary, oftentimes I wanted to kick people out, sounding something like Mr. Incredible: "Fly home, buddy. I work alone."

From the moment I stepped on the ship my radar was flooded with bogeys. Strong personalities collided from all over the globe, and to me, it was the greatest challenge of my life. Like a game of Agar.io, my task was to consume them all into myself, thus becoming the face of the ship. After the first week of sailing I felt very good about the squad I was surrounding myself with. I didn't have to compete with anyone, and I was the biggest noise. Then suddenly, like a shark attack in the surf line, someone had stealthily swum beneath my detection and ended up in my immediate circle. Squinting down at the center of my radar his blip was unnoticeable because it was directly on top of mine! His name has not made much of an appearance; how could I let him have any territory in my own book? But in all seriousness, Nic Swanger was the funniest person I had ever met, and I was terrified.

Anyone who is funny knows that the best aspect of a joke is its timing. Some can be blurted out at any time, but the real knee bucklers are ticking time bombs that only have a few seconds before they expire. Everyone beats you up if you pull the pin too early and you beat yourself up if you pull too late.

Nic dropped nukes.

He drove home the big risk jokes that I often steered away from. Taking the preposterous amount of thoughts that pop into my head and selecting the right one to leave my mouth at the proper time was a miracle in itself. But in the worst-case scenario, when I found myself holding onto a bomb past its due date, I'd chuck it to the side and just toss out something crass, desperately praying for any sign of amusement—cue Weston's, "Come on man!"

Even when a joke didn't require impeccable timing, Nic had an arsenal of anti-jokes. In my head they were so stupid that I couldn't fathom anybody would ever laugh at them, but they did.

Nic would say something like, "What did the kid with no arms or legs get for Christmas? Gloves and boots."—cue Jake lying on the ground laughing.

Strong arming Nic out of the squad was not an option and understanding the only thing worse than one bull in a china shop was two, I determined I needed to gradually whittle him down. Weeks went by of keeping score in my head. A successful joke or spectacle gained a tally. An explosion of Nic's bomb would start the fuse of my own. It didn't take long before I felt very uncomfortable when I didn't have the floor; anytime Nic was talking all I thought about was how I was losing ground. A month into the voyage constantly jockeying for position was starting to take its toll, but I was in too deep. I started to implement strategies so bizarre I was beginning to wonder if they were really my ideas.

Nearing the end of our time in Mauritius I was nauseated from keeping score and fatigued from holding in laughter, so I waved my little white flag and surrendered. Feeling naked and

Confronting Lions

ashamed for quitting, I stayed quiet and only spoke when I needed to. This was one of the worst periods in my life because I put my entire identity into something I had just given away.

So there I was, the day after exploring one of the most luxurious destinations on Earth, sitting in my cabin alone, at rock bottom. I remember having the thought that God was not real and that calling out to Him was a waste of my time. But this shadow of doubt followed by the temptation of omission was so intense I was immediately convicted of Satan's existence. The devil overplayed his hand. Naturally my next thought was: *If the devils real then God is certainly real.*

I leaned my head back and cried out, "God, please help me!"

The next moment, a sensation words cannot describe came over me. It was gone before it came. The only thing I knew when it had passed was how much I was loved. Not a word was exchanged but suddenly I had all the answers.

JP Beguhl once shared with me the term "nightwater": the indescribable quenching sensation of the water you chug when you wake up in the middle of the night. Now, without drinking anything, I had this feeling multiplied times infinity, then the deepest longing of my soul was quenched, resulting in the most intense peace I have ever encountered. A rest so overwhelming I wanted to dedicate my entire life to sharing Him with others.

In tandem with the epiphany that God loves me more than I'll ever know, He gifted me compunction, feeling guilty for my sins, and this incredible vision. Jesus and I were walking along the path of my past life surrounded by a beautiful prairie landscape. The path zig zagged all over the place, but somehow Jesus and I were able to walk straight whilst remaining on the trail. Jesus was carrying an enormous willow tree over his shoulder, and

I was empty-handed. We walked past all the times when I held in my laughter and poop where the spirit of control was at the root.

Since the voyage proved every day how little control I had over my life, my reaction was to control those around me. Friends or not, nobody could be as funny, outgoing, adventurous, or insane as me. To what lengths would I go to gain control? I'd go to the ends of the Earth! The gray space in my head was crystal clear, as if the frozen windshield of ice over my eyes had been scraped off. My extreme desire for approval was rooted in the lie that if I am not the center of attention, I am not loved. Simply knowing I am loved revealed my worth, and it's not correlated with the amount of time I spend in the limelight. I wonder if they call it limelight because spending enough time in it makes you sour.

Still in the vision, and marching deeper into my sinful past with Jesus, I felt the presence of something following us, but He did not change our pace. Spooked by the movements I was beginning to hear all around us I walked with my head down and giggled when I saw Jesus wearing rubber Birks, but I couldn't distract myself from my inflamed nerves. Another crackle snapped from the shrubbery, but I was too overwrought to open my eyes. I felt Jesus's hand on my head, so I looked up to him then quickly shut my eyes but not before I caught a glimpse of a lion snarling through the grass. I tugged on Jesus's clothes to stop but he continued on. The rustling grew louder until I could not deny we were being stalked. Utterly petrified, I shot open my eyes to see forty lions prowling around us in every direction. I was now face to face with my greatest and most hideous sin of all, my pride.

I despised my pride with all of my being, so I uttered a shrill cry hoping they would run off, but this only fueled their hunger. A few beasts were now within striking distance, so I swung my fist, but Jesus grabbed my arm saying, "No loud noises, no quick movements. Be still and know that I am with you." The entire pride seemed to be guarding a small portion of the trail where Jesus had fixed His eyes. He said, "Do not be afraid." Then we walked directly towards the lions, and they closed their mouths and bowed their heads letting out a symphony of deep moans. I was consumed with joy to be alive, and I wanted to thank Jesus for saving my life so I offered to help carry the tree on His back but he rejected saying, "You have yet to pick up your own."

Then Jesus looked down at my feet and pointed to the ground the pride of lions had been guarding. There, covered in drool, was my cross where I had dropped it early in my high school years. It was a splinter barely visible to the naked eye. "That's it? I can carry more weight than that, Jesus," I said proudly. But Jesus rejected, "No, this is all you can bear." I bent down and used all of my strength to lift the splinter off the ground. "This is your cross, Johnny. Embrace it. Your pride tempts you to let go as if it is as invaluable as a splinter, but then defends it with all their strength like it's the tree of eternal life. The more crooked your life of sin, the more places your pride has to hide and hunt you."

My pride told me there was nobody more important in my life than myself. My pride told me I could celebrate my friends' successes so long as they were less successful than me. My pride told me I needed to own the room at whatever the cost—there are owners and there are others—so forming a partnership was for the weak. My pride told me to use my gifts solely to promote my own kingdom until I got exactly what I wanted, thus becoming perfectly happy. All my life had been spent trying to make my name larger than His, to make myself the lord of my life. I hadn't even graduated from my teenage years, and I was exhausted.

Coming to such a conclusion I realized I had just met the God-man, Jesus, who Jeff, Mike, and JP were raving about. A few weeks before I set sail Jeff boldly invited me to live in a house of Catholic men the following school year. I declined his offer with something along the lines of, "Dude, I just lived in the fraternity house, that's way too extreme of a jump." A wave of disappointment crashed over me as I thought: *Damn, I blew my spot.* But just as quickly I thought: *If God wants me in this house, He'll make another spot.*

I needed to get ahold of Jeff immediately, so I purchased a calling card from the front desk. This card allowed me to place a call anywhere in the world from the corded phone in my cabin that had remained dormant all semester. I dialed my special number into the phone, but my spirits fell when the machine operator told me the lines were full. I ran back to the front desk and learned that only four people on board could be on the phone at the same time. Four people! Their advice was to continue dialing over and over in hopes that I would eventually be pushed through after somebody on the ship hung up.

After my thirty-second attempt my call was put through. I had never been so enraptured to hear the dial tone in my life. Five rings later I was directed to Jeff Crock's voicemail box, as to be expected considering we were on complete opposite time zones. I knew there was no guarantee I would get in the house, but I left a voicemail: "Hey, Jeff, it's Johnny Vrba...I'm not sure if you will get this message and I know you won't recognize this number because I am using a corded phone off the coast of Mauritius sailing to God knows where. But...I'm calling because I want a spot in that house you were talking about—I know I don't have all the details but if there's a spot I'm all in!"

Flexibility—Final Boss

"Whenever you do a thing, act as if all the world were watching."
—Thomas Jefferson

"THIS VOYAGE IS about to turn into a cruise," Dean Gene said gloomily in our Mauritius post-port reflection group. Making the fundamental switch from an intentional voyage to a lackadaisical cruise, I realized how thin of ice our ship was sailing on. We were back out to sea and headed for South Africa, but everyone knew the chances of our voyage continuing as planned were slim to none. Dean Gene speculated we wouldn't see many more ports. Instead we would finish all our classes early, and then try to make ship life as fun as possible. But ship life was already fun... if you wanted it to be.

After our session Angela and I spoke again about remaining optimistic in our situation. I said, "You know, at the beginning of the voyage I was very optimistic, but now I am far from confident about our future. I've just decided to choose joy." We shared a hug and Angela told me how much my presence has meant to our reflection group and her own perception of our voyage.

Leaving the union I saw a few students posing for a photo with a sign that read, "128, The World **Still** Awaits!" I chuckled at the modification of our tagline and then I thought back to day fourteen when I took headshots of as many of my shipmates as possible. Why did I start taking photos of people so early on? Did I jinx it?

The next afternoon I was on my way to meet the squad for lunch when I realized I forgot what it felt like to lose my balance. Apparently, others had a similar issue resulting in a few lost lunches on the carpeted entrance of Berlin. Walking past the library I saw a student who had created a petition with a couple hundred signatures for our voyage to end in Casablanca rather than Amsterdam. The hope was that the virus would be less of a threat to us in Casablanca rather than one of the largest travel hubs in Europe, the Netherlands. I did not sign, trusting the captain and the leadership's decisions.

In the afternoon I went to war with Professor Russ's final exam. Knowing his teaching style the class did not anticipate receiving a study guide. A week earlier it was like the heavens above opened up when we received a seamail titled "Study Guide." But I'm afraid we were even more intimidated staring into his 11,348-word document.

> Day 65 | Mar 9, 2020: Rather than the classic "take one and pass it back" Russ handed out every exam individually and repeated the same menacing, "Guud laak!"

Flexibility—Final Boss

By the end of the exam, my metacognition couldn't tell me if I had gotten an A or an F. Leaving the Four Seasons dining room, I headed up a few decks for a breath of fresh air and bumped into Scott Marshall, the CEO of Semester at Sea, on the pool deck. I immediately asked to steal some of his time, and he obliged. We pulled two chairs up to a small table and through a bit of conversation I learned that he was also an SAE! We shared a few stories and Scott made a point that "The voyagers of the one hundred and twenty-eighth Semester at Sea are currently being equipped with some of the most valuable skills which they will use for the rest of their lives, especially *flexibility*." I ended by honoring Scott for handling himself so well in the union the night before.

Now, Scott was not on board our ship all semester. To help diminish uncertainty and provide transparency from HQ back in Colorado, SAS flew Scott to the opposite side of the world while we were gallivanting around Mauritius. This may have been the only time COVID required an in-person meeting. The library even pre-popped dozens of bags of popcorn for the fiasco that was going to be this discussion after cringing through our last emergency meeting.

Once again, the questions flew across the room like gunfire, someone launching a bazooka here and there. He was like a juggernaut absorbing shot after shot. I was extremely impressed with his composure. The entire ship was on offence looking to score on him all night, but Scott defended SAS and its priorities without drawing a foul. At the end of the meeting Scott offered one-on-one time with anyone who still had further questions, assuring nobody's voice was left unheard.

Funny enough Scott had just assumed the position of CEO earlier that year—what impeccable timing. Passionate about the success of our voyage but also understanding the incredible effects our extensive on-ship time was going to have, Scott's dedication to our community was unwavering.

The sixty-sixth day of our voyage only six members of the squad showed up to eat together in Lido before heading downstairs for global studies. The vibe in the dining room had never been so low. Nic, of course, did his best to make light of the situation with jokes to which people responded, "Not now, Nic, not now."

Everyone was acting like our voyage was going to end tomorrow but we had an entire month to go! Still processing the mood of the ship in the union, I felt the urge to sit up on the balcony. Nobody else wanted to join me but I made the move anyway. The union looked oddly different one deck higher. Like any other global studies class, Michael pranced around the stage lecturing about the virus. He explained how the coronavirus's name comes from the Latin word *corona*, meaning *crown*, and if you were to look at the virus under a microscope, it looks like it's wearing a crown.

A few minutes into his lecture a very faint chatter started amongst the class. It was so soft I thought it was coming from someone's device. But moments later it was obvious the mumbling was coming from humans as I watched my class turn and whisper into their neighbor's ear. There was nobody else on the balcony, so I remained quiet until the chatter caught Michael's attention. The banter became so loud that he stopped lecturing altogether, saying, "What could possibly be going on out there?" A student in the front row shot up from her chair and said, "See for yourself," handing her laptop up to Michael on stage.

Flexibility—Final Boss

If someone were to have dropped a pin in the time between Michael's hand gripped her MacBook, and the first word out of his mouth, it would have sounded like a Hydro Flask on concrete. Michael looked at the screen and took in a sharp, shaky deep breath like when a doctor has their stethoscope on your back. I thought: *This has got to be another itinerary update, but I pray it's just something funny.* "OH FUCK!" Michael yelped, shattering the silence.

My pupils dilated, I gripped my chair tight, and slowly stretched my neck forward. Michael continued, "Whelp... I am afraid this lecture cannot continue... this is the email we've been waiting for... our voyage will terminate in four days in South Africa."

I let my head down into my lap as pandemonium broke out. Roaring screams of agony ricocheted off every wall, while shouts of joy pierced me like a double-edged sword. The news had such a polarizing response that I could hardly process the information for myself. My face showed no expression, but inside turmoil wreaked havoc on my heart. To call this moment stressful was to say almost nothing.

> Day 66 | Mar 10, 2020: When I heard the news, I couldn't feel anything. I think it's because I was feeling everything.

First, I was shocked; I figured we might not make it to Europe, but the southernmost tip of Africa was damn near the opposite side of the world. Second, I was furious how anyone could rejoice at such news. Third, I was nervous about what my life would look like after SAS. Fourth, I was depressed that the adventure of a lifetime with my friends was going to end with such a short runway for goodbyes. Finally, and by far the hardest to detect, I was at peace, because the unknown was finally known.

As Michael promised his lecture did not continue. Instead, he gave us a thirty-minute motivational speech. Not a single person shifted in their seat as Michael poured his heart out on stage. He opened up to us unlike anything we had ever seen, describing how this semester had been the most challenging of his teaching career. As hard as it was trying to learn in such an ambiguous environment, I couldn't imagine trying to teach in it. He asked for forgiveness for the lack of clarity regarding global studies exams and assignments which had been deteriorating his reputation. We forgave him and more. Michael began to break down and praised 128 for being the greatest, shortest voyage of all time.

"We must not define our experience by what we saw, but rather what we learned." Michael agreed we had a ship full of Gumbys—everyone had become masterfully flexible. Choking up and unable to continue on Michael ended his address with, "I love you all!" and if you weren't already crying, you were now.

I had never witnessed a professor be so vulnerable and I really wish it didn't have to take an epidemic to do so. And an epidemic we hoped it would remain—there were already rumors of the CDC potentially upgrading its classification.

Leaving class the ship was baptized in tears. If the other itinerary updates were a slap in the face, our voyages termination felt like I jumped in front of a bullet train. All of the other changes didn't affect the amount of time I had with the squad. In fact, they actually added to it! Since I had prebooked a SAS-sponsored field program in every country prior to the voyage, I wouldn't have been able to spend much time with the squad if I was on excursions all day in China, Malaysia, India, Ghana, and Morocco. Our extra time in Vietnam and Mauritius allowed me to spend time with the squad that would have otherwise been spent almost entirely on field programs. During our original six days in Vietnam I would have spent three fighting for my life in Cambodia, and our day in Mauritius whining down a waterfall.

This most recent update was the first one to take time away from my friends, not just by a few days, but over a month! The cherry on top of being kicked off the ship so early was missing out on the crew talent show and the alumni ball, two staples of Semester at Sea tradition. It seemed as if any sense of closure was becoming a fantasy.

Processing what my transition back to "real life" would be like, my soul was screaming like a jet engine, so I decided to seek out counseling for the first time in my life. Fortunately, it's free on Semester at Sea, so setting up an appointment was a breeze. However, walking into the room was a far more daunting task as I stared at the door and tried to collect my thoughts. I was nervous. I had no idea what happened in these types of conversations. The evil one whispered in my ear, "You are so weak. You can't even help yourself. Have fun venting your problems to a stranger to make you feel better."

Pulling together the courage to step through the door I was greeted with a warm smile, worn by a woman named Marvel. And what a fitting name she had.

"What's up!" she said buoyantly.

Her enthusiasm lifted my spirits right away. I quickly learned Marvel did not believe we were all on the same boat, rather experiencing the same storm. Some of our boats were sailing strong as ever, others were taking on water, and a few were capsized.

Marvel wanted to know how I was faring in these rough waters. She had seen me running around the ship all semester, so I was nervous she was going to think I had been operating behind a facade. But I was in her office, so it was time to spill the tea that had been fermenting in my brain all semester.

For the next thirty minutes, I threw up the contents of my heart onto Marvel's lap. I gave her my backstory, what I was feeling in that moment, and how Weston's words were amplified when he spoke into my life. I rubbed my shaved head as I retold the story of Neptune Day. Then I shared about how my ego threw a wrench between Nic and I's relationship. And finally how I ended up selfishly leading on Ashley the entire voyage.

Once Marvel was up to speed on my SAS experience we jumped back to my life before the voyage. We talked about my fraternity brothers and our lifestyle. Marvel was not surprised to hear that nearly every single one of my female friends came with benefits. Everything in me wanted to keep that inside, but I knew that meant it needed revealing. Admitting this to Marvel each swallow felt like a marble down my throat. I had never shared my lifestyle to any respectable adult, especially female, because it was "man's business." This dark and dusty drawer of my life had never seen the light of day. I reached in, clumped together the tangled string of thoughts inside my head, found an end, and surgically untied the knot.

Everybody's thirsty, and we all drink somewhere. For some its booze, others clothes, and for me it was women. Sure, I binge drank on occasion and felt the effects the next morning, but thirsting after hookups every weekend left me parched. I assumed that drawing from the same well enough times would eventually quench my thirst, but the well wasn't drying up, my

Flexibility—Final Boss

heart was. The lifestyle that culture put on a pedestal was actually a sinkhole.

You could fit all of my shipmates in a single classroom at ASU. It was so easy to feel less responsible for my actions back in Tempe. At one of the largest schools in the world being a small fish oftentimes comes with small repercussions; the gravity of my actions shrunk against the sheer size of the campus. Or maybe my actions just seemed less bad compared to the debauchery happening all around me. Semester at Sea put everything under a microscope, exposing much more than my bondage to my phone. Since our community was tighter than Arnold Schwarzenegger during yoga, sleeping around was not really as acceptable as it was back in the desert. My fellow voyagers might disagree with me on this, but they also didn't attend Arizona State University. For me, making decisions on SAS started with, "Would anyone have a problem if I did this?" as opposed to "Will anyone know I did this?" at ASU.

Extrapolating on Warren Buffett's front-of-the-newspaper test, if I were to write down every single thing I did each day and publish each chapter as a day in my life, would I be excited to sell the book? Maybe to a stranger, but there's no amount of money a relative could buy it from me. So why was I living in such darkness? Why couldn't I share every part of my day with my family? Was it because they weren't cool enough and wouldn't understand my lifestyle or was I just downright ashamed?

Marvel was still listening attentively, I could tell by the way she sat in her chair. She honored me for my vulnerability and trust in her. I finally took a breath and let Marvel speak into my life.

"Well, Johnny, it sounds like you need a backbone."

I jerked up from the terrible posture I was holding in my chair. *Did she really just say that?* Ding ding ding. Marvel rang my bell. Her first punch of the bout was so hard it didn't knock me down, it stood me up! And just like that, round one was over, but Marvel and I scheduled round two for tomorrow.

On my way out the door, frustrated I hadn't given Marvel more time to speak I asked, "How did you get so good at listening?"

"Well, when you're talking, you're not learning, and I like to learn," she replied merrily.

Stepping out of Marvel's office I had a strange inkling to find a quiet place and watch the ocean, so I obeyed. I found a seat near the aft, plopped down, and looked out. The moon was high, reflecting off the water just enough that I could faintly see the sea's whitecaps tackling each other. I pulled out my rosary and just held it in my hands while I let the weight of the day sink in.

> Day 66 | Mar 10, 2020: There have never been more extreme ebbs and flows in a day than today. The only thought that's been consistent is that *I am human*.

The morning felt like the entire sea was being poured over my head. Marvel helped put a regulator in my mouth so I could breathe again, and now, sitting there beginning to pray, the sea rushing over my head was now only a puddle of salty tears at my feet. I used to think praying was a good idea, but now I know it's a great one.

Dear Reader,

"I am not afraid of storms, for I am learning how to sail my ship."
—Louisa May Alcott

Day 67 | Mar 11, 2020: This afternoon the Voice announced that the CDC upgraded the coronavirus epidemic to a pandemic classification.

FOR LACK OF A better phrase, shit just got real. We were alive, just sailing past Madagascar during a *pandemic*. That word had so much weight to it when we heard it for the first time. Everyone in my immediate vicinity looked up at the speaker as if it had just foretold their death. The convenience of having the news read aloud to us overhead paradoxically left us wildly uninformed. I thought of my mom, so I seamailed her that everyone on board was safe and healthy. She shot me right back and said that the virus had already been brought back to ASU in January. I couldn't believe it. Students piled into the library searching for information about the most recent news.

"Thirty-six hours?" a student yelped. This was the total travel time it would take them to get home from South Africa. Both SAS and ASU instructed me to book my flight immediately after we ported in Cape Town. Since ASU already had a confirmed COVID case, staying in South Africa was technically safer than going home—the only worry was getting stuck there.

Once again, I was stressed out of my mind before entering Marvel's office, but this time I couldn't wait to burst through the door and continue rolling the elephant off my back. Since our last meeting less than twenty-four hours ago, I typed out a document listing all of the things I wanted to start and stop doing moving forward. Marvel made a point that as wonderful as these adjustments were going to be in my life and those around me, I couldn't make them standing still. To change my life, I needed to move away from the people/things/places leading me to darkness.

Aware of how serious our conversation was becoming I desperately tried to lighten the mood. "So, life is like a jet ski, you can't change directions if you're not on the throttle?" I asked.

"Precisely, but they also say it's impossible to frown on one, and I'm afraid my wrinkles might get even worse if I never stopped smiling," Marvel joked.

We shared a laugh, but my smile collapsed as Marvel began to outline the harsh reality I was soon to face back home. If I was a product of the five people I surrounded myself with, were those people positively contributing to my life? Well, they were my best friends—I know that they care about me, but to what

Dear Reader,

extent? How was I going to walk away from the guys I had been running with my first two years of college? Even if I despised the thing we were running toward, turning around now felt harder than stopping a locomotive by blowing at it.

A wave of doubt came over me and the father of lies barked in my ear, "You'll never be able to change, you're in too deep, but if you do, they will all say, 'We miss the old Johnny!' You're going to lose all your friends."

These thoughts depressed me. I just wanted to get home and disprove all those lies as quickly as possible, but I knew there was some truth in his final line. Marvel brought me back to the present and assured me I had already begun the fight. The ugliness I had kept in the dark for so long was finally brought into the light where it's hideousness was revealed. When I took my first step into her office, trumpets blared declaring war against the devil, and I took heart knowing God already secured the dub.

I told Marvel I wanted a platform to share this good news and to tell the world I was done using others as a means to an end and start giving myself to no end. I desired to share our conversations hoping it might help someone else, but Marvel reminded me that the greatest work to be done was inside my own heart. She kept my ask in the back of her pocket as the bell rang ending round two.

I was pent-up with energy as I made my way up to the basketball court to burn off some steam. My Birkenstocks failed me for the first time when I juked and ripped a strap going one-on-one with Nic. While we competed the squad began to gather at a table below on the pool deck. Joining our friends we sat around the table sweating and sulking. We were so blinded, feeling bad for ourselves that afternoon, we could not see we were actually the luckiest people in the world. When our pity party was over, we made a coherent commitment. Since ambiguity had walked the plank, it was crystal clear our number-one priority was to spend time with each other, so we vowed to stay awake for as many of the remaining seventy-two hours we had together as possible.

The following day our last global studies class took the form of a panel where all three professors reviewed the highlights of the semester. I heard that Jimmy tore out a scratch sheet of paper in the earlier session, wrote "BLITZ THE FRITZ!", took a picture, then airdropped it to everyone within range. The Fritz was the bar I was kicked out of on day one, but unfortunately the movement didn't gain any momentum.

When I got to class, it was packed to the brim unlike I had seen it all semester. When Scott finished his speech, he symbolically handed over an inflatable Earth beach ball for the next generation to take care of. Making its way around the room, we all signed the globe and then threw it back on stage for Scott to take home. What a phenomenal souvenir. Then, Sue brought the house down by executing one of her famous lullabies.

Shortly after class the Voice came on overhead. "President Trump has just restricted all travel from Europe into the United States."

Those who had connecting flights in Europe dropped to the floor with worry. The majority of the ship was already down there anyway, sprawling out to sign each other's world maps. This was SAS's rendition of yearbook signing. I felt like an eighty-year-old man getting off the floor for my final marketing class.

Dear Reader,

I arrived a few minutes early and wrote "Lance is a legend -->" on the mobile whiteboard at the front of the room. Everyone came in as usual and mumbled to each other about the sign. Like I planned, Lance strolled in without looking at the whiteboard and stood exactly where he always does allowing the arrow to point directly at his head. A few minutes into class Lance had yet to notice, and the class was wheezing as they whipped out their phones to take pictures.

"What? Do I look that good today?" Lance questioned.

Lance followed all of the fingers that were pointing beside him, and everyone erupted with applause. He blushed and stopped the class just to smile at us. It was a moment of pure bliss. I am certain all of us would have been content just smiling back at Lance for the remainder of the class. I wish every professor/teacher/leader's smile could convey the deep sense of appreciation Lance's did for us that afternoon.

> Day 68 | Mar 12, 2020: Lance smiled at us today the way Robin Williams did to his class at the end of Dead Poets Society.

Heading back to my cabin to start packing, I bumped into Marvel. Her smile was radiating, and she came bearing news.

"Remember that platform you wanted? You're live in a few hours!"

"LET'S GO!"

The counseling team on board created an event in the union for students to share what they are taking home from Semester at Sea. All I wanted was a platform to share my experiences and now I had a stage. I punted packing until tomorrow and began typing out what I was going to say. My testimony came out of me in a single stream of consciousness but reading it back I realized it was too raw. Too raw or too real? This was unlike anything I had ever shared publicly, so the devil growled, "Everyone is going to think you've been putting on your happy face when you drop this bombshell!"

Trying to shake off those thoughts I started memorizing my speech so I could deliver it in a personal way. But a few minutes in I was already struggling. I would always say the easy lines and skip over the hard ones. I feared bringing my notes on stage because I was talking about my own life, so why should I need a script? I decided I was just going to take my notes with me, that way I would say *everything* I wanted to say.

Time got away from me, so I quickly threw on my dress clothes and ran to celebrate Jimmy's birthday in the fancy dining room. He knew about my event but insisted that I come to dinner even if I couldn't stay the entire time. I was doing great on time after finishing my salad, but the main course was taking quite a while. I feared leaving before my entrée arrived would be unforgivable, but I was out of time. I waited a moment longer before I stood up, apologized, and sprinted over to the union.

Showing up right at the start of the event Marvel thought I had gotten cold feet. I forgot to tell her about Jimmy's dinner. The squad was already sitting front row, so I joined them as Marvel invited the first student on stage. After listening to three students share their testimonies, the butterflies in my stomach had mutated into falcons. Normally I would channel my butterflies into a source of motivation but these birds seemed untamable.

"And for our final speaker of the night, we have Johnny Vrba here to share his story," Marvel announced.

Dear Reader,

Simply standing up was challenging because the falcons laid bowling ball sized eggs in my stomach. Those same steps I had walked up many times before felt stories high as I made my way above the audience. The silence was deafening as I stood center stage, holding the same red muffed microphone I had screamed into all semester. Paralyzed with fear, the prince of darkness tried one final attack: "Why are you sharing all of this? Your words mean nothing! Nobody even cares!"

I took a deep breath, stomped on his neck, gripped the mic, and brought darkness into the light.

"Dear Shipboard Community,

"It turns out that I came to Semester at Sea with a heck of a lot more than just my blond hair and some luggage. I had much more baggage than I ever could have imagined. Let me set the scene. I am currently a sophomore studying at Arizona State University. During my freshman year, I became a founding father of a fraternity, through which has given me some of the greatest moments of my life. From summiting Mount Kilimanjaro to winning thirty thousand dollars in a dance competition for charity, I lived experiences beyond my wildest dreams for which I am forever grateful.

"However, my semester away from binge drinking and the high of chasing women has made me realize that way of life was not only robbing me of happiness, but who I was altogether. This shipboard community has opened my eyes to raw and authentic relationships that I quite honestly haven't had since grade school. The relationships I was able to form in just three incredibly short months have been deeper and more meaningful than I ever could've dreamt. Our culture, defined by flakey friend groups, is in deep need of genuine community. My circles back home act like they have brotherhood when they've hardly got friendship, and that's an incredibly sad and shocking pill to swallow. As I return to campus, I am eager to forward the good news that life is far more rich without the numbness of alcohol, drugs, hookups, and the facade of social media. Although we live within this culture, we do not have to succumb to its incredibly low standard of living.

"I am also going home with a brand-new meaning of the word *masculinity*. My previous view of masculinity told me that men don't share their deepest feelings with one another. That the strongest men make it all happen on their own. That the more sex you have the more of a man you are. The love I have experienced on this ship has helped me to grow instead of perpetuating pathetic pastimes. If we were to have visited every single country this semester, I'm not sure I would have reconnected with my true self. I am a firm believer that everything happens for a reason, and I could not be more grateful for our time spent at sea. Thank you so much and may God bless you all!"

My falcons, now flying in formation, carried me off the stage and into the embrace of the squad. I started to weep as the pressure of the group hug increased with each pair of arms. I squeezed Meg Jay whose '30 is not the new 20' Ted Talk is among the most viewed of all time, and who had just given an incredible keynote the night before. By the time I reached Marvel and her husband Chris I was bawling my eyes out. Hysterically crying over Marvel's shoulder she patted my back and whispered, "It's going to

Dear Reader,

be okay."

It's pretty hard to kick a bad habit or lifestyle on your own. It's pretty cool when you have people all over the world encouraging and praying for you. I'm convinced if you want to stop or start doing something...

let it be known.

Holy Spirit!

*"The day I started believing in Jesus
was the day I stopped believing in coincidences."*
—*Unknown*

OUR SECOND TO LAST day on the ship Jake and I rose at the break of dawn and conspired about what rules we could break knowing we'd be kicked off in less than forty-eight hours anyway. Something we both dreamed of from the beginning was flying the drone from the top deck—a felony as far as Captain Kostas was concerned. Drones were a prohibited item on board but Jake snuck his on anyway. It was like insulin to a diabetic, he *needed* it.

Up on the top deck, Jake calibrated his drone while I cleared the area and scouted for any movement. A few minutes later I signaled all clear, but Jake was having major complications achieving ready-to-fly status because of all the metal around us.

Holy Spirit!

Seldom does a seasoned pilot fly before their drone was ready and aware of its surroundings, but this was our only chance. We were going to fly no matter what.

Just before taking off Jake handed me a winter glove in case I needed to make a game-saving catch. With a jolt of excitement Jake pressed his thumbs into both of the joysticks of his controller. Holding our breath we watched the drone rise three feet into the air, but then, as if possessed by a demon, it made a beeline for one of the metal poles in front of us. Like a game of pinball the drone collided with four of the metal poles surrounding the deck. We were astonished it was still in the air. One final ricochet sent the drone in the direction of the pool. Inches before reaching the water one of the arms got lodged between a wooden pool chair slamming the drone down onto the deck.

Jake and I screeched, "That was totally wicked!"

By the time afternoon rolled around we were experiencing the greatest weather all semester. Dry heat in the high seventies called for a relaxing day lounging at the pool. The weather was so good a few of my fellow shipmates thanked God.

> Day 69 | Mar 13, 2020: No matter how gray some of us may have felt inside, there was no sadness that couldn't be unlocked by the power of the Son.

As evening fell, the squad dressed up for pictures on the pool deck before our last dinner together. We were one big family, but when it came to traveling, we were definitely not cheaper by the dozen. The background of our photos was photobombed by the southernmost tip of Africa, Cape Agulhas. This rocky headland was also the dividing line between the Atlantic and Indian

Oceans, which meant we sailed in three of the four major oceans in the world. Being so far south I figured we might as well continue down and check out Antarctica—our ship was ice rated so technically it was possible.

Before our final logistical pre-port meeting the kitchen threw the best they had our way. We were spoiled with cheeseburgers, ice cream, and three glasses of champagne which put everyone in a coma. During dinner and against the "better" judgment of the world, the squad mapped out our travel plans in South Africa. Our itinerary was *unreal*. Our families desperately wanted us to come home but understood the value of spending a few days together to cap off the nuttiest semester of our lives.

While the thirteen of us got situated in the union for pre-port, Ashley mentioned that her professor, Meg Jay, brought up my testimony during their last positive psychology class. Hearing this fixed my cheeks into a permanent smile I couldn't remove the remainder of the evening. This time, the leadership team took the stage to a massive round of applause before sharing their closing remarks and safety tips for our travels home. Our ship doctor, Mark, performed a dance for us with Kim, one of the nurses. Dean Sue cried through her speech so a handful of students followed her up by performing a comedy sketch to lighten the mood.

After the show, I stuck around to show my unopened seasickness patches to Kim. On the very first day of our voyage I told her that I would not touch them the entire semester, to which she scoffed. Kim took the box from me to inspect the packaging and confirmed that I had kept my word. I made a Tiger Woods-esque fist bump and Kim pulled out a Spiderman sticker, which of course was the official reward for earning your sea legs. Proudly slapping it on my chest I ran back to my cabin and threw all my remaining snacks into one of my rolling suitcases and pulled it throughout the ship like some sort of spring Santa Claus. I cringed as I handed out all my goodies that I couldn't take home, remembering how much time my mom spent calculating the amount of snacks I would need. At least none of them went to waste!

The ship played board games and cards throughout the night, and I finished an entire jar of Jif peanut butter in the process, adding a few more pounds of peanut butter to the more than two thousand our ship consumed over the past three months. Holding true to our promise to stay up as long as possible with each other, not many of us got more than an hour or two of shut-eye as we held each other tight for the grand finale tomorrow.

My body was exhausted but my mind was running at full speed on the morning of day seventy, our last full day aboard the ship. The fog was so thick Captain Kostas was forced to wait it out because the visibility made it unsafe to dock.

> Day 70 | Mar 14, 2020: It was almost like Mother Nature was fighting against the virus, allowing us to spend a few extra hours together. Some of us had never been so happy not being able to pull into port! Oh the irony!

Every single second was as precious as the toothpaste at the end of the tube. We gave every second the respect we gave a year.

Soon the fog began to rise, and we watched the sun shine on the *MV World Odyssey* for the last time as Captain Kostas safely brought our campus to its final resting position. We would no longer move again. Once the crew had secured our 22,496-ton home to the dock using a dozen nylon ropes, it was time for the famous ship photo.

The shipboard community filled every nook and cranny of the aft and smiled at the dock below for a photo that will withstand the test of time. Waiting for everyone to find the camera, I held "cheeeeeeeeeese" for several minutes—which dwarfed the agonizing amount of time my dad needed to take a picture. That was the largest group photo I had ever been a part of. There are very few instances when one thousand heads are all looking at the same camera.

After the photo, Jake and I went up to deck nine to hang out. We amused ourselves by reenacting how we met each other on that glorious afternoon seventy days ago. I leaned back on the same barstool, and Jake came whizzing around the corner. "Jake!" This time I added, "Can you believe we're going to become best friends?"

Jake responded, "No way! Can you believe were going to sail into a pandemic?"

It was a nostalgic moment and after sharing a few much-needed laughs, Jake showed me his finished Mauritius edit. Now, I have watched a fair amount of travel videos in my day, and I've been making them since I was fourteen, but none had ever made me shed a tear. Jake's video had that power. If a picture was worth a thousand words, then a video cannot be expressed with any.

The ship spent the remainder of the afternoon signing each other's world maps—there was such an abundance of Sharpies

Holy Spirit!

I basically got high walking into the library. In need of some fresh air I made my way to the aft of deck seven to work out. During one of my breaks I walked over to the wood guardrail for a breather and leaned over the side. Coming home to an air-conditioned gym was going to be quite the downgrade. Even if it meant having more than fifty square feet to work with.

Back in my cabin with all of my things I said a final goodbye to Jimmy and left my cabin for the last time. I embraced everyone in sight, and I could tell whether I was saying goodbye or see you later based on the duration of the hug. I squeezed the deans, my professors, Marvel, and then one of the mothers on the ship, Steph.

Steph told me I had no idea the impact I made on our voyage with the children in particular. She retold memories as if she was reading straight from my journal, events I knew she was not even present for! Then, Steph backed up herself up by airdropping me a picture she had taken in secret of me working out with Finn. "I never meant to share this with you, but I had a feeling you'd love to see it!"

Boy, did I! (I'd add that photo to this book along with many others, but it was way too expensive, if you'd like to see them text me 630-605-2110!)

It's a terrific feeling when you think you've got all the photos from an experience, and then someone shares one you had no idea existed. A few minutes away from stepping off the ship I watched students leaving with more luggage than they came with, except for Jimmy who strolled off with a quarter of his original haul. I ran over the mental list in my head of those I had not seen off yet. I was worried that every person I missed would somehow prevent me from experiencing closure. Then, right on cue, John turned the corner, with his arms wide.

To this day, I still wonder if John saw all of this coming considering the way he raced through his questions the first day we met. Approaching the end of his life, John did not live like the majority of his generation wasting away at country clubs and seeking every conceivable comfort money can buy. John, in his old age, decided to travel the world, which was an infinitely riskier endeavor for him than for a healthy teenager. Retiring was never John's plan, rather he was reenergizing.

John said everyone had the mindset that we must travel and see the world as fast as we can while we're young, but the world wasn't going anywhere. And as much as John loved travel, he loved home more than anything. He understood that there is a family underwhelmed and unappreciative with their life in the Midwest hoping to get to Paris for the thrills of big city life, just like the Parisian family longs for a bigger house, less noise, and a yard.

I knew I would be making connections with students on SAS, but never in a million years did I imagine bonding with anyone four times my age. Folks like John are bursting at the seams with incredible stories and wisdom, and all we have to do is run with scissors every once in a while. If you don't know whether or not to start a conversation, gray hair is usually a great sign, the whiter the better.

"It's been an absolute pleasure getting to know you, Johnny."

"Right back atcha, young man," I replied.

"I know you've been keeping a daily journal, every good man does. You'll look back on it for the rest of your life."

I held John with wet cheeks embarrassed thinking *real men*

don't cry. But John reassured me, "Real men have real emotions." John always said someone could write a book with all his wisdom, I'm sure he'd do it himself if he could sit down long enough. Would someone please send him a copy?

Now it was my turn to walk off the vessel that had allowed me to experience every kind of emotion. With my friends close behind the whole gang made their way off the gangway, but just before stepping onto South Africa I took a deep breath and thanked God for our voyage. I was only a summer away from moving into a house of fourteen Catholic guys. *Was Catholicism even the truth?* I had been pondering this question all voyage being surrounded by so many winsome non-denominationals.

While every drawer in my mind seemed to fly open, we posed for our last group photo next to the ship and I thought back to all the "first times" of the voyage. There were many; in fact, I used that phrase forty-nine times throughout this book and I'm about to use it once more.

For the *first time* all semester, I flipped through the pages of my journal I had been so diligently filling. I didn't realize how much I actually wrote down. Right before getting into bed, every day, I would set aside thirty minutes to decompress and document what happened. Ninety-nine percent of the time I was exhausted and had to fight hard just to sit down and write. On those days when I couldn't find energy to begin, like the Sea Olympics, I would just journal first thing the next morning. I wrote over a page every single day of the semester with the longest entry taking up five. I figured that I would have more to write about in-country but the longest entries were always from days on the ship.

Now it was time to sit down and write my final entry of the

voyage, but as I started writing something incredible happened.

My pen died.

My ballpoint pen I had been using all semester, the same pen I could have easily substituted for another at any point of the voyage, ran out of ink. I wrote down the final events of the semester and my pen wrote its last words as if it were destiny. I immediately thought back to the machete breaking in Vietnam. I've never been able to hold on to a pen long enough to see it die, so keeping one while traveling around the world was a miracle on its own. But out of all the pens in the world with all varying capacities of ink, I chose the pen that helped me journal from my first day meeting Jimmy in San Diego to stepping off the ship in South Africa.

Of all the people who've had their ink run out since the creation of the pen, I am fairly confident I was the happiest anyone has ever been. However, laughing over my joy I discovered an even more miraculous revelation. From the first day I landed in San Diego to disembarking in Cape Town, I created seventy-three journal entries, one per day. You know what other work has seventy-three books in total? The Catholic Bible. But still, it gets even crazier! Then I counted the books of the Old Testament to be forty-six, leaving twenty-seven in the new. My journal fell out of my hands when I counted forty-six days at sea, leaving twenty-seven days on land!

Just a few fortunate strokes of serendipity?

Fluke?

Or was it God's providential arrangement of circumstances?

When was I going to stop telling myself all of this was a coincidence and that it happened *on purpose*? I believe God knew I'd number the days of my voyage and discover they were synony-

Holy Spirit!

mous with the books of my greater story. If He has numbered the hairs on my head, He has numbered the days of my semester at sea. The squad, who stuck together through the thick and thin, amounted to twelve courageous souls, as did God's squad. Once again, I was overwhelmed with satisfaction similar to the night-water I had experienced before. So there I was, with my journal and a dead pen in hand. I closed my eyes and for the first time all semester nothing came to mind. My first thought came upon me in the form of a question.

Are there ever any coincidences?

~~~~~~

I was exhilarated to have read through my entire journal! Closing my manuscript I looked out the plane window to see the Chicago skyline, which sent a warmth down my body like a bowl of soup. I desperately searched for the energy to grab my bag from the overhead compartment. When I stood up my head was as light as a feather. After waiting a nauseating amount of time I was once again the last man standing at the baggage claim. I simply didn't have the brain power to comprehend where on earth my bag could have been. I tried to retrace my steps in my head as I do every time I lose something, but it's much harder when you're not the one who lost it.

I took a long deep breath. I could feel oxygen filling every nook and cranny of my lungs. Then, like a poorly thrown curveball, it hit me. My bag had flown on a completely different flight. Hobbling back over to the screens it appeared that the previous flight from Newark was unloaded at baggage claim seven. Just two claims down, I found my enormous bag circling around all alone; she must have been as dizzy as I was!

I thrusted the fifty-plus-pound bag off the belt and onto the floor which made me lose my breath. When I bent down to lift up the handle the blood rushing to my head almost pushed me over. *I think I'm about to die.* With all my luggage in hand I was bombarded by some of the strangest questions my conscience has ever asked.

Will my parents remember what I look like?

What kind of car do they drive?

The Windy City blew straight through me as I stepped through the automatic doors. Lifting my head to cross the street I locked eyes with both my parents. Approaching them at the fastest speed my legs would allow, my mom threw up her hands to distance herself. The rest of the life inside me was abruptly sucked out.

The back seat of our SUV had been quarantine-proofed with tarps, gloves, and a buffet of hand sanitizers. This was my first internal car wash. After the stinging sensation of Purell had cleared out my sinuses, I caught a clear whiff of food somewhere in the car. Like Mary Poppins, my mom whipped out a large Portillos bag out of thin air (the greatest food on earth). My stomach instantly stopped shuddering—I became full at the sight of it. The most depressing moment was realizing I was too tired to chew my roast beef sandwich.

On our drive home on the I-88 not many words were exchanged. I was away for so long I began to question why we drove on the wrong side of the road. My parents continually gave me permission to feel all kinds of emotions, but inside I felt

Holy Spirit!

pretty numb. In and out of sleep and fits of tears, I rested my head on the window and tried to stop thinking all together. But I couldn't. I had just conquered the world but now I couldn't even conquer my favorite food.

The curb into my driveway felt like a small crater. Stepping out of the car my house looked like it had grown substantially. Before going inside, my mom bluntly laid out some new ground rules. There was already a section of the house designated only for me. I was to stay in those areas and not touch anything outside of them. Food would be served with rubber gloves and conversations held on opposite sides of the room. The only person allowed inside my bedroom was myself. After two weeks, maybe we could talk about sharing a hug. I was heartbroken, and my parents were too. So *this is real life*, I thought.

Pressing my wrist downward on the handle while using my foot to push open the front door, I stepped into my home at 18:35 Central Standard Time, a total of thirty-eight and a half hours after stepping out of my stay in Cape Town. My final travel day truly was the cherry on top to a Semester at Sea during the COVID-19 pandemic.

~~~~~~

Afterword

WHELP, THAT WAS FUN! I hope you enjoyed *Seas the Day*, but I also hope its not the best book you've ever read (if it is you need to read more). I pray that *Seas the Day* encourages you to pick up THE book. The one that's got almost a million words and has been printed 5,000,000,000 times and is probably not too far from you at this current moment.

As selfish as this may sound, writing this book has done far more for me than it probably did for you. *Seas the Day* is a declaration of all the ways I wish to change, so if you don't see me implementing my own advice I want you to slap me across the face with my own book. The lessons sprinkled throughout were probably less revolutionary in your life as they were a reminder for my own.

Two years have passed since I stepped foot aboard the *MV World Odyssey*. Those relationships cultivated on Voyage 128 have continued to grow deeper, and some have already culminated in marriage! The squad has rendezvoused all across the United States: Zion, Las Vegas, Tuscaloosa, Tempe, Lake Powell, and Chicago.

Afterword

An Easy Decision

It took more than a day to fully unpack from my Semester at Sea and somehow my metal F-16 fighter jet penholder made it back in one piece and safely onto my dad's desk! I was so enraptured that it took me another two weeks before I realized my Sony a6000 and Tara's ping-pong paddle had been stolen. By some miracle I remembered the advice Jake told me about keeping my SD cards on me at all times, so all my footage was saved. But strangely enough, even to the writing of this very sentence, I still don't feel like I've settled in. Writing this book has certainly helped but some days it feels like fragments of my heart are still floating out at sea.

Thankfully, Semester at Sea has stayed afloat, which allowed them to offer some pretty tantalizing incentives. A $15,000 scholarship to any spring 2020 voyager who wished to sail during a future fall semester and $10,000 off a spring voyage. I calculated that it would actually be $7,500 cheaper to sail around the world my fall semester senior year than to study in Tempe. Of course, that excluded all the money spent traveling around the countries.

More than the money, there would be absolutely no one traveling the world when our ship would sail, so all of the top world destinations would not be jam-packed with tourists. COVID-19 took away our travel plans but now seemed to be handing them back to us on an even nicer plate. My pros and cons list was completely lopsided, so I decided to apply to the fall 2021 voyage.

First Semester Junior Year

On March 26, 2020, I finally reconnected with Jeff Crock over the phone. After talking his ear off about our voyage, I accepted the fourteenth and final spot in the Saint Paul's Outreach (SPO) household. That's right—fourteenth! A few days before my junior year I moved into the house from which the majority of this book was written. The master bedroom was renamed the six-pack because we had two triple-stack bunk beds along either side of the wall. Our house was the definition of countercultural: no television, no coed sleepovers, no alcohol, and everyone's lower body was stronger than their upper body. Time to start hittin' legs.

While COVID-19 surged around the globe, our house was building the radical brotherhood that I had dreamed of since I had first encountered it a few weeks before the voyage. You can't pray all day if you don't start in the morning, so all fourteen of us were out of bed at 6:00 a.m. Monday through Thursday. I laughed a few dozen times before the sun came up more than half the week. Do you have any idea how drastically this changed the course of my life? This precious early morning time was the elixir that produced a joyful day. My appetite for the truth had never been greater and my faith was coming alive, sparked by what I thought was just curiosity, but would later describe as tenacity.

If you are tenacious, you will find the truth.

Since ASU had switched to completely online learning every day was like an episode of *The Office*. Everybody had their desk in the same room, which made focusing in class a real doozy but it had its perks. Those who had to turn on their video camera to participate in Zoom University were subject to pranks at any time. Just having ten of us in the background of someone's video was strange enough, considering we were in the heart of the pandemic. No professor could believe any of us

Afterword

had thirteen roommates.

I was worried that after hanging around a dozen friends during my Semester at Sea I would miss the feeling of being surrounded by people all the time. But it was as if God said, "I'll give you one more." The thirteen of us plus myself needed three cars to get anywhere, so the Holy Trinity divided amongst us. Jesus frequently took the wheel of the car Mac was driving. (Sorry Mac) We rolled deep everywhere we went. Our joy for life was radiant whether we walked into In-N-Out or Mass.

When we took trips to California and filled up rows of churches we had never been to, priests would include us in their homily and sometimes outright thank us. As nice of a gesture as this was, thanking us for worshiping Jesus who was nailed to a cross for our sins was frighteningly disordered. What became very evident from these incredibly awkward interactions was the lack of righteous young men on fire, ready to go to battle for God. We need our elderly in the pews more than anything, but it's a bit strange to be taking pictures with them after Mass. I quickly understood that nobody wants to give an hour of their day to something they don't believe in, but they will give their entire life to something they do.

Our battlefield was the belly of the beast, Arizona State University. Arguably our school has devoured more souls than any other in the world, so it has become our mission to kick the devil off his own campus. We can't make any decisions for people, but we can love the hell out of them.

I wanted, so desperately, for my fraternity brothers to experience the brotherhood in SPO so at every chance I would make invitations to come and see. It was an adjustment for the guys to wrap their heads around the way I was living compared to how we used to spend time. When they saw my new way of life, it was evident I was living for something different, they just needed to want it for themselves. It was brutal to watch some old friendships slowly slip out of my life. Interactions in passing that used to feel like explosions spewing joy across the campus were now completely disarmed. Before the voyage I remembered giving our SAE salute anytime I saw letters, and now I was watching brothers walk past each other without even a head nod.

While the thought of many old relationships wilting away was in the back of my mind, there was an abundance of life front of mind. We got down in the trenches, developed real relationships, then invited men into our community. We went to war on the ultimate Frisbee field every single week. We went ice-blocking. We picked up guys around campus on our baby-blue tandem bicycle. We cooked hundreds of eggs for breakfast. We ate tacos out of a boat in our hot tub. We listened. We played softball, spike ball, real life Clue, Chess, Caton, and games of Fugitive so intense it took three cop cars to end our shenanigans. We spontaneously went on camping trips. We wrestled. We jumped off cliffs. We sprinted into the ocean.

The love was reciprocated when we found out a million-dollar house just across from campus sitting on nearly an acre of land was donated to us. We were no longer biking distance. Now we could walk to campus in two minutes. Our backyard was so large I couldn't even throw a baseball from our patio over the back wall, and I've got a good arm. Now we just needed to fill it. But I had already committed to sailing my fall semester next year, and I couldn't live in the house for just a semester; it was all or nothing.

Afterword

My first semester living in the house was coming to an end and the fourteen of us had rubbed up against each other sharpening, refining, and forming ourselves into the great men we desired to become. Men that might someday lead our families' households, parishes, or religious orders. With God as the master sculptor, constantly bending and molding us into His tools, we were never comfortable, never *content*. The Lord began to speak through the guys, Luke Swanson in particular, making it evident just what I was going to sail away from next year.

Luke said, "If you put the weight on your heart only God can carry on board that ship...she's gonna sink."

A Very Hard Decision

Through a series of phone calls with Semester at Sea HQ, I got word that SAS was going to make a decision whether they were even going to sail or not sometime in March 2021. It was January, so technically I could wait and see but I knew I needed to decide before they did and be *active* not passive in my decision. So I prayerfully reflected on my situation, with two incredible goods at hand. Should I participate in the greatest experience the *world* has to offer (in my opinion) or build something that is *eternal* yet does not have the curb appeal of a Semester at Sea? The Lord would permit me to do either, they were both *good* options, but I knew deep down in my heart that there certainly was a *better*.

On the morning of February 16, 2021, I decided to cancel my senior year voyage on Semester at Sea. A few weeks later, SAS announced that they would be setting sail with one of their most ambitious itineraries in the program's history. I was overjoyed for those who would sail, but I had already made peace with my decision.

We all know how much SAS loves applications, so similar to applying I actually had to de-apply from the program. The choices for cancellation included things like money issues, classes not transferring, schools rejecting permission, and other. My personal situation was best described by "other." I sure hoped my reason would be good enough. Below is the short essay I wrote on the form.

Why are you cancelling your Fall 2021 Semester at Sea Voyage?

> *On paper*, Voyage 128 was the least successful voyage in the history of Semester at Sea. *On board*, Voyage 128 will go down as the greatest experience of my life, and I wouldn't trade our time on the ship for the world. The life lessons I learned on board are now paying massive dividends in my day-to-day life on campus. There will be those that say our voyage was not wonderful or fair because we did not get to experience the same number of in-port days as our itinerary boasted. Alumni may also mention that they did not pay to have a semester at sea, they paid for a semester in port. However, I would argue that the community we built and the ever-valuable life lessons of flexibility were priceless additions to our voyage that infinitely outweigh our losses both personally and collectively. I had come to believe optimism was the rising tide that lifted all ships, but now I understand it was truly faith. As our ship continued to divert from entire continents, I realized just how little the actual destinations meant to me. I was truly captivated by

Afterword

ship life and the rich community being built. It was the community SAS showed me how to build that was now my reality at home.

Upon arrival back to ASU, I quickly became rooted in a household constructed of incredible men who are radically pursuing Jesus in all aspects of their lives. They too are an incredibly tight-knit community by proximity, but also in faith. And that difference means the world, so much so that I cannot afford to sail around the globe while so much is happening right in front of me. This house of men is the fruit of an extraordinary SAS experience so leaving them again would be like sawing off the limb I am standing on. I have committed to these brothers and the massive vision we hold for our city, state, country, and yes, the world. The time spent on campus next semester will continually yoke us together as one united front on a mission for a kingdom much bigger than words can describe. The sacraments mean more to me now than ever before; a ship without Mass and reconciliation is a deal breaker. I hope that I will sail again in my life, but not on my terms. I have given all my stresses, plans, hopes, and dreams to Jesus who was nailed to a tree for my sins, and he also happens to be my travel agent. Thank you for a truly life-changing experience. I pray that my spot will be filled by someone who has an equally transformative semester.

Closure

In June 2021, just two months before the fall 2021 voyage, I was at the University of St. Thomas in St. Paul, Minnesota for Saint Paul's Outreach training (that's a lot of saints) and I received an email from SAS that the fall 2021 voyage had been cancelled. I was speechless. If I would have gone through with the voyage, I would have forfeited my spot in the house and been left scrambling to find a place to live.

A Hard Drive

A few days before starting my senior year in August 2021 I was trying to work on an edit for my Instagram when I realized I misplaced my external hard drive. I searched for it all day, in denial that I actually lost nine hundred gigabytes of all the travel footage I have ever captured. I had not backed it up to the cloud, rather, another external hard drive that had also vanished. When night fell, I declared them missing, which opened the floodgates I had been holding in for hours.

    I decided to go for a drive to clear my head, and somehow, I ended up on the 202 Loop that circles Phoenix. Strangely, I put on Twenty-One Pilots' "Blurryface," which I had not listened to in many years. Then, after making an enormous loop, an hour later I pulled back into my driveway having come to a conclusion. I must delete all my social media *accounts*.

    I redownloaded all of the apps I had deleted back in Vietnam on the same date I began writing this book, April 10, 2020. But rather than feeling a sense of relief I felt like I was locking myself in chains. On this drive I screamed questions out loud, begging for answers. How will I be entertained? How will I stay connected with my friends? How will I get the word out about my book?

Afterword

Well, you're reading it now, aren't you?

Similar to how my confidence was so correlated to my physical appearance, my life was correlated with the desire to post. Looking back at all those times when I finished scrolling, not once did I say to myself, "That was a good use of my time, I feel better because I did that." And I was nauseated of having to brief myself the same way before I started scrolling: "Okay, just remember, it's a highlight reel, not real life, don't compare."

And maybe the reason it's so difficult to come up with a caption is because everyone is trying to find a different way to say, "Look at how happy I am!" I will say that deleting social media is not for everyone; I know plenty of people who set strict boundaries and use it to their advantage. But if you're anything like me, I couldn't tame the beast, so I killed it.

It's actually repulsive how hard it is to delete your Instagram account. They give you an entire month to think about it, sending you emails with a large blue button that will restore everything back to normal at a single touch. It needs us to survive just like a parasite.

Now, when you do something Instagram worthy, like riding a ranked bull, would you rather throw it up on the Internet for five hundred shitty impressions, or make a few of your best friends' day by sending personalized messages? For those who are inspired to kill the beast, the most immediate benefits are quicker poops and longer days. In less than a week, you will become a source of entertainment for your friends rather than a connection to it. And for those who want to go viral, as strange as it sounds, I promise you don't even need social media for that either. The internet has watched me lick chocolate off a stranger's face over 35 million times and that high was about as temporary as Flat Stanley in a hurricane.

We often buy the lie that social media is keeping us more connected, but the reality is seen every single day in the Starbucks line. No matter if we have a single notification to attend to, we automatically look down and find someplace to scroll, even old text messages. The next time you feel this urge, put it back in your pocket, turn around, and say, "Hey, what's this coffee gonna help you accomplish today?" Do this every day and your life will never be the same.

A few weeks after I had deleted all of my accounts, I got a call from my mom, she found both of my hard drives buried in a drawer.

Sometimes we lose something to lose something. Sometimes we lose something to gain something.

Jesus Calling

The first time I heard the Lord calling me to serve full time with Saint Paul's Outreach was at missionary training 2021. The fact that I was even considering the job was proof enough that God was supplying the grace, so I said yes. They say it takes a village to make a man and SPO is in the village building business, so this was a logical next step. In my previous job as a Financial Representative I sold invisible things to strangers, so I figured it was a solid pre-requisite to becoming a missionary. I was ready to *run* through walls for Jesus, but my roommates were way ahead of me.

Meet Stephen. Stephen, has a habit of doing extraordinary feats of human strength and endurance without telling anyone or himself! So naturally, Stephen was running a marathon he

Afterword

hadn't trained for, and nobody knew about, including his roommate Jeff. The morning of the marathon, Jeff heard the news, and with no bib, snuck into the race a mile in and ran alongside Stephen for twenty-five miles.

And they did it in four hours flat.

Our household constantly found ourselves saying, "I'll match your resolve." If you're going to go all out for something so am I. This is precisely why the relativist statement, "you do you" does not hold up. We are not a bunch of individuals, but rather a people living in community with one another. If you've been on a team before you know that you match the leader's energy to some degree. If the team captain is going all out in sprints, you're more likely to run faster. If the captain is lazy and slacking off its much easier to follow suit.

We never say "you do you" to someone who is struggling with a drug addiction, but we say it all the time to our friends addicted to alcohol and porn. "Well that doesn't affect me." One of the biggest lies we believe is that if we don't care about something it does not affect us. The same way we throw around the phrase, "nothing in life is free" we must add "nothing in life is free *of others*."

The Last Paragraph

As I graduate from Arizona State University, I am proud to have gotten straight A's, except for a few high seas. I am forever grateful to have sailed on Semester at Sea during the COVID-19 pandemic. Never again will any of us take domestic or international travel for granted, and we will take owner*ship* of our reactions. The leader*ship* we exhibited during one of the most stressful seasons of our lives will bid us well in our future careers. The hards*hip* we faced through an entire semester of ambiguity will prepare us for every uncertainty our lives will throw our way. The innocent cruise *ship* we boarded transformed into a war*ship* which wasted no time revealing what we wor*ship*ed. The relation*ship*s we formed with our *ship*mates forced us to shake our destination-oriented mindset, and focus on the joys of the journey, allowing us to truly **Seas the Day**.

    Amen.

Acknowledgments

First and foremost, thank you, Mom! You are the reason this book exists. In the midst of sharing all seventy-three of my journal entries in early April 2020, she stopped me and said, "You need to write a book!" and I wrote the first sentence that afternoon. Thank you for motivating me to write every day, especially when I deleted more words than I wrote. To my dad, a serial optimist, entrepreneur, and hype-man who raised me with the mindset that's infused in every page of this book, your joy is contagious, let's infect the world!

Thank you to my favorite brother, Luke, for pursuing your music/acting career and for not squandering your creative gifts. You call me outside of my comfort zone. I love our healthy competition, and I repent for all the times I've twisted it otherwise. Don't forget about me when you're famous, I'll need your money. ;)

This story would not exist if it weren't for my study abroad advisor Andrew Parady and my academic advisor David Calabrese. Thank you both for helping me realize my dream, and graduate on time.

To the highlight of Voyage 128, the friends who brought these stories to life, thank you for helping me find the end of myself: Jake Lattimore, Weston Bell, Nic Swanger, Chris Price, Jacob Johnson, Kate Lyons, Maddi Marshall, Ashley Farhat, Riley Durham, Jenna Klinkhammer, Lauren Brill, Dylan Chouinard, Zack Mays, Zara Salem, Emily Weisfield, and Eve Grill. Thank you, Jimmy Mernik for being an incredible cabinmate and your patience with my mildly obsessive-compulsive neatness.

Since sailing on Semester at Sea I have had the joy and privilege of living with some of the most extraordinary men on God's green Earth in Saint Paul's Outreach households. I have spent the last three years writing this book in the study room, dining room, bathroom, backyard, poolside, mountainside, oceanside, on campus, in cars, boats, planes, trains, and on the back of a tandem bicycle, and the following men have encouraged me in every setting and season: Aaron Acunin, Andrew Piazza, Christian Messner, David Pivonka, Jeff Zelkin, Luke Swanson, Mac Coomer, Owen Lamb, Roman DeCaro, Stephen Mikitish, Thomas Corzo, Ty Frigon, JP Beguhl, Thomas Hammen, Connor Joseph, Joseph Wright, Nicolas Casilli, Roger B. McCurdy III, Jacob Hoog, Scott Carney, Anthony Gagliano, Kenneth Salazar, Josue Reyes Diaz, Matt Schmid, Quinn Courteau, Ivan Yorobe, James Bartlett, Harry Zhang, Chris McLoughlin, Brett Braza, Mac Metzinger, Thomas Murphy, Gavin Gunkel, Brian Do, Will Mueller, Jonny DeMarais, John Patros, Sam Masek, Nick Hall, Francis Volkmuth, Dustin Goodchild, Kyle Devich, Michael Ennis, Lucas Shriver, Andrew Raschke, Angel Trejo, Charlie Appel, Will Leija, Adrian Salazar, David Switala, Mark Brenner, Miles Demko, Austin Redington, Nolan Bemiss, Michael Nichols, Matt Rodriguez,

Jonathan Ryan, Tobias Cossairt, and Brandon Ruiz.

Thank you to those who set aside their plans to put time and energy into my manuscript: Kristin Thurn, Grant Cloud, Nicole Johnson, Cory Fosco, Nicole Young, Monica Butler, Maggie O'Connell, Ella Penzkover, and Theresa Magalski.

A special thank you to Jared Kuritz and Strategies PR for guiding me through the book publishing process.

To Marvel Harrison, thank you for telling me what I needed to hear and giving me a shoulder to cry on. Thank you for opening up your home and network to me.

Finally, thank you God, the Author, for changing the trajectory of my life in the most unlikely circumstances, and for having a greater vision for my life than I ever could've imagined. Thank you, Jesus Christ, the Word, for pursuing me when I run from You, and for walking with me in this abundant new life which I live out every day using Your strength. Thank you, Holy Spirit, for the fire You fanned in me to serve as a missionary, and to finish this work so that others might come to believe.

About the Author

Johnny Vrba hails from Geneva, Illinois, an hour away from his favorite city in the world, Chicago. Which is strange considering he chose to study across the country at Arizona State University where he graduated summa cum laude with a degree in Management and a certificate in International Business. At nineteen, Johnny became a founding father of the Sigma Alpha Epsilon fraternity at ASU, led his fraternity to becoming the fastest growing SAE chapter in history, and spearheaded SAE's inaugural Climb for a Cause summiting Mount Kilimanjaro in Tanzania, one of the seven summits of the world, in support of the JP McNicholas Pediatric Brian Tumor Foundation (Live Like John). Johnny shot, edited, and produced a documentary of his climb to the roof of Africa which raised tens of thousands of dollars for pediatric brain tumor research. As a sophomore, Johnny taught WPC 101, an introductory business course, to twenty freshmen. As an upperclassman Johnny was a founding member of the nonprofits Consult Your Community (CYC), which offers free consulting work for local businesses and Sun Devil Dance Marathon (SDDM) which raises money for the Phoenix Children's hospital. The spring semester of his sophomore year, Johnny's thirst for adventure led him to apply to the world's most intense study abroad program, Semester at Sea. Disaster struck two weeks into the voyage when the coronavirus broke out. After 73 days and a rollercoaster of emotions Johnny retold the stories to his mom who said, "You could write a book!" So, equipped with a sixth-grade writing level Johnny set out to write his first book. When Johnny is not busy changing the world through the power of the Holy Spirit, he can be found starting an overly expensive hobby and then questioning this decision. Some of his talents include speaking, making a scene, and engaging in taboo conversations with strangers. Some of his greatest weaknesses are slowing down, multi-tasking, and spiders. Johnny currently serves as a Catholic missionary with Saint Paul's Outreach at the University of St. Thomas.

www.ingramcontent.com/pod-product-compliance
Lightning Source LLC
LaVergne TN
LVHW010309070526
838199LV00065B/5499